SUPER
TUESDAY

SUPER TUESDAY

Regional Politics &
Presidential Primaries

BARBARA NORRANDER

THE UNIVERSITY PRESS OF KENTUCKY

Copyright © 1992 by The University Press of Kentucky

Scholarly publisher for the Commonwealth,
serving Bellarmine College, Berea College, Centre
College of Kentucky, Eastern Kentucky University,
The Filson Club, Georgetown College, Kentucky
Historical Society, Kentucky State University,
Morehead State University, Murray State University,
Northern Kentucky University, Transylvania University,
University of Kentucky, University of Louisville,
and Western Kentucky University.

Editorial and Sales Offices: Lexington, Kentucky 40508-4008

Library of Congress Cataloging-in-Publication Data

Norrander, Barbara, 1954-
    Super Tuesday : regional politics and presidential primaries /
Barbara Norrander.
      p. cm.
    Includes bibliographical references (p.) and index.
    ISBN 0-8131-1773-9 (alk. paper)
    1. Presidents—United States—Election—1988. 2. Presidents-
-United States—Nomination. 3. Primaries—Southern States.
I. Title.
JK526 19881
324.973'0927—dc20   91-31263
                                    CIP

9-20-93

CONTENTS

ACKNOWLEDGMENTS

No book is ever written by the author alone, but in conjunction with the support and advice of friends and colleagues. This book is no exception. Numerous individuals contributed to the success of this book. Harold Stanley provided important information on the politics of Super Tuesday, as did Pat Stafford, Charley Williams, and Dan O'Connor of the Southern Legislative Conference. Clyde Wilcox helped with information on the Christian right and campaign finances, and Anthony Corrado provided insight on campaign strategy. John Geer and Patrick Kenney provided expert opinion on voter turnout and candidate choices in presidential primaries. As always, Bob Biersack of the Federal Election Commission provided timely assistance with financial records of presidential candidates. Also deserving thanks are Roy Christman, Peter Haas, John Kessel, Bill Lockwood, Hugh Winebrenner, Roy Young, and Neal Zaslavsky. Jim Moore's services as a graduate assistant were supported by a San Jose State University Foundation Research Grant. Secretarial support came from Kelli-Cheyenne Waldron, Stella Melgosa, and Linda Chromik.

The survey data analyzed in this book were made available through the Inter-University Consortium for Political and Social Research (ICPSR). The National Election Studies organization conducted the original Super Tuesday survey, as well as the 1980 panel, 1984 continuous monitoring, and the 1988 general election surveys. Exit polls originally gathered for the "CBS News"/*New York Times* Poll also were made available through the ICPSR.

1

Reforming the Reforms: Super Tuesday in a Historical Perspective

"When your dog bites you four or five times, it's time to get a new dog. We've been bitten and it's time for the South to get a new dog" (Gailey, March 8, 1986, 9). The new dog, so colorfully alluded to by Tennessee Democratic state party chair Dick Lodge, became Super Tuesday 1988, a one-day extravaganza on which fourteen southern and border states scheduled presidential primaries.[1] The old dog, a series of presidential primaries commencing in New Hampshire and ending in California, bit off a traditional base of the Democratic presidential coalition—the southern white voter. Only once in the past twenty years did a Democratic presidential candidate carry the South. The problem, according to southern Democratic leaders, lay in northern or liberal states having undue influence on presidential nominations.

The 1984 election, in particular, disappointed southern Democratic leaders. Southern Democratic voters, finding the Mondale-Ferraro ticket unpalatable, voted a second time for Ronald Reagan. The Democratic party felt the loss of these "Reagan Democrats" beyond presidential voting. In North Carolina, for example, the popular Democratic governor, Jim Hunt, was unable to defeat Jesse Helms for the Senate seat. Republicans also captured the North Carolina governorship and three "hotly contested" House seats (Galston 1988). Fearing the birth of a permanent Republican advantage, Democratic leaders felt compelled to act. Any change would be better than the existing system, but a change with pizzazz would grab the attention of both presidential candidates and the national media. A regional primary, in which all southern states would hold their presidential primaries on the same day, seemed to fit the bill. With Super Tuesday, the South hoped once again to rise to prominence within the Democratic party.

Super Tuesday emerged between 1986 and 1987 as eleven Democratically controlled southern and border state legislatures passed bills scheduling their 1988 presidential primaries on March 8, joining three southern states already holding early primaries. The event became more than a southern regional primary, as March 8 coincided with the Massachusetts and Rhode Island primaries, Democratic caucuses in four western states, and Republican caucuses in Washington. Even Democrats in American Samoa would select delegates on March 8. Super Tuesday became the biggest one-day event in presidential primary history. Nearly one-third of all 1988 Democratic and Republican national convention delegates would be selected on Super Tuesday.

Super Tuesday was not the first attempt to alter presidential nomination rules. Dramatic reforms occurred in the 1830s, 1910s, and 1970s, with more gradual modifications occurring with each election cycle. The founding fathers thought an inconclusive Electoral College would nominate presidential candidates, leaving the final choice to Congress. This system never materialized as the development of political parties led to decisive elections in the Electoral College. Instead, newly formed political parties nominated presidential candidates within their congressional caucuses. When congressional caucuses faced charges of being undemocratic, the parties switched to national conventions in the 1830s. While technically the same legal system exists today, conventions became increasingly constrained in their choice of candidates during the twentieth century. Presidential primaries, introduced by Progressives between 1905 and 1916, initially placed few restrictions on the conventions. Instead, changes in technology, such as public opinion polling, and campaign styles gradually reduced the convention's flexibility. In the 1970s, the proliferation of presidential primaries further restricted the freedom of conventions. In the 1980s, as a result of these changes, one candidate became the de facto nominee months before the convention convened.

Thus, Super Tuesday is only the latest change in presidential nominations, coming on the heels of a dramatic series of reforms in the 1970s. All reforms, even popular reforms, displease someone, since all political rules advantage some groups or candidates more than others. Additionally, all rule changes produce unintended consequences, as rules are only one of the forces shaping presidential nomination politics. By the 1980s, southern Democrats began to believe recent reforms had produced a presidential nomination process that ignored the South and advantaged liberal candidates. Something clearly needed to be done.

To understand their response, we need to gain a broader perspective on the changing presidential nomination system. We will first review the patterns of presidential nomination in the 1980s. Next, we will attempt to understand how this system developed by examining the influences of national reform movements, state parties and legislatures, the media, changing technology, and candidate strategies. These same forces will determine the fate of Super Tuesday. Finally, we will close the chapter by taking a detailed look at the regional primary movement and the creation of Super Tuesday.

PRESIDENTIAL NOMINATIONS IN THE 1980s

By the 1980s, candidates fought for the Democratic or Republican party's presidential nomination state by state through a long series of presidential primaries and caucuses commencing in Iowa and New Hampshire in February and ending in California, New Jersey, and several smaller states in June. No rhyme or reason dictated the order of these primaries. New Hampshire stumbled onto its early February primary in two stages. In 1915, New Hampshire moved its presidential primary to March to coincide with town meetings in order to save the state the costs of an extra election. Not many candidates, however, paid much attention to New Hampshire, since its primary only selected convention delegates. In 1949, the state added a presidential preference contest to its primary ballot. Thus, in 1952, New Hampshire began its historic role as the first scheduled contest between presidential contenders (Mayer 1987).

Since the 1950s, New Hampshire voters have found that a first-in-the-nation primary insured their state extensive media coverage, magnifying the effects of their primary. Even direct economic benefits accrued to New Hampshire. Candidate and media entourages spent considerable money on food, hotels, cars, and so forth. Pictures of candidates romping in the snow provided free publicity for New Hampshire's winter sports industry. Gradually, more and more states attempted to cash in on New Hampshire's primary bonanza by creating new primaries or moving the dates of their existing primaries forward. This caused the presidential nomination system to become front-loaded: that is, more and more delegates were being chosen earlier and earlier. Meanwhile, other states retained later presidential primary dates to coincide with their spring primaries for congressional and statewide offices, thus preventing the added expense of holding two elections. These late primary states, however, sometimes found the presidential nomination race over before their citizens had a chance to vote.

Technically, each state's presidential primary only selects delegates to attend the national party convention where nominations are officially bestowed. Yet in actuality, a race for media attention, public support, and campaign funds turned statewide contests into national events. Whichever candidate won a primary not only collected more delegates from a state but also received more media attention, which translated into increased public support and more campaign contributions. The state-by-state delegate selection process had been transformed into a national race for the presidency, with Iowa and New Hampshire apparently having the most influence.

In the past few elections, when a party had no incumbent president to renominate, six to seven candidates typically entered the race. Most candidates did not survive the first few primaries as losers were winnowed from the field. Meanwhile, one previously unknown candidate captured the "Big Mo," or momentum. Jimmy Carter in 1976, Bush in 1980, and Hart in 1984 all gained the media's attention by doing better than expected in Iowa or New Hampshire. With this increased media attention, these candidates became better known, attracting more votes and more campaign contributions.

By the middle of each primary season, two to three candidates remained in the race, turning their attention toward accumulating sufficient delegates to secure the nomination. This was not an easy task, but in every year since 1976, one candidate has concluded the primary season with the required number of delegates to win the nomination on the first convention ballot or else has had a huge lead in the delegate count. In 1984, Mondale controlled the needed 50 percent of convention delegates by the time the primary season ended in June. In 1980, George Bush withdrew as the sole remaining challenger to Ronald Reagan's nomination before the last series of primaries were even held. In 1976, Carter's delegate advantage led Udall, Humphrey, and Wallace to concede the race, though Carter did not yet control the required number of delegates guaranteeing selection at the national convention.

Fewer candidates contested the nomination if an incumbent president sought renomination. In the twentieth century, incumbent presidents were rarely challenged. Yet in the 1970s, two incumbent presidents, Gerald Ford and Jimmy Carter, fought off serious challenges from Ronald Reagan and Edward (Ted) Kennedy. After heated battles extending to the national conventions, both incumbent presidents won renomination. The highly popular President Reagan faced no opposition in the 1984 Republican primaries.

Just a quarter of a century earlier, presidential nominations were fought under a different system. About fifteen states scheduled presidential primaries, but results of these primaries did not dictate who would be the nominee. In 1960, five men sought the Democratic nomination, but only two, Hubert Humphrey and John Kennedy, competed in the presidential primaries. Lyndon Johnson, Stuart Symington, and Adlai Stevenson waited for a brokered convention, one in which no candidate had a lead coming into the convention and negotiations between candidates and state delegations would determine the final outcome. In 1988, all seven Democratic candidates competed in the primaries, and hopes of a brokered convention were fanned more by journalists, who dreaded another boring convention, than by party leaders.[2] On the Republican side in 1960, Vice President Richard

Nixon captured the nomination without significant competition.[3] In 1988, Vice President George Bush faced five competitors. By 1988, the path to the presidential nomination ran through the primaries, and no candidate, not even sitting vice presidents, could bypass them.

Not only were presidential primaries less important in 1960 than in 1988, but the dynamics of primary competition were different. In 1960, the New Hampshire primary defaulted to the politician from next door; John Kennedy's only competitor was Paul C. Fisher, a ball-point pen manufacturer. No one conceded New Hampshire to the Massachusetts Democratic governor in 1988. Michael Dukakis fought off all six competitors. Three Democratic candidates including Dukakis, spent within 95 percent of the $461,000 limit set by law for the New Hampshire primary, while two other candidates spent within 70 percent of this limit. Three of the 1988 Democratic candidates spent over fifty days campaigning in New Hampshire, two more over thirty days. Back in 1960, most primaries were not viewed as important enough to warrant such extensive candidate attention. John Kennedy entered seven primaries but concentrated mostly on Wisconsin and West Virginia, hoping victories in these two events would convince party power brokers to nominate him at the Democratic national convention (White 1961). Dukakis entered thirty-six primaries and won twenty-two to accumulate 1,393 delegates, two-thirds of the number necessary to earn the Democratic nomination. While winning these delegates in the presidential primaries, Dukakis's support in the Gallup Poll jumped from 14 percent preferring him for the Democratic nomination in 1987 to 66 percent by April 1988 (Gallup Poll, December 1987, 9-10, and April 1988). In contrast, John Kennedy was the first choice among Democrats in public opinion polls before the 1960 primaries and gained only seven percentage points over the course of the campaign (Beninger 1977). Primary victories helped Kennedy attain his nomination, but Dukakis's nomination came as a direct result of winning primaries.

Many of the recent changes in presidential nomination politics stem from one simple fact: the number of presidential primaries doubled between 1960 and 1980. Only sixteen states held presidential primaries in 1960, and candidates did not compete in every primary. Some primaries were conceded to regional favorites, as New Hampshire was to Kennedy. Other primaries, sometimes because of the presence of favorite-son candidates, failed to draw interest from any of the major national competitors. By 1988, thirty-seven states held presidential primaries. On one day—March 8, 1988, Super Tuesday—sixteen states held presidential primaries. Michael Dukakis competed in more primaries in one day than John Kennedy did in an entire season!

Presidential nomination practices in 1988 obviously differed from those used in 1960. The presidential nomination process throughout the course of

U.S. history has been altered by short dramatic changes and gradual evolution. Some of these changes were planned, such as the dramatic reform movement of the 1970s. Yet these planned changes often were accompanied by unintended consequences. Other changes in the nomination system were not part of a national reform package but occurred more gradually and haphazardly. No one planned to make New Hampshire the first primary, and, once it was in place, no one planned to make it so important. Rather, changing campaign styles and media practice merged to thrust New Hampshire to the forefront of nomination politics. In 1988, Super Tuesday would be one more attempt to alter nomination politics. Its success would depend not only on the astuteness of its planners but also on how it merged with the other forces shaping nomination politics.

REFORMING THE PRESIDENTIAL NOMINATION PROCESS

Reforms rarely materialize as their creators dream they will. Presidential primaries were introduced by the Progressives in the early 1900s with hopes of breaking the power of political bosses in the states, stopping the abuse of federal patronage at national conventions, and giving rank-and-file voters a voice in presidential nominations (Allin 1912). In 1912, Teddy Roosevelt won nine out of twelve primaries but failed to receive the presidential nomination. The Republican convention chose to renominate President Taft instead. After 1916, fewer and fewer states held presidential primaries, few serious candidates competed in them, and even fewer people voted. Not until after World War II would primaries play even a limited role in presidential nominations, and conventions retained some autonomy well into the 1960s.

Reformers of the late 1960s and early 1970s desired only to democratize procedures used in the then current mixture of primaries, caucuses, and national conventions. Members of the first Democratic reform commission, the McGovern-Fraser Commission, "believed that if [they] made the party's nonprimary delegate selection processes more open and fair, participation in them would increase greatly and consequently the demand for more primaries would fade away" (Ranney 1975, 206). Yet as we shall see shortly, for reasons of their own, state legislatures passed new presidential primary legislation instead. Whereas seventeen states held primaries to select half of the delegates in 1968, two election cycles later in 1976, thirty states held primaries to select three-quarters of the delegates. In 1988, thirty-seven primaries would select most of the delegates. Table 1.1 illustrates the growing number and importance of presidential primaries.[4]

Super Tuesday planners also had distinct goals. They wanted more clout for the South in presidential nominations. They planned to attain this clout by holding a regional primary. With 1,173 Democratic and 639 Republican

Table 1.1: Changing Number of Presidential Primaries

Year	Number of Primaries		% of Convention Delegates Selected	
	Democratic	Republican	Democratic	Republican
1912	12	13	32.9	41.7
1916	20	20	53.5	58.9
1920	16	20	44.6	57.8
1924	14	17	35.5	45.3
1928	17	16	42.2	44.9
1932	16	14	40.0	37.7
1936	14	12	36.5	37.5
1940	13	13	35.8	38.8
1944	14	13	36.7	38.7
1948	14	12	36.6	36.0
1952	15	13	38.7	39.0
1956	19	19	42.7	44.8
1960	18	17	47.6	48.3
1964	18	18	50.2	49.7
1968	17	17	47.0	47.6
1972	23	21	66.4	58.8
1976	29(1)	28(2)	75.8	69.1
1980	30(4)	33(2)	70.5	75.8
1984	24(5)	30(2)	61.3	69.6
1988	32(3)	34(3)	77.2	76.4

Values in parentheses are beauty contest primaries, whose delegates are not counted among those selected through a primary. Because of the difficulty of locating past primary rules, no attempt was made to designate beauty contests prior to 1976. Included in delegates selected through a primary are those states scheduled to hold primaries but which did not because no candidates filed.

Source: Arterton 1978 for years 1912 to 1956. 1960 to 1988 data compiled by Jim Moore for the author.

delegates at stake on one day, the southern regional primary could not be ignored. By holding Super Tuesday early, the planners insured that more candidates, including moderate or conservative candidates, would contest these primaries. Southern moderates would have a like-minded candidate to support in their primaries. Additionally, the stimulation caused by the media and candidate attention to Super Tuesday would increase the number of voters, making the electorate more representative of southern voters in general.

As mentioned before, reforms often fail to match the hopes of the reformers, but not because these reformers are naive amateurs. Reformers often are seasoned professional politicians. The McGovern-Fraser Commis-

sion included three senators, one House member, seven national or state
party officials, three state officials, three union leaders, and two political
scientists (Bode and Casey 1980).[5] Super Tuesday developed under the
auspices of the Southern Legislative Conference, composed of the presiding
officers of each state's legislature, and was supported by the Democratic
Leadership Council, composed of over seventy leading Democratic governors and congressional members. Every group of reformers harbors distinct goals and proposes plausible means to accomplish those goals. The
consequences of their reforms often do not match their goals because the
legal structures they reform constitute only one of the forces shaping
presidential nomination politics. Nationwide reform movements, such as
those of the Progressives at the turn of the century and the Democratic
party commissions of the 1970s, comprise one group. State politicians,
legislatures, and political parties comprise another. Presidential aspirants
are a third force attempting to mold the nomination process. Technological changes and modern media practices constitute the remaining two
factors. The combination of all five factors produced the expected and
unexpected twists and turns culminating in 1988 with Super Tuesday,
thirty-seven primaries, and emasculated conventions. We will now examine the role of each of these five forces in setting the stage for Super
Tuesday 1988.

NATIONAL POLITICAL TRENDS

The role of national reformers in changing presidential nomination politics is
well documented. (See, for instance, Ranney 1975; Crotty 1983; and Lengle
1987.) Most notable among the national reformers are the Progressive
reformers of the early 1900s, who created the first presidential primaries,
and the Democratic reform commissions of the 1970s, whose actions added
to the proliferation of the primaries. Both movements aspired to fairer results
by increasing rank-and-file involvement, reducing corruption, and making
the nomination process more democratic.

The 1970s Democratic reform commissions developed in response to
inequitable delegate selection procedures highlighted by the contentious
1968 Democratic convention. Supporters of Eugene McCarthy and the late
Robert Kennedy felt discriminated against by such delegate selection processes as (1) ten states with no rules; (2) ten states with inadequate rules, such
that county conventions were held in secret or, in the case of Virginia,
delegates were selected on buses headed toward the state convention; (3)
seventeen states allowing for the unit rule, in which all delegates were forced
to vote for the candidate preferred by the majority of delegates; and (4) six
states allowing delegates to run without stating their presidential prefer-

ences. In 40 percent of the states, party officials selected some or all of the delegates. One-third of all convention delegates were chosen prior to 1968 (Bode and Casey 1980; Fraser 1980).

To correct these problems, the national Democratic party created a commission to write guidelines states would have to follow when selecting delegates for Democratic national conventions. The McGovern-Fraser Commission established rules for the 1972 convention and was followed by the Mikulski Commission, which wrote rules for the 1976 convention. Rules written by these two commissions emphasized opening up the delegate selection process to all interested Democrats and selecting delegates to reflect the candidate preferences of rank-and-file participants. For the latter goal, proportional representation rules were encouraged and winner-take-all primaries banned. Quotas and affirmative action programs insured that delegates demographically reflected rank-and-file Democrats.

Subsequent reform commissions (Winograd Commission 1980; Hunt Commission 1984; and Fairness Commission 1988) modified the McGovern-Fraser and Mikulski commission rules in response to various objections voiced by states or candidates. For instance, larger states felt they lost much of their clout when they could no longer deliver a large bloc of delegates to a single candidate because of the ban on winner-take-all primaries. In response, later Democratic reform commissions allowed for more state variation in delegate selection procedures. Loophole primaries, in which direct voting for delegates often produces results similar to winner-take-all rules, were allowed. Bonus delegates could also be awarded to first-place finishers under a modified proportional representation scheme. Even under proportional representation, candidates could be required to receive as much as 25 percent of the vote before being awarded any delegates. Jesse Jackson complained, however, that the latter provision discriminated against black voters, who often constituted less than 20 percent of the electorate. In response, the threshold for 1988 was lowered to 15 percent.

Meanwhile, party and government officials began to feel locked out of the conventions. Super Delegate slots, to be filled by elected officials, were created in 1984 to provide the party elite with a renewed role in convention politics. The national Republican party chose not to impose specific delegate selection rules, leaving the choice up to the states.[6] Thus, a wider variety of rules are found on the Republican side, including winner-take-all primaries. This lack of structure, however, led to divisive battles over the rules in Michigan's and Hawaii's 1988 caucuses.

In the continuing battle over the rules, the U.S. Supreme Court upheld the right of national parties to require specific procedures for delegate selection, even when state laws allowed for other practices. In *Cousins v.*

Wigoda (1975), the Supreme Court validated the national Democratic party's right to refuse to seat fifty-nine Illinois delegates in 1972 because national party rules on representation of minorities and women were ignored. In *La Follette v. Democratic Party of the United States* (1980), the Court affirmed the national Democratic party's ban on open primaries. In both cases, the national party's First Amendment right to organization provided the legal grounds for the Court's ruling.

Not only were the political parties changing presidential nomination rules in the 1970s, the federal government changed the rules by imposing financial restrictions on presidential campaigns while simultaneously offering government funding. A post-Watergate reform package provided matching funds for individuals seeking the presidential nomination. Candidates must raise $5,000 in twenty states, in contributions of $250 or less, to qualify. After a candidate qualifies for matching funds, the first $250 from each citizen's contribution is matched by an equal number of government dollars supplied through the dollar check-off box on income tax forms. Many commentators feel federal matching funds encouraged more candidates to run for president. Yet the two elections immediately prior to the campaign finance reforms also had numerous candidates. Eight Democrats and five Republicans competed in 1968, while nine candidates vied for the 1972 Democratic nomination (Reiter 1985, 32). Nevertheless, matching funds facilitated the candidacies of thirteen individuals in 1988: seven Democrats and six Republicans. Lyndon LaRouche, who claims the Queen of England was involved in a drug-smuggling conspiracy and who himself was convicted of mail fraud in December 1988, and Lenora Fulani, who sought the New Alliance party's nomination, also qualified for matching funds. Additionally, finance rules may affect the length of candidates' campaigns. With individuals restricted to contributions of $1,000 or less, candidates must start their campaigns earlier and earlier in order to raise the huge sums of money needed to run a presidential campaign.[7] The Federal Election Commission provision cutting off matching funds to candidates who fail to draw 10 percent of the vote in two consecutive primaries brings an early close to some candidacies.

Changes in campaign finance laws as well as reforms instituted by the national Democratic party surely altered nomination practices. Some commentators tend to ascribe all recent changes solely to these national reforms (see, for instance, Polsby 1983; Shafer 1983; Kirkpatrick 1976, 1978). Yet as Reiter (1985) eloquently points out, current nomination practices evolved over a longer period of time. Recent national reforms constitute only one portion of this change. Changes in state and local parties, increasing roles for the media, and technological innovations all played a part in forming the presidential nomination system of the 1980s.

STATE PARTIES AND LEGISLATURES

National reform movements provided the idea for presidential primaries, but state parties and state laws put this idea into action. Florida, in 1901, enacted the first law allowing, but not requiring, national convention delegates to be selected through a primary. In 1905, Wisconsin Progressives, galvanized by their exclusion from the previous year's Republican delegation, passed the first law requiring direct election of convention delegates in a presidential primary. A greater role for rank-and-file voters typified the response of Progressives who sought to take power away from party elites. Oregon, in 1912, became the first state in which voters selected delegates with designated presidential candidate preferences. Oregon's primary became law through another Progressive innovation, the initiative process (Davis 1967).

By 1912, twelve states employed presidential primaries to select convention delegates. Nine states passed presidential primary laws between 1912 and 1916, but only one more state, Alabama, passed a new presidential primary law in the next thirty years. Meanwhile, eight states abandoned their primaries (Davis 1967). Presidential primaries were ignored by candidates, who had learned from the 1912 experience in which Theodore Roosevelt won nine out of twelve primaries but lost the nomination at the convention, that they could not win the nomination through primary victories. With few candidates competing, public interest waned and turnout fell.

Instead of presidential primaries playing a major role, state and local party elites maintained control over presidential nominations through the early twentieth century. Rank-and-file delegates came to national conventions uncommitted to any presidential candidate. Rather, delegates remained loyal to a state political leader, who bargained with leading presidential candidates. Several roll calls of all the states might proceed as candidates tried to build coalitions composed of various state delegations. At some point, one candidate would draw ahead, and a bandwagon effect would lead to his eventual nomination.

The decline in state and local party bosses had as much to do with the creation of the present nomination system as did changes at the national level (Reiter 1985). Power at national conventions began to center on candidates and national interest groups. No longer did state leaders control blocs of delegates. Dark horses and favorite sons became rarer and rarer. National political leaders replaced state leaders as the controlling forces at the conventions. Unlike in the nineteenth century, when presidential candidates could not even be assured of their own renomination, by the middle of the twentieth century sitting presidents regularly won renomination without any conflict.[8] (Only after presidential primaries began to dominate nomination politics after 1970 were sitting presidents once again challenged for the nomination.) Even unsuccessful presidential aspirants from previous years maintained influence in subsequent conventions. In the 1900s, four candidates who previously lost bids for the presidency (Bryan, Dewey, Stevenson, and Nixon) won second nomination bids (Pomper 1963). Senators and vice presidents, rather than governors, were the likely nominees. Besides national politicians, national interest groups challenged the authority of state party leaders. In Democratic conventions, over one hundred delegates would be attached to labor unions by the mid-1950s (Pomper 1963). The AFL-CIO's preprimary endorsement of Walter Mondale in 1984 helped him overcome Gary Hart's unexpected early primary victories.

These changes in the composition of the convention were recognized in the 1950s, long before the proliferation of the primaries (Carleton 1957; David, Goldman, and Bain 1960). William Carleton wrote in 1957 that "it is probable that by 1976 or 1980 all that a nominating convention will do will be to meet to ratify the nomination for president of *the* national favorite already determined by the agencies, formal and informal, of mass democracy; to ratify the nomination for vice-president of the second leading national favorite; to endorse a platform already written by leaders responding to national and group pressures; and to stage a rally for the benefit of the national television audience" (Carleton 1957, 237).

As state party leaders lost their role at the national convention, state legislatures started to play a more active role by passing new presidential primary laws. Part of the reason for the growth in primaries was the new rules instituted by the McGovern-Fraser Commission, but many other reasons were local in origin. For example, nine states considered switching to primaries before the McGovern-Fraser Commission held its first session (Bode and Casey 1980). Some states instituted primaries to insulate local politics from national politics. These state party leaders, fearing new national rules for local caucuses would make their meetings vulnerable to being overrun by small groups of ideologues, switched to presidential primaries to select convention delegates. With primaries being used to select national convention delegates, local party meetings and state conventions could continue to use their traditional rules (Ranney 1978). Other states switched to presidential primaries to bolster the fortunes of particular candidates. Both Texas and North Carolina adopted primaries in 1976 to aid the short-lived candidacies of Lloyd Bentsen and Terry Sanford. Georgia's switch to aid Jimmy Carter's candidacy proved more fruitful (Bode and Casey 1980). Other states switched to primaries, hoping to reap a financial gain. These states enviously watched New Hampshire receiving free media exposure year after year for its winter sports industry as network cameras focused on candidates tromping through New Hampshire's snow.

The goals of state party leaders often appear more tangible than those of the national reformers. State party leaders want to make candidates and media pay attention to their state, they want to help out favorite sons, or they want to comply with national rules with as few changes as possible. These same types of goals generated support for a regional primary in the South. Southern party leaders felt the media overlooked the South for New Hampshire's primary and Iowa's caucus. They felt the existing system hampered southern and conservative candidates. Yet the success of a southern regional primary would be affected by the remaining three forces shaping presidential nomination practices: media, technology, and candidate strategies.

MEDIA

The media contributed to the proliferation of primaries, the front-loading of the primary season, and the decline of national conventions. Yet ascribing all these changes solely to media effects would be as incorrect as ascribing all recent changes to the 1968 election, which begat the Democratic reform commissions of the 1970s. The media do give considerable coverage to presidential primaries and, except for Iowa, ignore caucuses. This attention led the public to view primaries as more legitimate than caucuses (Rubin 1981, 192). Media coverage also provided states with tangible reasons for switching from caucuses to primaries. Media coverage gives states free publicity, and media crews' daily expenditures add to a state's economy (Pomper 1979; Rice and Kenney 1984; Robinson 1980).

Besides adding to the proliferation of primaries, media coverage made primary campaigns feasible for potential presidential candidates. Media coverage turns state elections designed solely to select convention delegates into national events with the potential to affect public opinion. The influence of the media on the primaries, however, did not start after 1968 or even 1960. Harold Stassen ran the first media campaign in his quest for the 1948 Republican nomination. He was followed in 1952 by Democrat Estes Kefauver, who sought to capitalize on the name he had made for himself with the first televised Senate investigation, the 1950-51 investigation into organized crime (Beninger 1977; Davis 1967). Yet each of these candidates, despite the media coverage of their victories in the primaries, lost the nomination at the national convention. Primary campaigns and media coverage would not combine to a successful nomination strategy until the number of primaries proliferated and national conventions became weaker.

Media coverage of the national conventions, however, contributed to their decline (Robinson 1977). The 1988 Democratic and Republican conventions became well-staged media events with important speeches scheduled for prime time. Podiums, backdrops, posters, and "spontaneous" demonstrations of support for candidates were designed for maximum impact. Party unity rang out as the central theme of both conventions.

Important political decisions were no longer made on the floor of the convention. Conflict and division spoil the party's image, hurting its chances of victory in the fall. Media coverage alone did not reduce national conventions to free political advertisements, but it surely added to this trend.

By the 1980s, two additional transformations occurred in the media's coverage of presidential campaigns. First, television networks preempted newspapers in establishing the dominant themes of the media's coverage. In the 1960s and 1970s, network television regurgitated analyses of the major newspapers. In the 1980s, network news programs presented their own interpretations of primary results. The second transformation entailed the increasing number of journalists covering presidential campaigns. Thanks to satellite technology, local stations joined the networks in covering presidential candidates. Additional print journalists also swelled the ranks of the media entourage. The increased size of the press corps made relations between candidates and journalists more formal. Younger reporters, schooled on Watergate and other recent scandals, became more critical of candidates, viewing candidates' personalities and personal lives as legitimate campaign issues (Germond and Witcover 1989, 54-60).

TECHNOLOGY

Technological changes contributed to a reduced role for conventions and an increased importance for primaries. Perhaps the most significant technological change was the introduction of reliable public opinion polls in the 1930s. These polls indicated public preference for the nomination. Prior to this time, convention delegates could not be certain who was the most popular candidate and relied on a series of roll call votes to determine candidate support.[9] After the introduction of public opinion polls, conventions became more constrained in their choices. Conventions held between 1936 and 1968 nominated the candidate favored in the public opinion polls in all cases except in 1952, when the Democratic convention nominated Stevenson over Kefauver, who led in the public opinion polls (Keech and Matthews 1976, 215).[10] In thirteen out of the eighteen nominations, the winning candidate led the public opinion polls for up to three years. Obviously, nomination campaigns and primaries played no role in these nominations. In three of the remaining five nominations in which the candidates did not lead public opinion polls for three years prior to the convention (i.e., Wilkie in 1940, Stevenson in 1952, Humphrey in 1968), the candidates also did not win the nomination through primaries because they did not enter any primary (Beninger 1976). Thus, public opinion polls had an earlier and more effective influence on national nominating conventions than presidential primaries had.

Since 1972, primary results have affected polls standings. In 1972 only 3 percent of Democrats preferred George McGovern as their presidential candidate at the beginning of the primary season. An unexpectedly strong showing by McGovern in the New Hampshire primary led to a series of primary victories. Although the battle remained intense among McGovern, Wallace, Humphrey, and the undeclared candidacy of Edward Kennedy, by June, McGovern became the plurality favorite of Democrats (Gallup 1978). More dramatic effects occurred in later years. Before Iowa in 1984, Hart was recognized by only 5 percent of the public; eight days later, after his victory in New Hampshire, 50 percent knew of Hart (Beckel 1987). Similarly in 1988, winning candidates became more widely recognized. In 1987 less than 15 percent of Democrats preferred Dukakis, and over half of the remaining Democrats did not even recognize Dukakis's name. By April of 1988, two out of three Democrats preferred Dukakis as their party's presidential nominee (Gallup Poll, March 1988).

Pollsters in the 1980s formed an intricate part of each candidate's campaign staff. Louis Harris in Kennedy's 1960 campaign became the first pollster to be a key adviser to a candidate. Harris advised altering Kennedy's appearance when polls found the public viewed Kennedy as too youthful to be president. Kennedy subsequently changed his haircut and dressed in more conservative clothing (Bloom 1973). Patrick Cadell, Jimmy Carter's pollster in 1976, was not only a close adviser during the campaign but went on to play the same role in the White House. In 1988, polling was central to most candidates' campaigns. Bush's pollsters conducted three hundred interviews a night for a three-week period prior to Super Tuesday. Additionally, new marketing advances were incorporated. Pulse dials, small hand-held boxes on which participants pressed dials indicating their reactions, and focus groups, small numbers of individuals gathered to discuss their reactions, were both used to evaluate candidates' advertisements and debate performances (Hagstrom and Guskind, July 30, 1988).

Videocassette technology became the latest tool in presidential campaign strategy. By 1988, eleven of the thirteen major candidates produced videotapes, ranging in length from eight minutes (Kemp) to fifty-four (Robertson). Sometimes tapes were mailed directly to voters. Before the New Hampshire primary, Babbitt sent tapes to 450 uncommitted Democratic activists, and Robertson mailed tapes to every registered Republican. More often, tapes were played at video parties, where activists invited friends to their homes to persuade them to vote for and contribute money to a candidate (Luntz 1988). Videocassette technology even played a role in the demise of a candidate. The Dukakis campaign leaked to the press a videocassette containing footage of Joe Biden and British Labour Party leader Neil Kinnock giving the same speech. This visual evidence of plagiarism forced Biden to withdraw from the Democratic race before the first primary.

Cable television and satellite hookups also played a role in the 1988 campaign. Robertson initiated his campaign for the presidency with a request for signed pledge cards beamed to more than two hundred rental halls (Clendinen, September 13, 1986). More than three million conservatives responded positively (Jacoby, McCormick, Smith, and Warner, January 4, 1988). Robertson gained familiarity with satellite and cable television technology as the founder of CBN (Christian Broadcasting Network), the third largest cable network. Gore also recognized the usefulness of cable television. For Super Tuesday, a national spot on cable television cost less than buying time on a series of local stations.

Technology has changed presidential campaigning. Even such basic modern amenities as air travel shaped the 1988 campaign. With sixteen states to cover on Super Tuesday, candidates adopted "tarmac" campaigning. Candidates jetted across the South, stopping at several airports a day, rarely venturing beyond the runway tarmac. Robertson mastered this technique when on one day he visited eight cities in six different states (Feeney, March 1, 1988). Video technology beamed runway speeches to local television news studios. Without polls, planes, and satellites, candidates would not have been able to tackle the Super Tuesday campaign. But these technological devices allowed candidates to avoid grass-roots campaigning, in which they would have to come into personal contact with southern voters.

CANDIDATE STRATEGIES

Candidates adapted to and at times changed presidential nomination practices. Throughout the first half of the twentieth century, leading politicians played an "insider" strategy. These candidates courted the support of state and local party leaders who controlled blocs of convention delegates and had access to major financial contributors. Candidates pursuing an insider strategy often avoided primaries, especially if an opponent or favorite son hailed from that state. Insider candidates preferred to gain nominations through less contentious means, courting party and interest group leaders. Hubert Humphrey in 1968 became the last candidate to win a major party nomination using the insider strategy. Nevertheless, speculation mounted among journalists in early 1988 that Mario Cuomo or Sam Nunn might accept a convention draft, after a divisive Super Tuesday left the Democratic party with no apparent nominee.

By 1988, all candidates adopted what in the 1940s and 1950s had been called the "outsider strategy." This strategy, employed by long-shot candidates in earlier years, entailed running in primaries to demonstrate public support. Harold Stassen in 1948, Estes Kefauver in 1952, and John Kennedy in 1960 employed the outsider strategy of running in primaries, traveling the country, and using demonstrations of public popularity to gain support from party elites. The outsider strategy, however, was precarious. One primary loss doomed a campaign. Thus long-shot candidates in earlier years carefully selected primaries in which to compete, leaving many primaries without meaningful choices.

Neither the insider strategy of avoiding the primaries nor the pick-and-choose option of the outsider strategy were viable tactics by the 1980s. The proliferation of presidential primaries required candidates to compete in all of them. Few uncommitted delegates remained for candidates to court at the conventions. Even well-known candidates, such as Bush, competed in primaries in order to win committed delegates, while unknown candidates hoped primary victories would bring the media attention necessary to gain national recognition.

Leading candidates often attempt to alter rules in order to favor their campaigns. In 1980, Jimmy Carter convinced Georgia, Alabama, and Florida to hold early primaries. Carter feared early victories by Edward Kennedy in New Hampshire and Massachusetts would cast him as a loser. A set of early primaries in Carter's native South would counterbalance Kennedy's New England victories. Carter also persuaded the Winograd Commission to establish a window for Democratic primaries. This window limiting the dates of Democratic primaries to a short period of time should advantage an incumbent president running for renomination. Carter did not need time to build up his name recognition or gather money. More time could only help his opponents. In anticipation of the 1984 race, Mondale and Kennedy supporters on the Hunt Commission altered Democratic rules to their advantage. As leading national figures, both potential candidates preferred rules that advantaged front-runners in a state, such as loophole primaries and bonus proportional representation systems. The early selection of Super Delegates—national, state and local party and elected officials—would help Mondale maintain an early delegate lead over Hart in 1984.

The Fairness Commission, which established rules for 1988 Democratic primaries, was less affected by leading presidential candidates. Despite Jackson's and Hart's wishes for a reduced role for Super Delegates, the commission increased the number of these automatic delegate slots. Selection of these delegates, however, was delayed until later in the primary season. Minimum threshold votes necessary before candidates would be awarded delegates under proportional representation were lowered to 15 percent but not eliminated as Jackson had hoped (Lengle 1987).

The 1988 candidate most advantaged by the rules was George Bush. With South Carolina's primary three days prior to Super Tuesday, a Bush victory would give his campaign a boost right before the big event. Bush's strength in South Carolina was aided by his southern chairperson, South

Carolina's Governor Carroll A. Campbell, Jr., and his chief political strategist, Lee Atwater, who hailed from South Carolina. Bush's "hidden"
strength in South Carolina surprised both the national press and his rivals
seeking the conservative southern vote, such as Kemp and Robertson.

We have now seen how five forces combined to shape the presidential
nomination system of the 1980s. National reformers and state politicians
altered legal structures, hoping to fulfill goals as diverse as increased
fairness to advantaging specific candidates. Despite these national and state
officials being seasoned and astute politicians, their rule changes often did
not produce the expected results. Unexpected consequences emerged because other factors also shaped the nomination process. National media
coverage gave more clout to states holding primaries than those holding
caucuses and to New Hampshire rather than California. Candidates adjusted
their strategies to new written (legal) and unwritten (media) rules. Some
candidates even attempted to alter the rules to their own advantage. Finally,
technological advances facilitated modern mass-based campaigning, as
candidates employed airwaves and airplanes to reach the increasing numbers
of average Americans participating in presidential nomination politics.

BIASES IN THE 1980s NOMINATION SYSTEM

By the early 1980s, a thoroughly established system of sequential, state-by-
state primaries characterized the presidential nomination process. Candidates hopscotched across the nation to compete in each week's primaries.
Large numbers of candidates began the quest for the presidency, but many
were soon eliminated from the field. Others, buoyed by early victories,
captured momentum, leading to more victories. But as is true of all systems
of rules, the 1980s nomination process contained biases that displeased
reformers, candidates, and southern politicians.

Some of the biases arose from the sequential nature of the primaries and
the media's reaction to these primaries. New Hampshire and Iowa, both of
which chose less than 1 percent of the convention delegates, each appeared
to have the most influence on nominations because they held their primary
and caucus first. Voters in these two states selected among all the initial
candidates, and their decisions determined which candidates were winnowed out and which attained momentum. Extensive media coverage of
these first two contests exaggerated these effects. In 1980, 28 percent of all
primary stories focused on the New Hampshire primary or Iowa caucuses.
Southern states received approximately 11 percent of the primary coverage
on the "CBS Evening News" and 14 percent of news space in UPI reports
(Robinson and Sheehan 1983).

Besides dominating the media coverage, Iowa and New Hampshire seemed to have undue influence by causing some candidates to drop out of the race. Poor showings in these first two events caused many recent candidates to drop out of the race shortly after the New Hampshire primary. Included among this list are Birch Bayh in the 1976 Democratic race; Howard Baker and John Connally in the 1980 Republican race; and Reuben Askew, Alan Cranston, and Fritz Hollings in the 1984 Democratic contest. Other candidates greatly weakened by Iowa's and New Hampshire's results include Democrat Fred Harris in 1976, Republicans Robert Dole and Phil Crane in 1980, and Democrats George McGovern and John Glenn in 1984. Southern Democratic leaders in particular bemoaned the early demise of Glenn's campaign.

Meanwhile, victories in early primary and caucus states provided other candidates with momentum. But if these early victories came in small, unrepresentative states, candidates gaining the momentum advantage may not adequately reflect the preferences of every faction of the party. Alternatively, a candidate with momentum can rise in popularity and accumulate large chunks of delegates before the public becomes aware of his stands on the issues. In 1984, Gary Hart captured momentum by beating Mondale in the New Hampshire primary. His popularity soared, and he became Mondale's main competitor. But few people knew much about Hart or his "new ideas."

To capture more of the media's attention and assure themselves of a greater impact on nomination outcomes, many states moved the dates of their primaries forward, causing the system to become front-loaded. With more and more primaries being held earlier and earlier, two possible scenarios can arise. First, only candidates with huge campaign chests could afford to compete in a large number of almost simultaneous primaries. Second, a candidate who caught fire in Iowa or New Hampshire would ride momentum to quick victories in a number of primaries before voters had the time to contemplate the character and positions of the advantaged candidate (Bartels 1988, 262, 278-81).

The beginning of the race for the nomination kept creeping earlier and earlier, perhaps dissuading some potentially excellent candidates from running. Polsby and Wildavsky (1976, 222) assert the system restricted presidential candidacies to "wealthy athletes"—those individuals with the stamina and economic resources to spend two to three years on the road. Walter Mondale withdrew from the 1976 presidential race in 1974, saying he could not face another year of "sleeping in Holiday Inns" (Witcover 1978, 136).

Southern Democrats felt particularly displeased with the 1980s nomination process. More conservative candidates, such as Glenn in 1984, who might do well in the South were either eliminated from the field or badly scarred by losses in earlier primary states. Candidates continued to campaign more intensely in Iowa and New Hampshire than in the southern states, suggesting to southerners that these candidates ignored southern issues. As a result, the eventual Democratic nominee fared extremely poorly in the South during the fall presidential campaign. In 1984, Walter Mondale averaged only 38 percent of the vote in southern states, once the bedrock of Democratic support.

REGIONAL PRIMARY REFORMS

Southerners did not compose the sole group displeased with the biases contained in the sequential system of state primaries. At the national level two plans to fundamentally overhaul the system have been offered. The most dramatic, a one-day national primary, eliminates national conventions from the nomination process. Whichever candidate wins a majority of the votes in the national primary automatically becomes the party's nominee for president.[11] Representative Richmond P. Hobson (D-Ala.) introduced the first national primary bill in 1911 (Ranney 1978). The Progressive platform of 1912 called for a national primary, and Woodrow Wilson endorsed the idea in a message to Congress in 1913. Between 1911 and the 1980s, over one hundred bills were introduced, including five in 1977 (Ranney 1978). Douglas Applegate (D-Ohio) introduced two recent versions in the 100th and 101st Congresses (H2784 on June 25, 1987, H434 on January 4, 1989).

The second reform breaks the country into several regions with all states in a region scheduling their presidential primaries for the same date. Robert Packwood (R-Oreg.) introduced the first regional primary bill into Congress in 1972. His plan divided the nation into five regions. Sequential ordering of regions would be determined by lot, with announcements of primary dates withheld until seventy days before the actual election. A federal commission would determine which candidates appeared on the ballots, with a petition procedure available for excluded candidates. Proportional representation rules, with a minimum required vote of 5 percent, would be used to allocate delegates. Since Packwood's original bill, twenty-eight additional bills have been introduced. (See table 1.2 for a complete listing.) None have passed either house of Congress. Other unsuccessful suggestions call for the clustering of primaries by time zones (Davis 1983) or on a limited number of dates without states' date selections being dictated by region.[12]

In general, national proposals for regional primaries are quite similar. All break the country into four to six regions. All determine the ordering of regions by lot or rotation. Some plans require all states to hold primaries, while others only require states that do choose to conduct primaries to hold them on a specific date. Some proposals create a greater role for the federal government either in determining the candidates or financing the election

Table 1.2: National Legislation to Create a Regional Presidential Primary System

Congress	Bill number	Sponsor	Date introduced
92nd	S3566	Packwood	May 2, 1972
93rd	S2391	Packwood	September 7, 1973
94th	S1831	Packwood	May 22, 1975
	S2741	Mondale	December 4, 1975
	H11417	Brademas	January 21, 1976
	H11971	Brademas	February 19, 1976
	H12161	Ottinger	February 26, 1976
95th	S1207	Packwood, Hatfield	March 31, 1977
	H8322	Ottinger	July 17, 1977
96th	S964	Packwood, Hatfield	April 10, 1979
	H4212	Ottinger	May 23, 1979
	H125	Bennett	June 15, 1979
	H7753	Swift	July 2, 1980
97th	H105	Bennett	January 5, 1981
	S1149	Packwood, Hatfield	May 8, 1981
	H3583	Swift, Prichard	May 13, 1981
	S1336	Quayle	June 4, 1981
	H3905	Ottinger	June 11, 1981
98th	H43	Bennett	January 3, 1983
	S1595	Quayle	July 11, 1983
	S1984	Packwood, Hatfield	October 20, 1983
99th	H251	Bennett	January 3, 1985
	H3542	Nelson	October 9, 1985
100th	H62	Bennett	January 6, 1987
	S1786	Dixon	October 14, 1987
	H4004	Nelson	February 24, 1988
	S2319	Packwood	April 25, 1988
101st	S377	Dixon, Breaux, Boren, Sanford, Packwood	February 8, 1989

Source: Gorman 1976 for 92nd Congress to 94th Congress. Remaining years compiled by Jim Moore for the author.

costs. With a regional primary system, national conventions still ultimately
select the nominee. National conventions might in fact become more important if each region were to support a different presidential contender.

Benefits of Regional Primaries

Advocates of regional primaries claim both candidates and voters would
benefit. Candidates could better utilize their time and money if they could
concentrate their campaigning within one region for an extended period of
time. Better candidates, such as leading senators and representatives, might
be convinced to run for the presidency if they knew they would not have to
hopscotch across the nation for two to three years in the attempt. Regional
primaries also would force candidates to address a broader audience
(Stevenson 1984). Important national issues would no longer be ignored, in
contrast to the current system in which politicians may focus on parochial
issues to win in each state.

Regional primaries would also prevent the biases introduced by the
current sequencing of the primaries. New Hampshire, a small, unrepresentative state, would no longer have such a great effect on the nomination
outcome. If New Hampshire no longer held the first primary, the media
would not give its primary the inordinate amount of coverage that magnifies
its influence. With larger regions and a rotation of those regions, no one state
or area of the country would continue to unduly influence the presidential
selection process year after year. Yet with regional primaries, a sequential
element would remain, thus allowing voters to see how candidates react over
time and to a variety of circumstances (Davis 1983; Mann 1985).

The American public favors regional primaries. A March 1988 Gallup
Poll found 51 percent approved of the concept.[13] The popularity of the idea,
the simplicity of the process, and the possibility of better candidates and of
candidates addressing important national issues would, advocates argue,
lead more people to participate. A larger primary electorate would be a more
representative electorate.

Criticisms of Regional Primaries

Critics of regional primaries, however, are not convinced by these argu-
ments and assert that regional primaries will introduce their own set of
biases. First, regional primaries do not guarantee more people will participate. Ranney (1978) rejects claims of increased participation because all
primaries tend to have turnout rates of one-half that of the general election.
With presidential election turnout rates of 50 percent, regional primaries
would have turnout rates around 25 percent, very similar to the current rate
in the state-by-state presidential primaries. Furthermore, other evidence does

not support the claim that primary voters in recent elections have been unrepresentative (see, for instance, Geer 1988 and Norrander 1989). Increasing the number of primary voters, therefore, would not increase their representativeness.

Regional primaries may make the media even more important (Davis 1983; Ranney 1978). Without a series of state primary results to indicate popular preferences, the media will use their own criteria in determining the newsworthiness of various candidates. Media coverage would continue to affect public awareness of the candidates. Additionally, the media in their quest to provide the first news of the primary season would no doubt give the same undue media coverage to the first region as they now give to Iowa and New Hampshire.

State and local parties could be hurt by regional primaries (Mann 1985; Ranney 1978). Regional primaries will further restrict states as to how they can select convention delegates. If regional primaries are mandatory, state parties will not be able to use the caucus system, which some feel strengthens local parties by bringing more people into party meetings. National parties or the federal government may feel the need to insist on proportional representation rules or rules counting second and third preferences, further restricting state parties' abilities to experiment with different rules. Also, smaller states may feel squeezed out by a regional primary. With only a few delegates at stake, candidates may ignore these states for the larger states in a region.

Regional primaries could hurt the national party by heightening regional tensions. With diverse regional interests and regional favorites among the candidates, no candidate may have a significant lead in committed delegates, resulting in brokered conventions. However, these brokered conventions would not have the uncommitted delegates and party leaders who worked out compromises in the past. Delegates would be firmly attached to candidates, leading to long stalemates followed by unpopular choices (Davis 1983). Rather than unifying the nation by giving each region an equal role in the nomination process, regional primaries might divide the party along regional lines.

The loss of the long state-by-state sequencing of primaries with a regional primary system would also have consequences. Rather than drawing in better candidates, such a system might restrict viable candidacies to individuals with already established reputations. Without a long series of primaries, unknown candidates would not be able to build up their public recognition by victories in small states. New Hampshire might not be the microcosm of the nation needed for representativeness, but it is a small enough state that unknown candidates on shoestring budgets can compete on a nearly equal footing with better-known candidates. By winning or doing well in Iowa and New Hampshire, several unknown candidates—Gary Hart,

George McGovern, George Bush, Jimmy Carter—have become leading contenders for the presidency. The long series of primaries also allows the public to learn about the candidates and how they react in various situations (Stanley and Hadley 1987).

Rather than restrict the length of presidential campaigns, regional primaries might actually lengthen the time candidates have to run for the presidency. With only a few events, candidates would need to build their campaign resources—money and public awareness—in the preprimary period Arthur Hadley (1976) called the "invisible primary." Candidates would have to schedule numerous dinners and cocktail parties where they could meet individuals capable of contributing $1,000 to their campaign. Frequent trips to the larger states would be necessary to build a national reputation among party activists. These fund-raising and reputation-building events would occur with less public scrutiny of candidates than they would if they occurred during the regular primary season.

Finally, regional primaries would not change the fact that presidential aspirants have different appeal in different regions of the country. Even though the first region may be determined by lot or rotation, candidates with appeal in that region will do better than candidates from other areas of the country. If in 1988 the first region had been the South, Gore and Jackson could have used successes there to help them win in midwestern states such as Iowa, and Dukakis would not have had his New Hampshire win to give him publicity in the South. If the first region had been the West, perhaps Bruce Babbitt could have gotten his candidacy off the ground. As long as candidates have home regions, regional primary sequencing will help and hurt different candidates.

Despite this mixture of praise and criticisms for regional primaries, all national attempts have failed for a more practical reason. As Morris Udall (D-Ariz.) explained the fate of his 1972 bill to cluster primaries, congressional cycles do not fit with cycles of interest in reform: "You'll see a flurry of proposals while the thing is going on. By next year it's 3½ years from the next election and people say, 'Let's worry about it later.' The impetus to get some thing done only occurs in a year when you can't do anything about it" (Presidential Primaries, July 8, 1972, 1654).

CREATING SUPER TUESDAY

The nation's first regional primary was created not by national regional primary advocates but by a group of state politicians more interested in power than reform. Yet southern states were not the first to attempt to establish a regional primary. New England states tried to put together a regional primary for 1976. Leaders from these states felt candidates ignored issues of importance to New England, such as energy costs (Doyle 1975). New Hampshire, however, would not give up its first-in-the-nation status; Connecticut failed to adopt a primary; and Vermont created only a beauty contest primary, one in which convention delegate selection was not tied to primary results (Ranney 1978). A western regional primary also was attempted for 1976. Leaders at the 1972 Pacific Rim Conference agreed to hold their primaries on a common date in 1976, but only Idaho, Nevada, and Oregon eventually agreed on that date (Doyle 1975; Ranney 1978). An earlier attempt at a southern regional primary also failed. Carter supporters only succeeded in creating a southeast regional primary in 1980 with Alabama, Georgia, and Florida holding primaries on the same date (Stanley and Hadley 1987).

While other attempts had been made to create full-blown regional primaries, Super Tuesday 1988 constitutes the only successful attempt. Super Tuesday advocates possessed the same desires as other state reformers. Each group wanted more attention for its region and regional issues. Super Tuesday's creators also wanted to help conservative or southern presidential candidates. The overwhelming defeat of the Mondale-Ferraro ticket in the South added to southerners' desires for more influence on the selection of the Democratic nominee. The key to the success of southern efforts to create a regional primary lay in regional organizations, especially the Southern Legislative Conference, being able to coordinate activities across the states.

The idea of a southern regional primary surfaced in the early 1970s. Jimmy Carter, as governor of Georgia, advocated a southern primary at the 1973 Southern Governors Conference (Stanley and Hadley 1987). By 1974, members of the Southern Legislative Conference, a group representing southern state legislatures, began discussing the regional primary concept (Southern Legislative Conference, February 7, 1986).[14] Florida instituted the first early southern primary when it moved its primary from May to March in 1972. Alabama and Georgia adopted Florida's early primary date in 1980 at the urging of then President Carter. In 1982, the Southern Legislative Conference called for a regional primary in 1984, but the movement came too late for most state legislatures to act. Instead, Massachusetts and Rhode Island joined Alabama, Florida, and Georgia in 1984 to create the first Super Tuesday. Two additional "super" Tuesdays occurred in 1984 with four states holding primaries on May 8 and five primaries scheduled for June 5.

The major movement toward a southern regional primary, however, came in 1986 and 1987 as eleven southern or border states moved their primary dates or adopted primaries for the first time to form Super Tuesday 1988. (See table 1.3.) The success of the southern effort rested on the shoulders of the Southern Legislative Conference (SLC) and its chair, Texas

Table 1.3: Creation of Super Tuesday

Part A: Super Tuesday States with March Presidential Primaries in Earlier Years

Year	State	Date of primary
1972	Florida	March 14
1976	Massachusetts	March 2
	Florida	March 9
1980	Massachusetts	March 4
	Alabama	March 11
	Florida	March 11
	Georgia	March 11
1984	Alabama	March 13
	Florida	March 13
	Georgia	March 13
	Massachusetts	March 13
	Rhode Island	March 13

Part B: Dates Southern States Joined Super Tuesday, 1988

State	Date enacted
Kentucky[a]	February 25, 1986
Oklahoma[b]	March 14, 1986
Missouri[b]	March 18, 1886
Tennessee	March 24, 1986
Mississippi[b]	April 16, 1986
Maryland	May 27, 1986
Louisiana	June 17, 1986
North Carolina	July 7, 1986
Texas[a]	October 15, 1986
Arkansas[a]	March 9, 1987
Virginia[b]	March 26, 1987

[a]state switching back to presidential primary after holding caucuses; Texas's switch is for Democrats only
[b]state's first presidential primary law
Source of enactment dates: Stanley and Hadley 1987, 89.

State Senator John Traeger. In September 1985, the SLC established the Regional Primary/Caucus Task Force to work with state legislatures in passing presidential primary bills. The Southern Governors Association signed on to the idea at their September 1985 meeting. The Democratic Leadership Council, a group of over seventy southern and western governors and members of Congress, also advocated regional primaries in hopes that Super Tuesday would lead to the nomination of more moderate Democratic candidates.[15]

The growth of Super Tuesday developed mainly as a result of the SLC's

Regional Primary/Caucus Task force members working with state legislatures to pass the necessary bills. With each new bill, the Southern Legislative Conference issued a press release. Coordination and publicity kept the
movement on track, until all southern states except South Carolina agreed to
hold their primary on March 8, 1988. South Carolina Republicans scheduled their primary for March 5, three days prior to Super Tuesday. South
Carolina Democrats continued their tradition of holding caucuses, with the
first round set for March 12.

While the goals of national regional primary advocates centered on
democratizing and rationalizing the nomination process, the goals of state
regional primary advocates and Super Tuesday's creators centered on power
and influence. According to the Southern Legislative Conference, Super
Tuesday was created:

—To strengthen the region's impact in the nominating process of both parties;
—To assure that issues of interest to the South play a major role in the presidential
   campaigns of the future;
—To simplify the presidential nominating process and to encourage greater par-
   ticipation by southern voters, and;
—To assure that candidates for president are forced to take the South seriously and
   campaign early and frequently in the southern states. [Southern Legislative
   Conference, January 27, 1986]

By holding Super Tuesday early in the primary season, southerners
hoped to diminish the influence of Iowa and New Hampshire on presidential
nominations. While Iowa and New Hampshire selected 2 percent of convention delegates, a fourteen-state regional primary would select over a quarter
of all delegates. Candidates could not overlook the large pool of delegates
available on Super Tuesday. In order to win these delegates, candidates
would have to focus on southern issues such as textiles, farming, and energy.
As the regional primary process and the importance of Super Tuesday
became clearer to voters, and as candidates paid more and more attention to
the South, more southerners would vote.

While the Southern Legislative Conference's participation was officially nonpartisan, many of the most ardent regional primary advocates
were Democrats. After all, Republicans hardly had any complaints about a
process that nominated presidential candidates who captured the bulk of the
southern votes over the last two decades. In contrast, Democratic supporters
of Super Tuesday wanted a different kind of presidential nominee. They
wanted a nominee who was not a northern liberal. Even a moderate Democrat would do, if a southerner such as Sam Nunn chose not to run. To
influence the Democratic party to choose such a nominee, Super Tuesday
would have to be held early, before moderate and conservative candidates

were knocked out of the race by losses in northern primaries. In 1984, John Glenn, whom many southern leaders supported, was so wounded by losses in Iowa (5 percent of the vote) and New Hampshire (12 percent) that he could only limp into the Alabama, Florida, and Georgia primaries before officially calling it quits. Southern Democrats also hoped that added attention from candidates and the media would stir voter interest in the primaries. As more "mainstream" Democrats participated, the electoral fortunes of moderate and conservative candidates would rise. Super Tuesday, southern leaders hoped, would lead to the nomination of a Democratic candidate capable of carrying the South in the subsequent presidential election.

Enthusiasm swelled for Super Tuesday. Statements of support employed rhetoric couched in a Civil War theme (Stanley and Hadley 1987). "You can go back home and gather up your Confederate money, 'cause the South is going to rise again!" averred Mississippi State Senator Bill Harpole (Treadwell, April 19, 1986,4). "We will nominate the next president of the United States," declared Thomas Murphy, Speaker of Georgia's House of Representatives (Carlson, December 17, 1985,35). Even some national commentators lent their support. Tom Wicker, writing in the *New York Times,* saw the South as providing a good example to other areas of the country on how to develop a nationwide system of regional primaries (Wicker, September 16, 1985).

While Super Tuesday was the child of the Democratic party in the South, Republicans were not necessarily displeased. They speculated that Super Tuesday would backfire on the Democratic party. Noting that white southerners had been voting for Republican presidential candidates in the general election, southern Republicans hoped that these voters would fall further into the Republican camp through participation in Republican presidential primaries. To persuade southern Democrats to vote in Republican primaries, Republican leaders tried to paint the Democratic primary as the liberal primary and the Republican primary as the conservative primary. Republican leaders created the Southern Republican Primary Project, headed by Haley Barbour of Mississippi, to spread this message. These leaders hoped for their best results in the eight southern states holding open primaries, in which anyone can vote in either party's primary. In closed primary states, where party registration dictates in which primary a person can vote, Republican leaders hoped to reregister wavering Democrats as Republicans. Not only did Republicans feel that they could win the 1988 battle for the presidency, they thought that by drawing Democrats into their presidential primaries they could lay down a base of support for future elections, at both the national and state levels (Stanley and Hadley 1987). If the Republicans succeeded in drawing off conservative white Democrats into their party's primaries, the Democratic Super Tuesday electorate would be composed of blacks and liberal whites. These groups, the Republicans speculated, would only support the type of candidate who could not win in the South. Such an electorate might nominate Jesse Jackson.

Both political commentators and political scientists expressed skepticism about the Democratic plans. Stanley and Hadley (1987) speculated the importance of Iowa and New Hampshire would increase, not decrease. The large number of states holding primaries on Super Tuesday would require a large campaign chest or considerable free publicity. Free publicity would go to the winners of New Hampshire and Iowa. Losers would not have time to recover. A southern candidate might not fare well in these northern states, but to avoid them would cast doubts on whether he was a truly national candidate.

Stuart Eizenstat, President Carter's chief domestic policy adviser, expressed concerns over the composition of the Super Tuesday electorate. Describing the 1984 Democratic party electorate as composed of white liberal activists and blacks, he saw no reason for that to change in 1988, unless all southern states scheduled their state and local primaries on the same date as their presidential primaries. Traditional interest in these latter contest among more conservative Democrats would bring them to the polls (Eizenstat, March 5, 1988). But instead of most states scheduling presidential and congressional primaries jointly, only five states did so, and two southern states, in fact, separated their previously jointly held primaries as they moved their presidential primaries to Super Tuesday. Don Fowler, South Carolina's Democratic National Committee member, also agreed with Eizenstat's appraisal of the Democratic electorate. He averred Super Tuesday advocates were "psychologically in another era" and had missed the changing composition of the party in the South (Ingwerson, March 28, 1986,3). Republicans might be correct in their predictions of liberals and blacks voting in the Democratic primaries even without drawing Reagan Democrats into their primaries.

Predictions of victory for more conservative candidates might be in error even if the electorate is composed of more moderate voters. Merle Black, a noted political scientist specializing in southern politics, pointed out that a number of moderate candidates could split the vote, leaving a liberal candidate as the plurality winner (Ingwerson, March 28, 1986). Super Tuesday's planners apparently forgot that Georgia's and Alabama's primaries rescued Mondale's candidacy in 1984, after Gary Hart captured momentum with his New Hampshire victory. Southern states moved the 1984 nomination toward a liberal northerner!

The breadth of Super Tuesday could dilute its effects. Super Tuesday's advocates hoped it would force candidates to address southern issues. But southerners do not agree on all issues. Those involved in textile manufacturing in the Carolinas favored protectionist legislation, but southern farmers feared retaliations against such legislation by other countries would make their products more difficult to sell abroad (Gailey, April 8, 1986). The South contains a core of traditional conservative voters, but it also contains liberal voters centered in high-tech industries around the Research Triangle in North Carolina and Austin, Texas, and in enclaves of northern retirees in Florida. Diversity, rather than uniformity, characterizes the modern South.

The hopes of the southern creators of Super Tuesday might also be dashed because Super Tuesday became more than a southern regional primary. Six nonsouthern states would choose delegates on Super Tuesday. Massachusetts and Rhode Island would hold primaries. Democrats in four western states and American Samoa would hold their caucuses, while Washington Republicans also scheduled caucuses for March 8. (Republicans in the other three states held their caucuses on a different date than did the Democrats.) With the addition of these nonsouthern states, candidates might not be forced to address southern issues. Issue positions might even clash among the regions. For instance, the South is a producer of energy while New England is a consumer of energy. These different roles lead to different positions on energy matters. Candidates who appealed to voters in nonsouthern states on March 8 would benefit in the media scorecard of Super Tuesday winners, diluting the impact of southern votes.

Others felt that, regardless of what benefits it had in the South, Super Tuesday would harm the presidential nomination system. Super Tuesday's early date would contribute to the front-loading of the primary season. If other states countered by moving their primary dates forward, the U.S. would end up with a de facto national primary. Candidates would win the nomination before voters had any real chance to know them. Money would become paramount. Only candidates who raised significant sums of money before the election year began could compete in Super Tuesday and all the other early primaries (Hyping Hyper Tuesday, March 28, 1986).

SUMMARY

Southerners gambled on Super Tuesday. Dissatisfied with the presidential nomination process of the 1980s, southern legislatures adopted new primary laws or established new dates for existing primaries to make March 8, 1988, the nation's first regional primary. With a fourteen-state extravaganza, southern leaders hoped to give the South more clout in presidential nominations, forcing candidates to campaign in the South and giving southerners more choices and more inclination to participate. Democratic leaders hoped Super Tuesday would result in the nomination of a more conservative Democrat. If Super Tuesday produced less than desired results, it would not be the first time in history that astute politicians were surprised by the results of their reforms. After all, these politicians could only change one of numerous factors that shape our presidential nomination system.

Super Tuesday was an experiment. While enthusiastic claims were made by some, others recognized the risk. Mr. Lodge, whose statement about the South being bitten by the old dog began this chapter, recognized that "nothing is without risk and our friends in the Washington political community are happy to tell us why it's a bad idea. But it can't be any worse than now, and if this doesn't work, we'll change it again" (Gailey, March 8, 1986, 9). Super Tuesday reflected the experimental nature of previous reforms. Problems in the presidential nomination system were cited, solutions were proposed, and subsequent politicians, journalists, and scholars were left to question the intended and unintended consequences of the reforms.

2

The Structure of the 1988 Campaign

Who won the 1988 Democratic nomination depended on who played the nomination game and how their actions fit the shape of the playing field. The architects of Super Tuesday hoped to change both the playing field and the players. They hoped to change the playing field so that the South would have more clout. They hoped the new set of players would include southern, or at least more moderate, candidates. Of course, Republican leaders had different expectations for Super Tuesday. Still, the structure of their playing field and who became their players also would determine who won the Republican nomination. In this chapter we will explore these expectations by examining how Super Tuesday affected the playing fields and the players in 1988.

STRUCTURING THE PLAYING FIELD

The Election Calendar

With convention delegates selected state by state over a six-month period, the election calendar influences candidate strategies and election outcomes. Candidates must begin their campaigns in Iowa and New Hampshire, where the first contests are held, even though a western candidate, such as former Arizona Governor Bruce Babbitt, might prefer to demonstrate his strength in his own area of the country first. Furthermore, because Iowa and New Hampshire are first, candidates often spend disproportionate amounts of time and effort in these two states, beginning as early as two to three years before the election. Once the campaign year begins, candidates rarely have the luxury of campaigning extensively in any one state. Rather, candidates crisscross the nation: a few days in Illinois followed by a trip to Michigan, then off to Wisconsin and back east to New York.

The election calendar also affects the election outcome. Victories in early primaries or caucuses may lead to momentum, that increase in publicity, name recognition, and campaign contributions that facilitates subsequent primary victories. For example, two weeks before the 1976 Florida primary, Ford edged out Reagan in the New Hampshire primary. Surveys conducted by Richard Wirthlin, Reagan's pollster, indicated that the New Hampshire victory turned Ford's early three-point margin in Florida into a seventeen-point margin by election day (Bartels 1988, 216-17). On the Democratic side in 1976, Carter's nomination would never have materialized if all primaries had been held on the same day, such as in a national primary. Carter would even have lost most of the southern primaries, as he would not have had victories in Iowa and New Hampshire to support his claim that he was more electable than fellow southerner George Wallace (Bartels 1988, 201-202).

The election calendar, with some states holding their primaries and caucuses earlier than others, also affects results by eliminating some candidates from the competition before many states select their delegates. As noted in Chapter 1, Reubin Askew, Alan Cranston, and Fritz Hollings left the 1984 Democratic race after the New Hampshire primary, while John Glenn's poor showing left him limping into the March 13 southern primaries. Failing to regain credibility with dismal performances in these states, Glenn soon withdrew from the nomination race, as did McGovern. After six primaries, but with eighteen still to go, the candidate field narrowed to three: Hart, Mondale, and Jackson. As the election calendar influences candidate survivability, it ultimately affects the nomination outcome.

Over the past twenty years, each new nomination contest has brought a restructured election calendar as more and more states adopt presidential primaries or move the dates of their primaries, mostly to earlier points in the nomination season. States undertook these actions in hopes of attaining more clout in the nomination process. The movement to earlier dates sprang from envy aroused by the excessive attention paid to Iowa and New Hampshire by both candidates and the media. For example, in 1980 the Iowa caucus and New Hampshire primary received over one-fourth of all media coverage for the entire nomination season, despite the fact that these two states selected only 2 percent of convention delegates (Robinson and Sheehan 1983). In preparation for the 1984 campaign, candidates spent 283 days in Iowa (Winebrenner 1987). Politicians from many states, not just southern states, attempted to encroach on Iowa's and New Hampshire's territory by selecting earlier primary or caucus dates.

Since 1980, national Democratic party rules have restricted the movement of caucus and primary dates by imposing a "window" on delegate selection dates.[1] For 1988, all delegates to the Democratic national convention were to be chosen between the second Tuesday in March and the second Tuesday in June, with exceptions granted for Iowa, New Hampshire, Maine, and Wyoming (Lengle 1987). Against national party wishes, Minnesota and South Dakota rescheduled their 1988 delegate selection events outside the window. The national party, in return, required that South Dakota's primary results be ratified by participants at a March 12 caucus and that official results from Minnesota's caucus not be released until March 8.[2] The Republican party does not impose a window on delegate selection, leading to a wider variety of dates. Michigan's January 14 county conventions constituted the opening round in 1988, but the initial selection of delegates to these conventions began in August 1986.[3]

By scheduling Super Tuesday at the beginning of the Democratic window, southern Democrats expected to provide the South with maximum impact on the nomination process and to guarantee that a larger number of candidates would contest their primaries. By doing so, however, Super Tuesday contributed to the "front-loading" of the delegate selection process. With the front-loading of the election calendar, more and more convention delegates are being chosen earlier and earlier in the nomination season. Table 2.1 demonstrates the front-loading of the presidential nomination process from 1976 to 1988.[4] Back in 1976, the selection process had begun for only 17 percent of Democratic delegates by the middle of March, and only 15 percent of Republican delegates had been available for selection. The percentage of delegates chosen early inched upward in 1980 and 1984, with most of the increase coming in the late March period. Super Tuesday in 1988, however, caused an explosion in early delegate selection, with the designation of over 50 percent of convention delegates being initiated by the second week in March.

The front-loading of the delegate selection process may forebode negative consequences. For the public, front-loading may not allow sufficient time to become aware of all aspects of the candidates before most of the delegate are selected. A candidate with an early victory might ride the momentum bandwagon long enough to capture a significant chunk of delegates before the nation has had time to consider seriously his or her merits. Other candidates may be eliminated from the race at a faster pace before they have had the opportunity to demonstrate their merits before a wider audience.

Front-loading taxes all candidates' resources, though front-runners are assumed to have an advantage over lesser-known candidates. With the front-loading of the 1988 nomination calendar, candidates needed at least $5 million on January 1 to be able to compete in Iowa, New Hampshire, and the South. With only three weeks between New Hampshire and Super Tuesday, candidates could not wait until after New Hampshire to lay the groundwork

Table 2.1: Front-Loading of the Nomination Calendar, 1976-1988, Indicated by the Cumulative Percent of Delegates for States That Have Begun Their Selection Process by the End of Each Period Given

| | % Democrat | | | | % Republican | | |
	1976	1980	1984	1988	1976	1980	1988
January-February	8	5	2	6	7	9	14
March 1-15	17	22	19	51	15	20	56
March 16-31	25	39	42	57	25	34	58
April	50	59	62	76	45	50	75
May	80	79	86	87	82	78	87
June	100	100	100	100	100	100	100

Note: 1984 and 1988 figures exclude Super Delegates.

for their Super Tuesday campaigns. Yet not all of the 1988 candidates possessed sufficient funds to campaign in the South without an earlier campaign victory to spark increased donations. Thus, better-financed and better-known candidates would be advantaged by the front-loaded 1988 nomination calendar.

The 1988 Calendar

The 1988 presidential nomination calendar can be divided into five segments: the Big Two Openers, the Lesser Antilles, Super Tuesday, the Big State Showdowns, and the Finale. In 1988, three Republican contests preceded the traditional Big Two Openers in Iowa and New Hampshire. The Michigan county conventions on January 14 and the Hawaii caucuses on February 4 both resulted in intensive battles between Robertson, Kemp, and Bush forces, augmented by confusing rules.[5] Kansas also held local Republican caucuses during the first week in February, but with native son Dole as a candidate, most of the other candidates ignored this event. None of the three early events overshadowed the Big Two. Once again, Iowa and New Hampshire received extraordinary attention from the media and candidates, as we will see in later chapters.

Between the Big Two and Super Tuesday fell a half dozen caucuses or primaries in small midwestern, eastern, or Rocky Mountain states. Democratic consultant Peter Hart nicknamed these contests the Lesser Antilles, as their small size reminded him of the tiny Caribbean islands where his family vacationed (Mashek, February 21, 1988). Several candidates, notably Simon, Gephardt, and Dole, attempted to use these Lesser Antilles events as springboards for Super Tuesday. A more significant springboard existed on the Republican side. South Carolina's primary, scheduled a mere three days

Table 2.2: Democratic Calendar for 1988

| | | Delegates | | |
		Selection Method	Number	Percent of Total
February 8	Iowa	C	58	1.4
February 16	New Hampshire	P	22	.5
February 23	Minnesota	C	86	2.1
	South Dakota	P[a]	19	.5
February 28	Maine	C	27	.6
March 1	Vermont	P[b]		
March 5	Wyoming	C	18	.4
Super Tuesday				
March 8	Alabama	P	61	1.5
	American Samoa	C	4	.1
	Arkansas	P	43	1.0
	Florida	P	146	3.5
	Georgia	P	86	2.1
	Hawaii	C	25	.6
	Idaho	C[c]	23	.6
	Kentucky	P	60	1.4
	Louisiana	P	71	1.7
	Maryland	P	78	1.9
	Massachusetts	P	109	2.6
	Mississippi	P	45	1.1
	Missouri	P	83	2.0
	Nevada	C	21	.5
	North Carolina	P	89	2.1
	Oklahoma	P	51	1.2
	Rhode Island	P	26	.6
	Tennessee	P	77	1.9
	Texas	P	198	4.8
	Virginia	P	85	2.0
	Washington	C	72	1.7
March 10	Alaska	C	17	.4
March 12	South Carolina	C	48	1.2
March 13-27	North Dakota	C[d]	20	.5
March 15	Illinois	P	187	4.5
March 19	Kansas	C	43	1.0
March 20	Puerto Rico	P	56	1.3
March 22	Democrats Abroad	M	9	.2

Table 2.2, continued

		Delegates		
		Selection Method	Number	Percent of Total
March 26	Michigan	C	151	3.6
March 29	Connecticut	P	59	1.4
April 2	Virgin Islands	C	4	.1
April 4	Colorado	C	51	1.2
April 5	Wisconsin	P	88	2.1
April 11-20	House Super Del.		210	5.0
April 12-19	Senate Super Del.		43	1.0
April 16	Arizona	C	40	1.0
April 18	Delaware	C	19	.5
April 19	New York	P	275	6.6
	Vermont	C	19	.5
April 24	Guam	C	4	.1
April 25	Utah	C	27	.6
April 26	Pennsylvania	P	193	4.6
May 3	Indiana	P	85	2.0
	Ohio	P	174	4.2
	Washington, D.C.	P	24	.6
May 10	Nebraska	P	29	.7
	West Virginia	P	44	1.1
May 17	Oregon	P	51	1.2
June 7	California	P	336	8.1
	Montana	P	25	.6
	New Jersey	P	118	2.8
	New Mexico	P	28	.7
	Total		4,160	

[a]Technically, the South Dakota primary had to be a beauty contest primary because it was scheduled outside the Democratic window. However, participants at the March 12 caucuses could vote to reconfirm the primary results and be bound by them in delegate selection.
[b]Vermont selected delegates in caucus procedure starting on April 19.
[c]Idaho held a nonbinding primary on May 24.
[d]North Dakota held a nonbinding primary on June 14.

C = caucus/convention
M = ballot by mail
P = primary

Source: Cook 1987.

Table 2.3: Republican Calendar for 1988

		Delegates		
		Selection Method	Number	Percent of Total
January-May	Virginia	C[a]	50	2.2
January-May	Arizona	C[b]	33	1.4
January 14	Michigan	C[c]	77	3.4
February 1-7	Kansas	C	34	1.5
February 4	Hawaii	C[d]	20	.9
February 8	Iowa	C	37	1.4
February 9-24	Wyoming	C	18	.8
February 16	New Hampshire	P	23	1.0
February 18	Nevada	C	20	.9
February 23	Minnesota	C	31	1.4
	South Dakota	P	18	.8
February 26-28	Maine	C	22	1.0
February 27-March 1	Alaska	C	19	.8
March 1	Vermont	P[e]		
March 5	South Carolina	P	37	1.6
Super Tuesday				
March 8	Alabama	P	38	1.7
	Arkansas	P	27	1.2
	Florida	P	82	3.6
	Georgia	P	48	2.1
	Kentucky	P	38	1.7
	Louisiana	P	41	1.8
	Maryland	P	41	1.8
	Massachusetts	P	52	2.3
	Mississippi	P	31	1.4
	Missouri	P	47	2.1
	North Carolina	P	54	2.4
	Oklahoma	P	36	1.6
	Rhode Island	P	21	.9
	Tennessee	P	45	2.0
	Texas	P	111	4.9
	Virginia	P[a]		
	Washington	C	41	1.8
March 15	Illinois	P	92	4.0
March 20	Puerto Rico	P	14	.6
March 29	Connecticut	P	35	1.5

Table 2.3, continued

| | | Delegates | | |
		Selection Method	Number	Percent of Total
April 1-30	Delaware	C	17	.7
April 4	Colorado	C	36	1.6
April 5	Wisconsin	P	47	2.1
April 19	New York	P	136	6.0
	Vermont	C[e]	17	.4
April 25	Utah	C	26	1.1
April 26	Pennsylvania	P	96	4.2
May 3	Indiana	P	51	2.2
	Ohio	P	88	3.9
	Washington, D.C.	P	14	.6
May 10	Nebraska	P	25	1.1
	West Virginia	P	28	1.2
May 17	Oregon	P	32	1.4
May 24	Idaho	P	22	1.0
May 28	Virgin Islands	C	4	.2
June 7	California	P	175	7.7
	Montana	P[f]		
	New Jersey	P	64	2.8
	New Mexico	P	26	1.1
June 14	North Dakota	P	16	.7
July 7	Montana	C	20	.9
	Total		2,273	

[a]Virginia's delegates were selected through a caucus process beginning in January. On March 8 a beauty contest primary was held.

[b]Arizona's precinct delegate elections were held on September 16, 1986.

[c]Michigan's precinct delegate elections were held on August 5, 1986.

[d]Hawaii caucuses were originally scheduled for January 27, 1988.

[e]Vermont's delegates were elected in caucus procedure that started on April 19, 1988. On March 1 a beauty contest primary was held.

[f]Montana's delegates were selected at state convention on July 7. A beauty contest primary was held on June 7.

C = Caucus
P = Primary

Source: Cook 1987.

before Super Tuesday, was positioned to foretell the fortunes of Bush, Robertson, and Kemp in the other southern primaries.

Super Tuesday, the third period of the 1988 election calendar, presented candidates with the first opportunity to accumulate large numbers of delegates. The Big Two Openers and Lesser Antilles selected only 230 Democratic delegates (6 percent of the national total) and 406 Republican delegates (18 percent of the national total). Furthermore, most of these initial events were caucuses, meaning that while the delegate selection process had begun in these states, most of the national convention delegates would be selected at later county, district, or state conventions. Candidates' fates change between the initial caucuses and the state conventions, such that the number of projected delegates for each candidate often do not match final delegate counts. For instance, in 1976, the estimates of national delegates won after the initial round of the Iowa caucuses gave thirteen delegates to Carter, six to Bayh, five to Harris, three to Udall, and two to Shriver and designated eighteen as uncommitted. By the time of the district and state conventions, where national delegates were actually selected, Bayh and Shriver had left the race. As a result, the actual delegate count became twenty for Carter, twelve for Udall, two for Harris, and thirteen uncommitted. At the national convention, Iowa's delegation cast twenty-five votes for Carter, twenty for Udall, and one each for Kennedy and Brown (Winebrenner 1987, 80-85). In contrast to earlier caucus states, Super Tuesday would select one-third of the delegates and most of these through primaries. Actual delegate totals would be known that night.

After Super Tuesday came the Big State Showdowns in Illinois, Michigan (Democrats), Wisconsin, New York, and Pennsylvania, all with primaries or caucuses (Michigan) scheduled from mid-March through April. At this point in any election year the initial winnowing of candidates is complete. Two to three candidates remain to battle it out, each attempting to add new groups of supporters while not alienating members of their original coalition. With fewer candidates, each candidate is more heavily scrutinized by the media, who now start to question the feasibility of each candidate's issue positions and his or her qualifications for the presidency.

The May and June primaries would provide the finale to the 1988 presidential nomination season. Normally during this time period, one candidate emerges as the apparent nominee, either by acquiring the required number of delegates needed for victory at the national convention or by accumulating significantly more delegates than the second place candidate. Jimmy Carter in 1976, Ronald Reagan in 1980, and Walter Mondale in 1984 all became de facto nominees at the close of the primary season. Yet despite these recent precedents, many commentators speculated that the 1988 Democratic race might result in a brokered convention, one in which no candidate has enough delegates to win on the first ballot (see for instance

Apple, January 3, 1988; Barnes, March 21, 1988; Barnes, March 19, 1988; Udall, January 10, 1988; and Wicker, February 19, 1988; but see Glen, November 14, 1987, for a contrary view). Super Tuesday played a role in these speculations for a brokered Democratic convention. Most commentators expected Jackson to win the sizable black vote in the South and Gore to pick up another segment because of regional ties. The rest of the vote would be split by the remaining candidates. With no single winner on Super Tuesday and with Super Tuesday front-loading the nomination calendar, commentators asserted no candidate would be able to accumulate a majority of the delegates by the end of the primary season. To select the Democratic nominee, deals would be struck between the remaining candidates, party leaders, and important constituency groups, such as labor, either before or at the convention. Errant speculation about the possibility of a brokered convention, however, was not unique to 1988. In 1976 when the Democrats also had no front-runner at the start of the race, many speculated no candidate would win the nomination through primary victories. Jimmy Carter, nevertheless, emerged from the pack and, with the help of momentum and the attrition of other candidates, secured the nomination in the closing round of primaries.

The Rules

Beyond the election calendar, delegate selection rules structure the playing field and modify candidates' strategies. Once again the national Democratic party places restrictions on states as to the procedures they use to select convention delegates. In most primaries, voters cast ballots for one of the presidential candidates, though the legal purpose of the primary is to select that state's delegates to the national party convention. These delegates will in turn cast their ballots for a specific candidate during the presidential nomination roll call vote. Thus some set of rules must be employed to translate primary votes into convention delegates. The simplest procedure, awarding all delegates to the first-place candidate, seemed unfair to Democratic reformers since in multicandidate races the winning candidate often led the second place candidate by only a few votes. Therefore, the Democratic party banned such winner-take-all primaries prior to the 1976 election.

The Democratic party instead encouraged states to employ proportional representation rules, in which each candidate receives the same proportion of a state's delegation as he won in the primary vote. Under proportional representation rules, a candidate is often required to receive a minimum vote before being awarded any delegates. In 1988, this threshold was set at 15 percent of the vote, a concession to Jesse Jackson, who complained that higher thresholds in 1984, as high as 25 percent, unfairly deprived him of his full share of convention delegates. The Democratic party in 1988 also allowed bonus proportional representation systems, in which the first-place candidate in each congressional district is awarded an additional bonus delegate.[6] While national party rules urged proportional representation, larger states often felt they could have more influence on the nomination if they could award a large bloc of delegates to one candidate. This is a possibility under the third type of rule allowed by the Democratic party: loophole primaries. In loophole primaries, voters in each congressional district cast ballots for individual delegates, not for the national candidates.[7] Since each voter tends to select delegates committed to one presidential candidate, winner-take-all results often occur. For example, in New Jersey's 1984 loophole primary Walter Mondale won 45 percent of the vote but 98 percent of the delegates. (See Lengle 1987 for a summary of national Democratic rule changes over the past twenty years; and Cook 1987 for procedures used in each state for 1988).

The Republican party does not impose national standards on delegate selection procedures. States may use winner-take-all, proportional representation, bonus, or loophole primaries to select Republican delegates. For many of the Republican caucuses, no formal rules exist for delegate selection, and some delegates are chosen as uncommitted to any of the national candidates.

Besides requiring proportional representation, bonus, or loophole rules to select convention delegates, the Democratic party designates four different types of delegates. The bulk of each state's delegates are district delegates selected according to the primary vote in a relatively small election district, almost always coinciding with U.S. House of Representatives districts. An additional 20 percent of the delegates are chosen according to statewide voting results. PEOs, pledged party and elected officials, constitute another 15 percent of each state's delegation.[8] These PEO delegates are Democratic officeholders, such as big-city mayors, and party officials. As pledged delegates, their votes at the national convention must reflect their states' primary or caucus results. The final 643 delegates to the 1988 Democratic national convention were Super Delegates, including 80 percent of Democrats in Congress, all Democratic governors, and all Democratic National Committee members. Super Delegates are unpledged and thus free to support any presidential candidate. While the number of Super Delegates increased by seventy-five over 1984 figures, their selection date was moved back until April.[9] Hart complained that Mondale accrued an undue advantage in 1984 as House Super Delegates selected before the Iowa caucuses overwhelmingly supported Mondale, giving the former vice president an early boost in the delegate count. While the preponderance of early primary and caucus dates front-load the election calendar, actual delegate selection lags behind, especially in caucus states and for at-large and PEO delegates. For example, the four hundred at-large delegates for the Super

Tuesday states were not chosen until May or June (Barnes, March 19, 1988), after Gephardt and Gore left the race. These candidates' shares of the at-large delegates were redistributed to the remaining candidates: Jackson and Dukakis.

The selection of rules for Super Tuesday primaries followed in the footsteps of a twenty-year battle, mostly within the Democratic party, over the desired rules for delegate distribution and voter participation. Underlying this battle were disagreements over basic values and candidate advantages. Before the reforms of the 1970s, the purpose of a presidential primary was to select a monolithic delegation representing the state political party. In the post-reform era, the purpose of primaries—and caucuses—is to select delegates reflecting the candidate preferences of individual voters (Pomper 1979, 786). The question is how best to reflect these preferences, since no system of rules is unbiased. Lengle and Shafer's (1976) analysis suggests that winner-take-all rules advantage moderate candidates, whereas proportional representation rules advantage more liberal candidates. Lengle and Shafer further argue that winner-take-all rules provide larger states with considerable clout over the presidential nomination, whereas proportional representation rules would make medium-sized states the most attractive to candidates. Included among the latter group would be most of the southern states. Hammond (1980) and Pomper (1979, 792) disagree with the specifics of Lengle and Shafer's findings but not with the general conclusion that certain candidates or specific regions may be better served by different rules.[10] Finally, Kamarck (1987) and Ansolabehere and King (1990) note that the tendency of the two parties to employ different rules colors the whole nature of the fight for each party's presidential nomination. The proliferation of proportional representation rules on the Democratic side allows a divisive battle for the nomination to linger longer, crippling the eventual nominee in the fall election against his Republican opponent. In contrast, the absence of proportional representation rules on the Republican side allows a swifter close to the nomination battle, while at the same time decreasing the importance of the earliest primaries and caucuses.

Table 2.4 lists delegate distribution rules for southern Democratic primaries held on Super Tuesday. All states, except Maryland, used some form of proportional representation. Nine states held strict proportional representation primaries with 15 percent thresholds, while four states adopted bonus proportional representation rules. In Maryland, voters cast ballots directly for convention delegates in a loophole primary. The pattern of Democratic rules on Super Tuesday matched that in the rest of the nation, where eleven states held proportional representation primaries, four scheduled bonus primaries, and four more conducted loophole primaries. With mostly proportional representation rules on Super Tuesday, no Democratic candidate could expect to sweep the delegate count.

Table 2.4: Rules for Democratic Primaries

| | Selection Rules | | | Number of Delegates | | | | |
	Open/Closed	District	State	District	State	PEOs	SD	Total
Alabama	O	PR-15%	PR-15%	37	12	7	5	61
Arkansas	O	PR-15%	PR-15%	25	8	5	5	43
Kentucky	C	PR-15%	PR-15%	36	12	7	5	60
Louisiana	C	PR-15%	PR-15%	41	14	8	8	71
Mississippi	O	PR-15%	PR-15%	26	9	5	5	45
Oklahoma	C	PR-15%	PR-15%	30	10	6	5	51
Tennessee	O	PR-15%	PR-15%	46	15	9	7	77
Texas[a]	O	PR-15%	PR-15%	119	40	24	15	198
Virginia	O	PR-15%	PR-15%	49	16	10	10	85
Florida	C	BPR-15%	PR-15%	89	29	18	10	146
Georgia	O	BPR-15%	PR-15%	50	17	10	9	86
Missouri	O	BPR-15%	PR-15%	50	17	10	6	83
North Carolina	C	BPR-15%	PR-15%	53	18	11	7	89
Maryland	C	Direct	PR-15%	44	14	9	11	78

[a]Texas's state delegates and PEOs selected through caucus-convention process, separate from the primary results

BPR-15% = one bonus delegate awarded to top candidate, rest of delegates allocated by proportional representation with a 15% minimum threshold
C = closed primary
Direct = direct election of delegates, winner-take-all results possible

District = congressional district, except Texas Democrats where state senate districts used instead
O = open primary
PEOs = pledged party and elected official
PR-15% = proportional representation with a 15% threshold
SD = unpledged Super Delegates
State = at-large delegates selected on the basis of statewide outcomes
Source: Cook 1987.

Since the national Republican party does not impose restrictions on delegate selection procedures, a wider variety of rules were employed for Republican primaries in the South. (See table 2.5.) Only five of the fourteen states held proportional representation primaries, and these states used a variety of thresholds from a low of 4 percent to a high of 15 percent. In contrast to the Democrats, the majority of Republican primaries on Super Tuesday were winner-take-all. Two of these primaries, in Alabama and Texas, only awarded all of the delegates to the leading candidate if he won over 50 percent of the vote. If no candidate won a majority, a second procedure would come into play. In Alabama, at the district level, the top

Table 2.5: Rules for Republican Primaries

	Selection Rules			Number of Delegates		
	Open/Closed	District	State	District	State	Total
Arkansas	O	PR-3.7%[a]	PR-3.7%	12	15	27
Kentucky	C	PR-15%	PR-15%	21	17	38
Missouri	O	PR-15%	PR-15%	27	20	47
North Carolina	C	PR-10%[a]	PR-10%	33	21	54
Tennessee	O	PR-15%	PR-15%	27	18	45
Florida	C	WTA	WTA	64	18	82
Maryland	C	WTA	WTA	24	17	41
Georgia	O	WTA	WTA	30	18	48
Oklahoma	C	WTA	WTA	18	18	36
Mississippi	O	WTA	PR-10%	15	16	31
Louisiana	C	WTA	PR-20%	24	17	41
Alabama	O	WTA; 2D,1D	WTA; PR-15%	21	17	38
Texas	O	WTA; PR-20%	WTA; PR-20%	81	30	111
Virginia	O	beauty	beauty	30	20	50

[a]District threshold based on statewide vote totals instead of district vote totals

2D, 1D = top candidate receives two delegates, second candidate receives one delegate
beauty = beauty contest primary, delegates allocated on basis of caucus-convention process
with no formal rules
C = closed primary
District = congressional district
O = open primary
PR-——% = proportional representation with a given percentage threshold
WTA = winner-take-all
WTA; = winner-take-all if top candidate gets majority vote, otherwise rule listed after semi-
colon applies

Source: Cook 1987; except Louisiana from Katz, March 7, 1988.

candidate would be awarded two delegates and the second candidate one delegate. In Texas, and for state-level delegates in Alabama, if no candidate won an absolute majority, delegates would be awarded on the basis of proportional representation. Because it was a beauty contest primary, Virginia's Republican primary did not determine the allocation of delegates. Instead, delegates would be selected in a caucus-convention process that had no formal rules. Also unlike their Democratic counterparts, the rules used in Republican Super Tuesday primaries differed from those used in the rest of the nation. Southern states were more likely to hold winner-take-all primaries; only five of the twenty-one other Republican primary states used similar rules. The remaining Republican primaries included nine proportional representation, one bonus, and six loophole primaries. With the predominance of winner-take-all primaries on Super Tuesday, one candidate could amass a huge bloc of delegates, giving him a formidable lead in the delegate count.

As delegate distribution rules affect the ultimate outcome of each primary, these rules also should affect candidate strategies. Winner-take-all primaries present both a bigger payoff and a greater risk. Candidates with a reasonable chance of winning these primary states should spend lavishly to insure victory, while candidates with little chance of winning should avoid these states. With proportional representation, both favored and less favored candidates should allocate similar resources to the states, as any candidate winning at least 15 percent of the vote is awarded some delegates. Tad Devine advised his candidate, Michael Dukakis, to seek out the nonproportional representation delegates on the Democratic side in order to accumulate a larger delegate total. For instance, he suggested that the Dukakis campaign target states using bonus proportional representation or direct election of delegate rules, while also urging Dukakis to court unpledged Super Delegates. Trying to win a majority of delegates through a proportional representation system would simply be too difficult (Black and Oliphant 1989, 100-103).

The Demographic Base of Super Tuesday

Besides the rules and the timing of Super Tuesday, the outcome of the southern primaries would depend on the people living in that area of the nation. Different people prefer different types of candidates. Bartels (1988) demonstrated that state economic and political characteristics affected primary outcomes in 1976, 1980, and 1984. Therefore, if residents of the southern Super Tuesday states do not match the characteristics of other Americans, southerners may have different candidate preferences, and Super Tuesday would produce a different result than a regional primary held in another section of the country. Additionally, Super Tuesday may eliminate candidates preferred in other areas of the country while advancing the candidacies of others with less support outside the South.

The basic economic, demographic, and political traits of southern Super Tuesday states are compared with those of states in other regions of the country in table 2.6. Figures given are averages for states in the two regions. The first four entries indicate that the South remains different in terms of economic characteristics. Southern states have lower per capita incomes, more people living below the poverty line, and fewer union members than other parts of the nation. The second set of numbers in table 2.6 indicates that southern states also have significant demographic dif-

Table 2.6: Characteristics of the Southern Super Tuesday States Versus Rest of the Nation

	Southern Super Tuesday	Rest of Nation	significance
Economic characteristics			
Per capita income	$11,302	$12,746	.032
% Union members	15	21	.003
% Unemployed	7	6	.090
% Below poverty line	16	11	.000
Demographic characteristics			
% 12 years education	60	70	.000
% Black	17	6	.000
% Asian	2	5	.284
% Hispanic	3	5	.448
% Urban	64	64	.983
% Jewish	1	2	.460
% Catholic	9	23	.001
% Evangelical	1	2	.020
% Pentecostal	2	1	.033
% Fundamentalist	2	1	.000
% Southern Baptist	20	2	.000
Political characteristics			
% Democratic identification	47	35	.000
% Independent identification	29	37	.001
% Republican identification	18	24	.003
% Normal Democratic vote	61	49	.000
% Liberal	17	21	.007
% Moderate	38	40	.019
% Conservative	34	32	.242
% General election turnout	47	54	.001

Sources: Barone and Ujifusa 1987; *Churches and Church Membership in the United States, 1980* 1982; U.S. Bureau of the Census 1989; U.S. Department of Education 1988; Wright, Erikson, and McIver 1985.

ferences with southern states having more blacks, residents with lower educational levels, fewer Catholics, more fundamentalists, and more Baptists. These demographic traits coupled with a unique historical tradition produce a South with different political characteristics. Southern states have fewer liberals and moderates, more Democrats and fewer independents and Republicans, more citizens who vote Democratic but also more citizens who do not vote at all. The composition of the southern Super Tuesday electorate remained distinct from the rest of the nation and may forebode different voting patterns.

The South, however, has changed since the 1950s, and even since the 1960s. Under the old southern politics, one found "one-party political systems, highly depressed rates of white political participation, the relentless subordination and exclusion of blacks from politics, and state politics devoted principally to advancing and protecting the interests of 'haves' rather than the much larger group of 'have nots'" (Black and Black 1987, 3). The old South no longer exists. Even though the South still has lower turnout rates than the rest of the nation, these differences are not as prevalent as in the past. In fact, turnout rates have steadily risen in the South (Black and Black 1987, 177). The civil rights movement brought blacks into the southern electorate, such that blacks now constitute one-third of Democratic voters in southern and border states (Oreskes, March 2, 1988). Women also have emerged as a vital component of the new southern electorate. Whereas in the past southern women were more likely than their northern counterparts to refrain from politics, southern women are now as likely to vote in elections as southern men. The one-party politics of the old South also began to disappear as transplanted northerners and, more important, younger southerners began to vote for Republican candidates. Conservatism remains the preferred ideology in the South. Arising out of a traditionalistic and individualistic political culture, southern conservatism values rewards for individual achievement and rejects large-scale government "hand-out" programs. Meanwhile, southern blacks are decisively liberal in their orientation (Black and Black 1987). The South remains different from the rest of the nation but not as different as it once was. The contemporary southern electorate is quite diverse, with blacks and whites, women and men, and even a few liberals intermixed with the moderates and conservatives.

Super Tuesday established a playing field with distinct political characteristics. The large number of delegates to be selected on Super Tuesday greatly front-loaded the selection process. The selection of over 50 percent of convention delegates began by the middle of March, and half of these were southern delegates. The Democratic party, with a preponderance of proportional representation rules on Super Tuesday, could find itself in a bind with delegates scattered among several presidential candidates and no one candidate being able to negotiate a victory through the remaining primaries. In contrast, the Republican party, with eight winner-take-all primaries on Super Tuesday, could conclude its race a mere month after it formally began. All these scenarios would depend on how the South voted. Would the South's unique political history and remaining economic and political differences lead its voters to cast ballots in a unique manner?

THE PLAYERS

Presidential Candidates and Their Assets

In recent years when no incumbent president sought renomination from a party, six to seven candidates often entered the fray. Twelve Democrats fought for the 1976 Democratic nomination, seven Republican vied for the 1980 Republican position, while eight Democrats battled in 1984 for the chance to oppose Reagan in the fall election. The unusual aspect about 1988 was that for the first time since 1968 neither party had an incumbent president to renominate; both parties therefore found themselves with numerous competitors. Seven Democrats and six Republicans entered 1988 as candidates for their parties' nominations; only two would win the honors.

Besides these thirteen candidates, several individuals contemplated running but never officially declared themselves as candidates.[11] Most notably absent from Super Tuesday was Georgia's Senator Sam Nunn. When southern Democrats created Super Tuesday, many hoped one of their own would run. Nunn, known as a moderate to conservative Democrat with a strong reputation on defense matters, represented the ideal candidate for many of Super Tuesday's supporters. Yet Nunn announced in August 1987 that he would not seek the nomination. Nunn's stated reasons for deciding not to run centered on his obligations to the U.S. Senate and his family. In the Senate, Nunn chaired the Armed Services Committee. He averred he could not meet his obligations to that committee and spend the inordinate amount of time on the campaign trail necessary to win the nomination. Nunn also was wary of subjecting his college-age children to the confines of being presidential offspring, such as Secret Service protection. In addition to these reservations, Nunn apparently questioned the structure of Super Tuesday. He calculated that the South would be better served by having a couple of smaller states hold early primaries, with the larger primaries being held off for a few weeks (Dart, March 5, 1988).

Other southerners deciding not to contest the Democratic primaries included Senator Dale Bumpers and Governor Bill Clinton, both from Arkansas. Charles Robb, former governor of Virginia, was frequently mentioned as a possible candidate. With Nunn, Robb, Bumpers, and Clinton failing to declare, Senator Al Gore of Tennessee became the sole southern Democratic candidate. Republicans also found that one of their leading southern candidates decided not to run. Tennessean Howard H. Baker, Jr., who ranked third in early public opinion polls behind Bush and Dole, opted to become President Reagan's White House Chief of Staff in the wake of the Iran-Contra scandal.[12]

New York Governor Mario Cuomo led the field of nonsouthern noncandidates. Cuomo's keynote address at the 1984 national convention brought him into the national limelight. His theme of family unity appealed to more conservative Democrats. Therefore, despite Cuomo being the governor of an eastern state, some felt he might be the preferred candidate of a significant number of southerners. Cuomo's surprise announcement in February of 1987 that he would not run, followed by Hart's misfortunes in May, left the Democratic party with no clear front-runner at the beginning of 1988.

Two announced candidates folded their campaigns before the election year began: Senator Paul Laxalt of Nevada and Senator Joseph R. Biden, Jr., of Delaware. Paul Laxalt, a longtime friend of Ronald Reagan, contested the Republican nomination until August 1987. Overconfidence in his ability to raise funds misled Laxalt to start his campaign at a relatively late date. In the end, raising only $2 million of the $10 million needed for a serious campaign, Laxalt wisely chose to withdraw from the race (Runkel 1989, 19). Joe Biden's campaign ended abruptly in September 1987 when a videocassette leaked to the media juxtaposed Biden and British Labour politician Neil Kinnock using the exact same words in their speeches.[13] This led to further allegations of Biden plagiarizing parts of Robert Kennedy's and Hubert Humphrey's speeches. Coming in the wake of the Hart controversy, and subsequent heightened concerns over candidates' moral and ethical values, the plagiarism charges forced Biden from the field.

The Active Candidates in 1988

Seven Democrats and six Republicans entered 1988 as presidential candidates. Two prominent, well-financed candidates led the Republican side: Vice President George Bush and Senate Majority Leader Robert J. Dole of Kansas. Meanwhile, Representative Jack F. Kemp of New York, one of the original advocates of supply-side economics, would fight Delaware Governor Pierre "Pete" S. du Pont IV, television minister Marion "Pat" Robertson, and former Secretary of State Alexander M. Haig, Jr., for the right to lead the conservative wing of the Republican party. Former Senator Gary Hart of Colorado reentered the race in December 1987, with high poll ratings but lingering doubts about whether he would be taken as a serious candidate or merely as a celebrity. Hart's lesser-known Democratic opponents found themselves saddled with such nicknames as the Seven Dwarfs (including Biden) or the Not Ready for Prime Time Candidates. Former Arizona Governor Bruce Babbitt, Massachusetts Governor Michael S. Dukakis, Representative Richard A. Gephardt of Missouri, Senator Albert Gore, Jr., of Tennessee, and civil rights activist Reverend Jesse Jackson vied with Hart for the Democratic nomination.

Super Tuesday's creators hoped to attract a new type of candidate to the race—a moderate, preferably southern, candidate. The question becomes whether the 1988 candidate list matched those of previous years or whether

Super Tuesday changed the type of individual seeking the presidency. Three aspects of the 1988 candidates can be compared to previous candidate fields. These include the career paths individuals took prior to seeking the presidency, the home states of the candidates, and their ideological positions.

Career Patterns.   The background of who becomes president has varied throughout U.S. history. Through the 1820s, successful presidential candidates often served first as secretary of state, including Thomas Jefferson, James Monroe, and John Quincy Adams. The last secretary of state to advance successfully to the presidency was James Buchanan in 1857, not a good omen for Haig's candidacy. Cabinet members dominated the list of early presidential candidates because both parties nominated their presidential candidates through congressional caucuses. This small group of Washington's elite looked to their colleagues in the infant national government. When presidential nominations moved to national conventions around the 1830s, state party leaders controlled the nominations and chose a different breed of candidate. Concerns over state and local elections dominated the thinking of these state party leaders. They wanted presidential nominees who would attract votes for state offices. Military men, especially after the Civil War, fit the bill for the Republican party. These military heroes could attract votes in an era before the mass media. Because of the southern basis of the Democratic party, Democrats had no national heroes to nominate and instead chose governors of large states. This pattern continued after the turn of the century, with Democratic nominees through 1956 often being governors from large swing states such as New York, New Jersey, Ohio, and Illinois. After running out of Civil War heroes around the turn of the century, Republicans turned to a wide mix of nominees: two cabinet members, two Supreme Court judges, two governors, two vice presidents, a lawyer, and a general (Moxley, January 17, 1976).

The 1960s and early 1970s found Washingtonians once again dominating the nomination ranks, although this time senators and incumbent vice presidents edged out other competitors. The development of national television coverage of the Washington scene may account for this change (Moxley, January 17, 1976). Since the proliferation of presidential primaries in the 1970s, governors once again may have returned to the forefront of presidential nominees. Jimmy Carter in 1976, Ronald Reagan in 1980, and Michael Dukakis in 1988 held governors' posts prior to their nomination victories. The other successful candidates have been former or sitting vice presidents: Mondale in 1984 and Bush in 1988. The key to the success of these candidates is that these posts either allowed candidates the time to campaign extensively (Reagan and Carter as ex-governors) or gave them the ability to

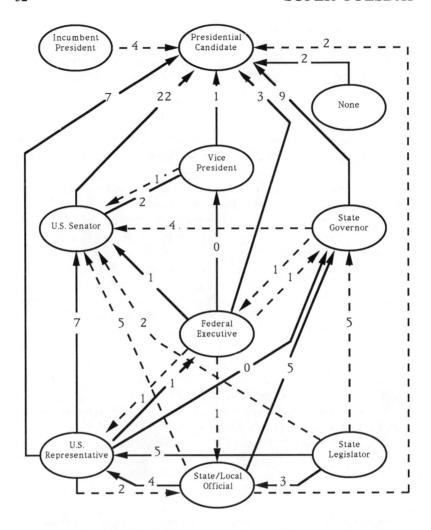

Figure 2.1: Previous Governmental Offices of 1988 Presidential Candidates

raise considerable sums of campaign money (Bush, Mondale, Reagan, and Dukakis).

Figure 2.1 illustrates the career patterns of the 1988 presidential candidates, while figure 2.2 presents the same data for candidates from 1972 through 1984. As is usual in recent times, most of the 1988 candidates were governors or senators. Senators are more likely presidential candidates than representatives, as senators are more likely to have national reputations than are House members. Secondly, representatives suffer an electoral disadvantage. Senators' six-year terms allow them to seek the presidency without

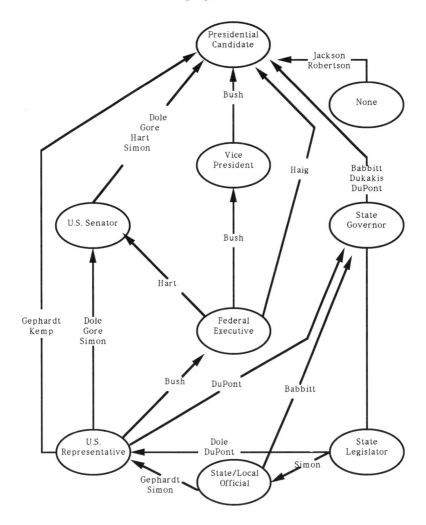

Figure 2.2: Previous Governmental Offices of Presidential Candidates, 1972-1984

jeopardizing their congressional careers. Representatives, at some point, must decide between continuing to run for the presidency and running for their seat in the House. Gephardt in 1988 exited the race as the filing date for his House seat fast approached. Along with senators, governors also predominate as presidential candidates, with three in 1988 and nine from 1972 to 1984. Some governors, such as Ronald Reagan, possess a national reputation. Ex-governors Carter and Babbitt, along with Reagan, had the time for extensive pre-election-year campaigning.

The 1988 crop of candidates closely matched their predecessors. Figure

Table 2.7: Comparing Immediate Prior Career Positions of 1988 Presidential
Nomination Seekers with Candidates from 1972 to 1984

	1972–1984	1988	t-test
Incumbent president	8% (4)	0% (0)	−1.05
Senator	44% (22)	31% (4)	−.85
Governor	18% (9)	23% (3)	.41
Vice president	2% (1)	8% (1)	1.09
U.S. representative	14% (7)	15% (2)	.01
Federal executive	6% (2)	8% (1)	.26
Local office	4% (2)	0% (0)	−.73
No government office	4% (2)	15% (2)	1.46

None of the tests of significance meet the .05 cutoff point. Values in parentheses are
numbers of cases in each category.

2.2 illustrates a few paths that did not reoccur in 1988, depicted with dotted
lines, but mostly the pathways to candidacies and the numbers along each
path match those in figure 2.1. Table 2.7 recapitulates the occupations of
candidates prior to seeking the presidential nomination. No statistically
significant differences exist between the 1988 candidates and their predecessors in 1972 through 1984. As far as career paths are concerned, Super
Tuesday did not alter the type of candidate seeking the nomination.

Home Regions.   The creators of Super Tuesday hoped that a southern
regional primary would increase the willingness of southerners to run for the
presidency. But as tables 2.8 and 2.9 illustrate, no lack of southern candidates existed in the 1970s and 1980s. In fact, the South provided the most
Democratic candidates during this period. Not all of these candidates were
serious contenders—i.e., Wilbur Mills or Terry Sanford—and others did
not make it past the New Hampshire primary—i.e., Reubin Askew and
Ernest "Fritz" Hollings—but these traits are not unique to southern candidates. Most candidates are winnowed early. The three southern candidates in
1988 represent both a typical number and a typical fate for southern candidates in recent years. In fact, the East, the home of the New Hampshire
primary, produced the fewest Democratic candidates in this era. In terms of
successful candidates, each area, except the West, produced a presidential
nominee, with one southerner, one easterner, and two midwesterners winning the Democratic nomination.

On the Republican side, the three southern candidates in 1988 matched
the three candidates in the last open race in 1980. Bush and Haig, being
transplants from the East, might not be considered true southerners. Nev-

Table 2.8: Home States of Democratic Presidential Contenders, 1972-1988

	South		West		Midwest		East	
1972	Mills	AR	H. Jackson	WA	Hartke	IN	Chisholm	NY
	Sanford	NC	Mink	HI	Humphrey	MN	Lindsay	NY
	Wallace	AL	Yorty	CA	McCarthy	MN	Muskie	ME
					McGovern	**SD**		
1976	Bentsen	TX	Brown	CA	Bayh	IN	Shapp	PA
	Carter	**GA**	Church	ID	Shriver	IL	McCormack	NY
	Harris	OK	H. Jackson	WA				
	Sanford	NC	Udall	AZ				
	Wallace	AL						
1980	**Carter**	**GA**	Brown	CA			Kennedy	MA
1984	Askew	FL	Cranston	CA	Glenn	OH		
	Hollings	SC	Hart	CO	J. Jackson	IL		
	J. Jackson	SC			McGovern	SD		
					Mondale	**MN**		
1988	Gephardt	MO	Babbitt	AZ	Simon	IL	**Dukakis**	**MA**
	Gore	TN	Hart	CO	J. Jackson	IL		
	J. Jackson	SC						

The winning candidates are underlined. Jesse Jackson was assigned two home states because of personal and business connections to both South Carolina and Illinois.

Table 2.9: Home States of Republican Presidential Contenders, 1972-1988

	South		West		Midwest		East	
1972			McCloskey	CA	Ashbrook	OH		
			Nixon	**CA**				
1976			Reagan	CA	**Ford**	**MI**		
1980	Baker	TN	**Reagan**	**CA**	Anderson	IL	Bush	CT
	Bush	TX			Crane	IL		
	Connally	TX			Dole	KS		
1984			**Reagan**	**CA**				
1988	**Bush**	**TX**			Dole	KS	**Bush**	**CT**
	Haig	VA					du Pont	DE
	Robertson	VA					Kemp	NY

The winning candidates are underlined. Bush claimed two home states—Connecticut, where he was born, and Texas, where he served as a U.S. representative.

ertheless, once again the East, not the South, produced the fewest presidential candidates in recent years. As was true for the Democrats, recent Repubiican nominees came from every region: Bush, who claimed to be both an easterner and a southerner; Reagan and Nixon from the West; and Ford from the Midwest. With southern nominees on both sides, neither party neglected the South in recent years.

Ideological Positions. Ideology may be the most controversial and least understood aspect about potential presidential nominees. Super Tuesday's architects wanted a more conservative Democratic nominee, but what did they mean by "conservative" and who would determine which candidates fit the bill? Issue positions adopted by candidates during the campaign might be used to determine ideological classifications. Yet, as Gephardt and Gore demonstrated in 1988, campaign positions do not always match congressional records or previously held positions. Equally perplexing is that a candidate might be considered a moderate on one set of issues and a conservative on another. Would it be enough for a Democratic candidate to take a hard-line position on defense issues to satisfy the desires of Super Tuesday's Democratic creators? Classifying the ideological positions of presidential candidates is much more difficult than tracing their career paths or assigning their home states (although Bush claimed so many home states that for him the latter was not an easy task either). Political commentators often speak of the candidates as being liberal, moderate, or conservative. Whether or not voters classify candidates in these terms is less certain.

To try and gauge the ideological positions of the 1988 candidates and compare them with candidates from previous years, three types of measures will be employed. First, we will compare the congressional records of the presidential candidates. The rating scheme by the Americans for Democratic Action (ADA), a liberal group, will be used to measure the ideological nature of their congressional roll call votes. Second, we will examine classifications of the candidates by various "experts" (i.e., scholars and journalists). Finally, we will investigate how the public rated these candidates.

Table 2.10 lists the ADA ratings for the various presidential candidates. These measures are only crude indicators of the voting patterns of representatives and senators. No measures were undertaken to assure that a 100 percent rating in one year indicates as liberal a voting pattern as a 100 percent rating in another year. Additionally, not all candidates served in the U.S. Congress, such as Ronald Reagan and Jerry Brown, and their exclusion does affect the overall average liberalness rating for the years in which they were candidates. Given these caveats, the 1988 candidates do not appear to be ideologically distinct from those of previous years. On the Democratic side, the overall average for 1988 falls slightly more moderate than in previous

Table 2.10: Liberal Voting Patterns (ADA scores) in Congress of Candidates
Seeking Presidential Nominations

	% Democratic candidates			% Republican candidates		
1972	Humphrey	99	(60-64)	McCloskey	56	(68-72)
	Mink	97	(65-72)	Ashbrook	4	(61-72)
	Muskie	84	(60-72)			
	McGovern	83	(60-72)			
	Chisholm	80	(69-72)			
	McCarthy	78	(60-70)			
	Hartke	72	(60-72)			
	Lindsay[a]	70	(60-65)			
	Mills	27	(60-72)			
	average	77		average	30	
1976	Udall	81	(61-76)	Ford	10	(60-73)
	Bayh	80	(63-76)			
	Church	77	(60-76)			
	Harris	70	(65-72)			
	H. Jackson	68	(60-76)			
	Bentsen	48	(69-76)			
	average	71				
1980	Kennedy	90	(64-80)	Anderson	28	(61-80)
				Baker	14	(67-80)
				Dole	9	(61-80)
				Bush	7	(67-70)
				Crane	6	(70-80)
				average	13	
1984	Mondale	92	(65-76)			
	Cranston	86	(69-84)			
	McGovern	82	(60-80)			
	Hart	77	(75-84)			
	Glenn	64	(75-84)			
	Hollings	37	(67-84)			
	average	73				
1988	Hart	77	(75-84)	Kemp	11	(71-88)
	Simon	74	(75-88)	Dole	8	(61-88)
	Gore	64	(77-88)	Bush	7	(67-70)
	Gephardt	60	(77-88)			
	average	69		average	9	

Numbers in parentheses are years on which ADA averages are based.

[a]Lindsay was a Republican congressman at the time of the rating.

years, but the difference is not significant. The 1988 candidates had none of the very liberal candidates of the past—i.e, Mondale, Kennedy, or Humphrey—nor any of the extremely conservative candidates—i.e., Hollings, Lloyd Bentsen, and Mills. Only in this sense could one claim that the 1988 candidates were more moderate than Democratic candidates in the past. On the Republican side, once again the 1988 candidates matched the ideological positions of previous candidates. The only exception is the lack of a very liberal Republican candidates, such as Paul "Pete" McCloskey in 1972, or a moderately liberal Republican, such as John Anderson in 1980. Based on congressional voting records, both the 1988 Democratic and Republican candidates mostly reflected the ideological positions of candidates from previous years.

The ideological classification of candidates by scholars or journalists are often highly subjective and do not always match more objective standards. For instance, in 1984 Mondale was viewed as a mainstream candidate, with Alan Cranston, George McGovern, and possibly Hart viewed as liberal candidates. Yet ADA ratings in table 2.10 demonstrate Mondale to have the most liberal voting record. With these reservations, a synthesis of ideological classifications of the candidates by leading political scientists and journalists is listed in table 2.11. In each year without an incumbent president seeking renomination, generally four or five liberals vied for the Democratic nomination. The 1988 contest was no exception. The remainder of the Democratic field is often composed of moderates or conservatives, usually two or three. Once again, 1988 was no exception, although the more objective ADA ratings reported Gore and Gephardt as having fairly liberal congressional voting records. The last time a truly conservative Democrat played a major role in the nomination contest was in 1976 when Wallace accumulated 13 percent of the vote, compared to 39 percent for Carter (The Primaries: Raw Vote and Regional Vote, July 10, 1976).

On the Republican side, 1988 represents the typical pattern of several candidates vying for the conservative position. The remainder of the field falls to mostly moderate Republicans, with an occasional liberal. Of course, a Republican liberal is not as liberal as a Democratic liberal, just as a Democratic conservative is not as conservative as a Republican conservative. These expert placements are relative and highly subjective. Dole, who was classified as a conservative in 1980, became a moderate by 1988.

Some commentators began to speculate that ideology was becoming less important in separating candidates in recent years (Dionne, February 10, 1987; Germond and Witcover 1989). Gone were the battles between the hawks and doves over Vietnam, between proponents and opponents of the civil rights movement, and between party regulars and party reformers. By 1984 and 1988 the lines appeared to be between traditional Democrats, i.e, Mondale and Simon, and new technocrat Democrats, i.e., Hart and Dukakis

(Dionne, January 17, 1988). By 1988 it became harder to find an ideological classification of the Democratic candidates, although Gore's military positions received more attention from the press than his domestic positions because the former served to classify him as the most conservative Democratic candidate (Germond and Witcover 1989, 228). Discussions of conservative and moderate Republicans also occurred.

Whatever the political commentators thought of the candidates, the American public was even less clear about candidates' ideological positions. Figure 2.3 lists the ideological placements of Democratic and Republican candidates as ascertained through National Election Studies polls conducted at the time of the presidential primaries.[14] In 1988, Republican respondents placed du Pont as the most "liberal" of the Republican candidates, in contrast to his markedly conservative positions. The placement of Hart moved from a moderate position in 1984 to the most liberal position in 1988, even more liberal than Jackson's classification. Obviously something was happening to cause these anomalies in the rating schemes. As for du Pont, his moderate classification most likely occurred as voters assigned an unknown candidate the neutral, or "guessing," middle position on the scale. This moved du Pont's average position toward the center of the scale, giving him a more moderate rating. For Hart, his apparently liberal lifestyle, based on the Donna Rice incident, either led people to assume his political positions were as liberal as his lifestyle or caused people to respond to the ideology question on the basis of personal characteristics rather than political positions. All in all, the public may be less willing than journalists or political scientists to classify candidates as liberals, moderates, or conservatives. Ideological classifications, whether by the public or by experts, did not distinguish 1988 candidates from their predecessors.

We have now examined three aspects of the 1988 candidates: their career paths, their home states, and their ideology. In all three areas, the 1988 candidates resembled the 1976, 1980, and 1984 candidates. Super Tuesday did not draw out a new or different type of candidate. Of course, 1988 may have been too early to look for these differences. Many candidates decided to run in the 1988 primaries simultaneous with the South's move toward a regional primary. Other candidates—Hart and Bush—decided to run long before the reality of Super Tuesday emerged. With much of Super Tuesday in place for 1992, those who think they can be advantaged by a southern regional primary may be more willing to run.

THE RESOURCES OF THE CANDIDATES

The ability of the 1988 candidates to win the nomination would depend on the structure of the calendar, FEC state and national spending limits, the

Table 2.11: Ideological Placement of Candidates by Experts

	Democrats	Republicans
1972		
Liberals	Chisholm Lindsay McCarthy McGovern	McCloskey
Moderates	Humphrey H. Jackson Muskie	Nixon
Conservatives	Mills Wallace Yorty	Ashbrook
1976		
Liberals	Bayh Brown Church Harris Shriver Udall	
Moderates	Carter H. Jackson	Ford
Conservatives	Wallace	Reagan
1980		
Liberals	Brown Kennedy	Anderson
Moderates	Carter	Baker Bush
Conservatives		Connally Crane Dole Reagan

various delegate allocation rules, and the resources of each candidate. Candidates do not have the same assets, and some have more of one asset than another. Some candidates have very few assets, but no candidate has unlimited resources. Each candidate must make strategic decisions about how best to deploy his finite resources to win the maximum benefits. The

Table 2.11, continued

	Democrats	Republicans
	1984	
Liberals	Cranston Hart J. Jackson McGovern Mondale	
Moderates	Glenn	
Conservatives	Askew Hollings	Reagan
	1988	
Liberals	Babbitt Dukakis Hart J. Jackson Simon	
Moderates	Gephart Gore	Bush Dole
Conservatives		du Pont Haig Kemp Robertson

Sources: Kessel 1980, 17-20; Kessel 1988, 20-28; Morrison 1988, 50-57; Reiter 1985, 112-115.

resources candidates have may be both tangible and intangible, but time, money, and name recognition tend to be the most important.

Name recognition helps win elections both directly and indirectly. Direct effects accrue because voters are reluctant to vote for candidates of whom they have not heard. Patterson (1980) estimated Jimmy Carter gained 12 percent in the 1976 Pennsylvania primary simply because he was better known than the other candidates. Indirectly, name recognition helps to win primaries by aiding in the collection of campaign contributions, which in turn can be converted into television commercials and campaign visits, further increasing a candidate's name recognition.

Table 2.12 lists the recognition levels of candidates in April, July, and October 1987, before most of the public became aware of the campaign. Thus, these figures represent the baseline on which candidates were able to

Democrats

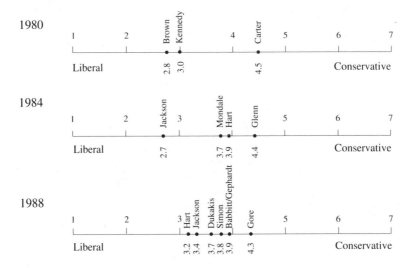

Republicans

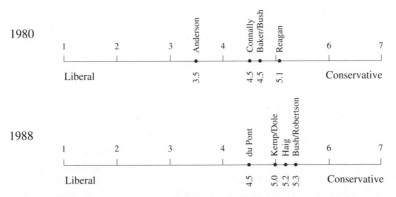

Figure 2.3: Ideological Placement of Presidential Candidates by the American Public

Table 2.12: Percentages of National Poll Respondents Who Recognized
Candidates' Names in 1987

	April	July	October
Democrats			
Babbitt	24	36	38
Dukakis	21	43	49
Gephardt	25	39	44
Gore	22	40	46
Jackson	92	94	96
Simon	—	45	46
Republicans			
Bush	96	97	98
Dole	79	83	83
du Pont	31	33	34
Haig	85	83	82
Kemp	65	61	58
Robertson	79	72	80

— = candidate's name not included in poll

Source: Gallup Poll, December 1987.

attract funds and also represent the need for some candidates to build up recognition as a prerequisite for a successful campaign. Using October 1987 figures, four Republicans (Bush, Dole, Haig, and Robertson) were recognized by over 80 percent of the population. The other two candidates, Kemp and du Pont, obviously were at a disadvantage before the campaign even began. They would first have to catch up with their fellow Republican candidates. The Democratic side presents the opposite picture. Only Jesse Jackson was universally recognized. Hart, who is missing from these polls taken during the period he suspended his campaign after the Donna Rice incident, also was widely known. The remaining five all went unrecognized by over half of the American public.

Time is a resource theoretically equally divided among all candidates. Yet some candidates have other obligations that distract them from the campaign trail. Dole's duties as the leader of the Senate Republicans often kept him in Washington, D.C. and off the campaign trail. Dukakis's duties as governor of Massachusetts drew him back to Boston. In recent campaigns, candidates with fewer obligations often seemed to be at an advantage. Both Carter and Reagan first won their nominations when they were ex-governors. With this in mind, several candidates relinquished government posts in order to run in the 1988 campaign. Gary Hart did not seek reelection to the Senate in 1986. Similarly, many people felt Howard Baker left his Senate seat to run for the Republican nomination, though Baker later accepted a position in the Reagan White House instead. Of the seven Democratic candidates in 1988, four held current government positions. Besides Hart, Babbitt no longer held a government post, while Jackson had never occupied a government position. On the Republican side, three candidates (Bush, Dole, and Kemp) held current government positions, though Kemp announced he would not seek renomination to his House seat. Du Pont and Haig no longer held their government jobs, while Robertson stepped down from his position as the chairman of CBN and host of the 700 Club television show. Ironically, in 1988 the successful candidates held government posts, with Bush occupying the vice presidency and Dukakis holding down the governorship of Massachusetts. Perhaps the most essential asset in a front-loaded nomination season is money, not time.

Money is the mother's milk of political campaigns, or so it is often said. Money greatly affects the strategies employed by each of the presidential candidates. Since 1974, strict rules have existed for raising money in a presidential campaign. Candidates can receive no more than $1,000 from any individual or $5,000 from any political action committee (PAC). During the nomination phase of the presidential race, candidates qualify for a system of matching funds by raising $5,000 in each of at least twenty states in contributions of $250 or less. Once qualified, each candidate receives one dollar from a federal fund for each dollar raised. Only the first $250 from an individual's contribution is matched by federal funds.[15] A candidate loses his matching funds if he fails to win 10 percent of the vote in two consecutive primaries.

Once candidates accept matching funds, they must abide by strict national and state spending limits. Each state has a specific spending limit based on its population size. In 1988, state limits varied from $461,000 (in sixteen states, two territories and the District of Columbia) to $7,509,505 (in California). The national limit of $23 million in 1988 is smaller than the total of all the state limits.[16] Both state and national spending limits require even wealthy candidates to make strategic decisions on where to expend their resources. Candidates are not bound to accept matching funds, though they remain bound to the individual contribution limits. John Connally, in 1980, refused the federal matching funds so as not to be subject to the national and state spending limits. After spending an estimated $13.7 million, Connally won only one delegate (Alexander 1983). Pat Robertson considered declining matching funds. He accepted the first matching-fund payment in January 1988 but placed the money in an escrow account with the possibility of returning it to the federal government. However, the Robertson campaign then proceeded to borrow against these funds, raising legal questions as to whether the money could be returned as unused. Speculations arose that Robertson wanted to avoid accepting matching funds so that he would not be confined to the overall national spending limits. Robertson hoped to be able to afford an all-out media blitz on Super Tuesday, which would put him over the national limit, as he had spent over half the limit in 1987 alone (Wilcox 1991). In the end, Robertson accepted and used the matching funds and came close to spending the national limit by the close of Super Tuesday.

Presidential campaigns are costly affairs, and raising the millions of dollars needed for a successful campaign is not an easy task. Having to raise funds in sums of less than $1,000 makes the task especially onerous, since methods that can accomplish this, such as direct mail, are costly and time-consuming. Many of the 1988 candidates evaded some of the costs of raising funds by establishing PACs before they became legally declared presidential candidates. Monies raised by these precandidacy PACs do not count against FEC spending limits once the candidate declares his candidacy. Legally, these precandidacy PACs are created to help other candidates, such as those running for House or Senate seats, or to strengthen party organizations.[17] Yet less than 10 percent of this PAC money is ever contributed to House or Senate candidates. Instead, precandidacy PACs subsidize travel by the potential presidential candidate and pay the salaries of future staff members. Most important, these PACs are used to develop mailing lists of potential contributors for the presidential campaign. One campaign official estimated that the Campaign for Prosperity PAC saved Kemp's presidential campaign $2 million in fund-raising costs (Corrado 1990; Wilcox 1991).

In 1988 all of the Republican candidates and four Democratic candidates established precandidacy PACs. (See table 2.13 for a complete listing.) Three of the remaining four Democratic candidates relied on some other vehicle to finance their pre-election campaigning. Hart created a tax-exempt foundation, the Center for a New Democracy, which legally was to house a think tank for new policy ideas but served to finance Hart's appearances across the country. Robertson employed a similar tactic with his tax-exempt foundation, the Freedom Council.[18] Jesse Jackson financed his activities in 1987 with an "exploratory" committee. Finally, the FEC allowed Dukakis to transfer $380,000 and the list of contributors from his 1986 gubernatorial campaign to his 1988 presidential campaign. Only Gore had no precandidacy organization (Corrado 1990).

Bush built the wealthiest precandidacy PAC, his Fund for America's Future (FAF). Two years before the election, this PAC employed fifty people with Lee Atwater as its chair. FAF "included the personnel needed to raise funds from large and small donors, develop national and state political structures, recruit volunteers, engage in policy research, conduct polls, develop direct mail programs, and monitor compliance with federal regulations" (Corrado 1990, 19-20). FAF provided Bush with a ready-made campaign organization once he formally declared his candidacy. For his own campaign fund, Bush raised most of his money in $1,000 contributions. His

Table 2.13: Precandidacy Political Action Committees (PACs) Associated with
the 1988 Presidential Nomination Seekers

	PACs	Money raised in millions
Republicans		
Bush	Fund for America's Future	$10.8
Dole	Campaign America	6.5
Kemp	Campaign for Prosperity	4.2
Haig	Committee for America	1.1
Robertson	Committee for Freedom/Freedom PAC	.7
du Pont	GOPAC[a]	
Democrats		
Gephardt	Effective Government Committee	$1.2
Simon	The Democracy Fund	.5
Babbitt	Americans for the National Interest	.2
Biden	Fund for '86	.1

[a]Du Pont's GOPAC contributed money solely to state and local races and thus was not required to report spending to the Federal Election Commission

Source: Corrado 1990.

vice presidential status made his $1,000 a plate dinners successful. One Houston dinner raised $750,000 (Wilcox 1991).

Dukakis raised the most money on the Democratic side with the help of Robert Farmer, the finance chairman for Dukakis's 1982 bid for governor. Farmer sought out upper-middle-class professionals who could raise $10,000 for the Dukakis campaign by soliciting contributions from friends and relative. "It was Tupperware on a grand scale, with a political twist" (Black and Oliphant 1989, 106). Nearly 1,000 individuals raised $10,000 or more for the Dukakis campaign. In addition, about 16 percent of Dukakis's money came from Greek Americans (Berke, December 27, 1987). Farmer raised the maximum allowed by law, while refusing all PAC money and contributions from lobbyists, state contractors, and those seeking ambassadorships in return for hefty contributions (Black and Oliphant 1989).

Dole raised most of his funds in much the same manner as Dukakis. The difference was that Dole's team of fund-raisers promised to collect $50,000 from friends and business acquaintances. While Bush, Dukakis, and Dole relied on $1,000 contributions, Jackson, Simon, Kemp, and Robertson collected money in much smaller sums. As in 1984, Jackson once again raised money through collections at black churches, but in 1988 he supplemented this with mail and phone solicitations. Kemp, Simon, and especially Robertson relied on direct mail, a costly method of raising funds. Contributions solicited by direct mail rarely exceed twenty-five dollars, and mailings

Table 2.14: Financial Status, in Dollars, of the Presidential Candidates
as of February 29, 1988

	Total Raised	Total Spent	Cash on Hand	Debt
Republicans				
Bush	27,397,118	20,516,839	6,704,924	1,123,325
Dole	22,674,153	21,837,703	836,445	716,107
Kemp	14,245,571	14,185,891	59,686	765,233
Robertson	32,702,667	25,290,344	7,412,321	8,398,916
Democrats				
Dukakis	17,772,687	14,852,259	2,920,431	569,344
Gephardt	8,014,125	7,500,695	450,037	1,034,506
Gore	7,260,594	6,919,668	342,964	91,858
Hart	4,453,403	3,472,410	488,966	34,661
Jackson	4,633,892	4,204,918	428,974	845,857
Simon	8,047,922	7,287,167	760,755	825,199

Source: Federal Election Commission, April 12, 1988.

are quite expensive. Kemp's direct mail costs ate up forty cents of every dollar raised (Wilcox 1991).

By the time Super Tuesday approached, the 1988 candidates possessed very unequal monetary resources. Of course, some spending for the Super Tuesday campaign occurred in 1987 as well as 1988, but last-minute campaigning in the South would depend on candidates' financial resources at the beginning of March. Table 2.14 provides each candidate's assets as of February 29, 1988. The cash-on-hand figures provide the best indication of a candidate's ability to compete on Super Tuesday. The debts of most candidates, except Dukakis and Bush, arose as they borrowed against future matching funds to pay for current expenses. Gore borrowed $1 million to help finance his Super Tuesday campaign. Of course, some Super Tuesday campaigning occurred prior to March 1 and thus is represented in the amount of funds already spent.

On the Republican side, Robertson raised the most money and spent the most. Robertson's large amount of cash on hand came from a $6 million loan he took out at the end of February (Wilcox 1991). Robertson's heavy spending during the early part of the campaign brought him close to the overall national limits by the close of Super Tuesday. By the end of February, Robertson as well as Dole had already spent 80 percent of the national limit (Wilcox 1991). Even if Robertson and Dole had done better at the polls, both would have been hard-pressed to compete with Bush under such restrictive financial conditions. Bush held the best financial position as Super Tuesday approached. Having raised $27 million and spent $21 million, he still had nearly $7 million on hand, while owing only $1 million. Such monetary resources would allow Bush considerable leeway in his final preparations for Super Tuesday. Dole raised nearly as much money as Bush or Robertson but by Super Tuesday had few dollars left. Dole, as Gephardt, did not benefit financially from his victory in Iowa (Wilcox 1991). Kemp never played in the same league as the other three Republicans, raising only half as much money and having almost no money in reserve for the March campaign.

On the Democratic side, Dukakis led the financial race, raising twice as much as any other Democrat, although his figure was still $10 million less than Bush's or Robertson's. Dukakis, as Bush, had a rosy future for Super Tuesday with nearly $3 million on hand at the beginning of March. Gephardt, Gore, and Simon, lagging behind Dukakis, raised and spent roughly equal amounts. Gephardt and Simon, however, were saddled with much larger debts than Gore, who had significantly reduced his pre-Super Tuesday campaigning outside the South. As mentioned previously, Gore borrowed $1 million to complete his Super Tuesday campaigning. Hart and Jackson raised only one-fourth as much as Dukakis, and half as much as Gephardt, Gore, or Simon. Jackson had less need for a large campaign war chest. His strong support among black voters and the free media attention his campaign engendered allowed a low-budget campaign to produce significant votes. Hart, however, without financial support was soon forgotten by the media and voters.

At the onset of Super Tuesday, Bush and Dukakis led their respective parties with the most resources available for the grueling twenty-state campaign. Bush enjoyed widespread recognition and ample financial resources, but Dole and Robertson also enjoyed recognition and sizable campaign chests. On the Democratic side, Dukakis was less widely recognized than Bush or Dole, but he led the Democratic pack in terms of finances. His ample resources gave Dukakis a head start on his Super Tuesday campaign. Dukakis could afford to jet down to the South in the midst of the Iowa campaign (Walsh, December 5, 1987). Meanwhile, Gephardt had spent as much as he had raised in the early part of the campaign and was forced to spend most of the first week of March raising funds rather than campaigning. Simon similarly lacked the funds to approach the mega-state campaign, and moreover had failed to attain the early victories necessary to encourage more contributions. Only Gore could challenge Dukakis financially as Super Tuesday approached.

SUMMARY

Super Tuesday altered the playing field for the 1988 presidential nomination contests. The front-loading of the delegate selection process increased, with the selection of over 50 percent of the delegates initiated by the second week in March. One-third of all convention delegates were chosen on Super Tuesday. But in order to win these delegates, Democratic and Republican candidates had to play on different fields. The Republican field, with a preponderance of winner-take-all primaries, opened the possibility for one candidate, with a sweep of these primaries, to tie up the nomination. Democratic proportional representation rules divided delegates among several candidates, making a clean sweep less likely. In addition to having to follow a distinct set of rules, candidates on Super Tuesday had to court a unique set of voters in order to win delegates. Southern voters remained poorer, less likely to belong to a union, more likely to be black, more likely to be members of a conservative religion, and more likely to be Democrats but less likely to be liberals than voters in other regions of the country. All in all, the Super Tuesday playing field presented candidates with a unique set of circumstances.

Still, the characteristics of the 1988 players matched those of presidential candidates in recent years. Senators and governors predominated. Sam Nunn did not run, but three other southern or border state Democrats (i.e., Gephardt, Gore, and Jackson) did. In fact, southern candidates have not been a rarity in recent years. The hoped-for conservative Democrat did not run in 1988, but then few conservatives have run or done well in the past. Mostly liberal candidates contest the Democratic primaries while mostly conservative candidates vie for the Republican nomination. The public, nevertheless, tends to have great difficultly in describing candidates as liberal or conservative. Ideology may not be as important to voters as it was to Super Tuesday's architects.

The seven Democratic and six Republican candidates began their quests for the presidency at different starting lines. Bush outpaced the other Republicans in name recognition and financial resources. On the Democratic side, Jackson led in public recognition, while Dukakis led in financial assets. The playing field was not even for the rest of the candidates. In Chapter 3, we will investigate the campaign strategies of the 1988 candidates in face of their competition, their varying resources, and a playing field altered by the presence of Super Tuesday.

3

Candidates' Strategies: Iowa, New Hampshire, & Super Tuesday

"I feel like my home is Hartsfield Airport in Atlanta," lamented Lanny Griffith. John Dukakis learned to "work y'all into a sentence better than anyone in Boston," and Ron Daniels visited fourteen communities in three days (Etherton, March 1, 1988, 6). Such frenzied activity characterized the preparation of these Bush, Dukakis, and Jackson campaigners for Super Tuesday. Having to compete in sixteen primaries and four caucuses on the same day resulted in frazzled candidates and campaign staffs stretched thin. Strategic decisions about where to expend campaign resources became all the more important with so many delegates at stake at one time.

Super Tuesday placed enormous time constraints on the candidates. While the candidates laid the groundwork of their Super Tuesday campaigns in 1986 and 1987, with early visits to the South and the development of state and local campaign organizations, election year campaigning was squeezed into the three-week period between the New Hampshire primary and March 8. During this short time period, candidates faced competing not just in sixteen states but rather in 121 media markets for television advertising and in 171 congressional districts, the basis upon which most delegates were selected.[1] Illustrating this point were the two maps that covered the office walls of Gore's chief delegate tracker, Rick Hutcheson. One map designated each election district, including the number of delegates to be selected. Circles outlining media markets filled the second map. Hutcheson's job required him to calculate which election districts Gore might be able to win and to coordinate these with the nearest media market. Mismatches between the two maps often occurred, but once a match was made, Gore would be sent to campaign in the area. A quick airport stopover would net local television coverage, which might also be augmented with additional television advertising (O'Byrne, March 6, 1988).

The vast geographical size of Super Tuesday coupled with the short time frame led to "tarmac campaigning," in which candidates jetted across the South, making numerous short stops on each day but rarely venturing far beyond the airport runways. For example, Robertson scheduled visits to nine cities for February 25: Louisville, Kentucky; Bristol, Tennessee; Birmingham, Alabama; Columbus, Mississippi; Springfield and Kansas City, Missouri; Tulsa and Oklahoma City, Oklahoma; and Dallas, Texas. With an average stopover of sixty-five minutes at each airport, Robertson hoped to reach 5.2 million households via local television coverage (Sack, February 25, 1988). With tarmac campaigning, cities with airports and television stations received a parade of candidates. Small towns and rural areas, where over 40 percent of Southerners live, were ignored (Phillips, February 24, 1988). By contrast, Robertson crisscrossed Iowa in a bus, scheduling stops from Pocahontas to Strawberry Point (Roberts, January 19, 1988). The entire Democratic and Republican field descended on Oskaloosa, Iowa, population 10,000 (Apple, January 28, 1988).

The condensed format of Super Tuesday forced candidates to rely on the media to contact most voters. The in-person campaigning used in Iowa and New Hampshire became infeasible with thousands of miles to cover. When relying on media, candidates face three options: national news media, local news media, and paid media. With eight major candidates on Super Tuesday, no one candidate could expect much attention from the national media, except perhaps with a decisive or unexpected victory in Iowa or New Hampshire. Still, most candidates could not rely on extensive national coverage in the weeks prior to Super Tuesday, so they turned their attentions to the local media, hoping to capture a few seconds or even a minute on local nightly newscasts. Candidates were aided in their quests by the advent and widespread usage of satellite television technology. By videotaping a speech and relaying it through a satellite transmission or by establishing a live hook-up with a group of local television stations, each candidate could multiply his audience. For example, by the beginning of March, Gephardt had been seen in sixty of Super Tuesday's media markets, though he actually visited only twenty. Gephardt reached the other forty through satellite appearances (Risen, March 4, 1988). Similarly, Dukakis used satellite technology to schedule interviews with nearly two dozen local stations, covering every Super Tuesday state, on the final day of the campaign (Drogin, March 8, 1988).

The other media option open to Super Tuesday candidates required purchasing television time to broadcast campaign advertisements. With paid media, candidates control the message being sent, but that message is very expensive with 121 media markets to cover. No candidate could afford to blanket the South with campaign commercials. Dukakis's $2 million advertising budget allowed him to run commercials in eleven of the twenty Super

Tuesday states (Drogin, March 8, 1988). Al Gore topped Dukakis with a $3 million blitz, but Gephardt's depleted treasury allowed only $1 million for advertising in the South. Jackson's low-budget, two-commercial campaign cost a mere $100,000. With little time or money to develop elaborate media packages, many candidates resorted to broadcasting negative commercials in attempts to dissuade people from supporting their competitors. Yet Republicans began running negative advertisements even before the Iowa caucuses, and Democrats soon followed suit in New Hampshire.

Super Tuesday's size led candidates to rely on airplanes and airwaves to contact voters, but the elements of candidate strategy remained the same as in previous campaigns. Candidates plan how to use their limited resources to win the presidential nomination given the nature of the competition, the election calendar, and their intermediate goals. This chapter will explore how each candidate approached Super Tuesday with its wealth of delegates but staggering costs.

CANDIDATE STRATEGIES IN 1988

Ultimately, all presidential nomination seekers need to gain the support of 50 percent of convention delegates to win the nomination. But candidates can choose varied paths in attempting to fulfill this goal. These varied paths are the campaign strategies of the candidates. Candidate strategies take into account the structure of the playing field (i.e., the election calendar, delegate distribution rules, and FEC state and national spending limits) and the structure of the candidate field. According to John Aldrich (1980), candidate strategies depend on the number of other candidates. In a two-candidate race, each candidate calculates both his own and his opponent's strength in each upcoming event. Candidates expend more resources in a primary if both candidates are evenly matched in a state and fewer resources if one candidate has a big lead or a huge deficit. However, a candidate might allocate a few resources to a state favorable to his opponent if the state uses proportional representation rules, which allow the second-place finisher to pick up a few delegates. Both candidates will seek out states with more delegates at stake or holding earlier primaries. Determining the most rational strategy when a large number of candidates compete is not as easy to define, but Aldrich proposed some possibilities. In multicandidate races most candidates should contest most primaries, but each candidate may choose certain states as more crucial and target them. Unlike in two-candidate races, in multicandidate races each candidate tends to concentrate on the states most favorable to his own candidacy so that winning somewhere will boost his image.

In multicandidate races, the candidate field often becomes subdivided into smaller contests between select groups of candidates. Aldrich (1980) and Brams (1978) assert that candidates fall into three ideological groups, with only one candidate from each group surviving the initial round of primaries. For instance, in 1980, Reagan beat out Crane, Connally, and Dole to become the surviving conservative candidate; Bush bested Baker as the moderate candidate; while Anderson alone represented the liberal wing. In 1988, a number of the Republican candidates also competed along an ideological division, as Kemp, Robertson, du Pont, and Haig vied to be the conservative alternative to Bush. Ideological divisions on the Democratic side in the 1980s, however, seem less clear-cut. The 1984 Hart-Mondale race was not between liberals and conservatives but between more traditional New Deal Democrats and newer technocrat Democrats. By 1988, battles to emerge as the leader of a regional division overshadowed any ideological cleavages. Simon's loss to Gephardt in Iowa doomed the rest of his campaign as Gephardt emerged as the candidate of the Midwest.

While all candidates hold the same ultimate goal of winning the nomination, three intermediate goals may be adopted. Some candidates seek momentum, others pursue delegates, while a third group may aim to eliminate a competitor from the race. The goal of capturing momentum often characterizes lesser-known candidates (Gurian 1986) or candidates in the early part of the race (Kessel 1988). The goal of accumulating a larger bloc of delegates may be foremost for better-known candidates or for all surviving candidates in the later stages of the campaign. The goal of eliminating a competitor arises when another candidate is competing for the same groups of voters, whether on the basis of ideology or geography.

When the goal is momentum, a candidate allocates most of his resources to the early primary and caucus states. Because these contests are in small states, even relatively poor candidates can garner support through frequent visits or a relatively low advertising budget. Though only a few delegates can be attained by winning these early contests, election victories bring candidates more publicity. This publicity in turn raises their standings in public opinion polls and may convince more people to contribute money to their campaigns. Such momentum, however, does not guarantee ultimate victory. Bush's triumph in the 1980 Iowa caucus placed him on the front cover of *Newsweek,* while *Time's* main campaign article proclaimed in a subtitle that "Bush Soars" (Surprise Harvest in Iowa, February 4, 1980). Nevertheless, Reagan bested Bush in the New Hampshire primary and went on to claim the Republican nomination. The momentum strategy sets up a difficult road to success, as rising expectations require constant victories at the polls. Campaign funds may not arrive quickly enough to meet the increasing demands of a growing campaign. Furthermore, by concentrating so much energy on the first two contests, the momentum-seeking candidate enters the remaining primaries well behind in candidate organization and groundwork. For example, in 1984, Hart found he did not have full slates of delegates filed in Florida and Illinois after capturing momentum by winning the New Hampshire primary.

Delegate-seeking goals characterize better-known, better-financed candidates. These candidates can afford to run in the larger states where more delegates are at stake. Better-financed candidates also can withstand a few losses, as Reagan did in 1980 and Mondale in 1984. However, these candidates too must win an early contest to maintain their credibility. A long shot candidate, such as Carter in 1976, who successfully plays the momentum strategy becomes an established candidate and switches to a delegate-maximizing strategy in the latter part of the campaign. The delegate-acquisition strategy, however, also is not an easy task. To acquire large blocs of delegates, candidates must win the votes of a wide variety of individuals. Conflicts may arise among these diverse groups of supporters. Jimmy Carter alienated many of his black supporters when he promised to support white working-class desires for ethnic neighborhoods prior to the 1976 Pennsylvania primary. Additionally, candidates with the status to seek large blocs of delegates receive more intense scrutiny from the media, fellow candidates, and the public. Mondale derailed Hart's bid for a growing portion of the delegate totals by asking the simple question, "Where's the beef?"

Eliminating a rival becomes a central goal when another candidate stands in the path to victory. This other candidate often is pursuing the same groups of voters. The fight between rival candidates might be along ideological lines, as a couple of Republican candidates fight to remain the conservative candidate in the race or two or three Democrats battle to become the liberal alternative. On the other hand, the rivalries may fall along regional lines, as Jimmy Carter and George Wallace fought in Florida to become the southern candidate in 1976. With the goal of eliminating a rival, a candidate often targets a state or a group of states to demonstrate his superiority. Gephardt and Simon poured resources into the early primaries and caucuses in the upper Midwest in their quest to establish credibility in their own region. Controlling one ideological or regional faction of the party, however, will not win the nomination. The surviving candidate will need to turn his attention toward capturing the support of other groups within the party in order to accumulate the required number of convention delegates.

We will now review the strategies of the Democratic and Republican candidates in 1988 to gain insight into how the changing landscape of Super Tuesday affected their plans. We will begin with the stories of three candidates—Haig, du Pont, and Babbitt—who never made it to Super Tuesday, and follow with those of three more candidates—Simon, Hart, and Kemp—who did so poorly in the early primaries and caucuses that they were no longer considered serious candidates as Super Tuesday approached. We will then consider the stories of the major contenders on Super Tuesday, before examining in more detail the overall pattern of resource allocation in 1988 and in previous years. With the latter analysis, we will see whether Super Tuesday changed candidate strategies.

CANDIDATES DEFEATED BEFORE SUPER TUESDAY

Alexander M. Haig, Jr.:
The Anti-Bush Candidate

Former army officer, NATO commander, and secretary of state Al Haig led a low-budget, late-starting, "if only" campaign. If only some crisis would shake people's confidence in Bush. If only some candidate would drop out of the race so that Haig could pick up his supporters. If only voters would look at the issues instead of at personalities. If only Haig could erase from the public's memory the phrase "I am in control here"—Haig's misstatement about his authority as secretary of state when President Reagan was shot in 1981 that led the public to view him as a Rambo-like figure (Germond and Witcover 1989, 69). Additionally, Haig had to hope that the media would stop considering the Republican race as a two-man contest between Bush and Dole. Then if Haig could survive Iowa and New Hampshire, he could move on to what he perceived as friendly territory in the southern Super Tuesday primaries.

None of Haig's "if onlys" came true. In October 1987, the financially strapped Haig campaign decided to forgo Iowa and concentrate on New Hampshire, dreaming of a third- or fourth-place finish. On February 13, 1988, three days before the New Hampshire primary, Al Haig withdrew from the race after calculating that he would receive only 3,000 votes. Endorsing Dole, Haig hoped his supporters would help Dole beat Bush in New Hampshire (Runkel 1989, 10-12). A primary motive of Haig's presidential bid had always been to prevent Bush, whom Haig considered unelectable and ineffective in his previous government positions, from winning the nomination (Warner, January 25, 1988; Weinraub, February 13, 1988). Even Haig's withdrawal "if only" did not come to pass, as Bush bested Dole 38 percent to 28 percent. Haig's momentum-seeking candidacy failed on all fronts.

Pierre S. "Pete" du Pont IV:
The Alternative to the Alternative to Bush

Pete du Pont also pinned his hopes for the presidency on someone beating Bush in Iowa and New Hampshire. Such a dual loss, du Pont speculated, would force Bush from the race, and someone else would take over as the front-runner. Du Pont did not expect to be the new front-runner; his limited resources would not be enough to win in Iowa or New Hampshire. But if du Pont did respectably well in these contests, he felt he could emerge as the conservative alternative to the new front-runner (Runkel 1989, 1-2). Du Pont planned to attract support with his unique set of conservative issue positions: a voucher system for education, allowing pupils and parents to choose their own schools; an option for individuals to have their own retirement plans in lieu of Social Security; random drug testing of high school students; required work in return for welfare benefits; and elimination of $25 billion in farm subsidies. Du Pont never had the opportunity to be the alternative to the alternative to Bush because, even though Bush faltered in Iowa, Bush's New Hampshire victory kept him as the front-runner heading into Super Tuesday. Du Pont, finishing fifth in Iowa (7 percent of vote) and fourth in New Hampshire (10 percent of vote), withdrew from the race on February 18, two days after New Hampshire, eliminating the second momentum-seeking candidate from the Republican race.

Bruce E. Babbitt:
All His Eggs in the Iowa Basket

Bruce Babbitt's campaign manager, Frederick Du Val, admitted that all Babbitt's eggs were in one basket—Iowa (Runkel 1989, 5). He also admitted that this was not a novel idea. It was the classic momentum strategy. Jimmy Carter's victory in the 1976 Iowa caucus gave him momentum heading into the New Hampshire primary.[2] Babbitt's momentum-seeking plan contained two parts. First, he would present himself as the successful governor of a state. Unfortunately for Babbitt, the better-financed Dukakis also claimed that theme. Second, Babbitt would run as the uncandidate—the awkward television personality who told the hard truth about the issues. Once again, Babbitt's plan misfired as this theme played better with the media than with voters. With losses in Iowa and New Hampshire, and no western primaries until May, Babbitt became the third candidate to withdraw from the race before Super Tuesday.

CANDIDATES LIMPING INTO SUPER TUESDAY

Jack F. Kemp:
The Third Alternative to the Alternative to Bush

Jack Kemp's strategy, as those of Haig and du Pont, hinged on someone crippling Bush in Iowa and New Hampshire. If that happened, Kemp could compete in Super Tuesday, win a few states, and move west as the alternative to Dole or a weakened Bush. Just as the strategy failed for du Pont and Haig, the strategy failed for Kemp.

Kemp had hoped to win support as the "progressive conservative," advocating supply-side economics and maintaining a tough anticommunist stance while trying to attract blacks and blue-collar workers to the Republican party (Silk, March 6, 1988). Instead, Kemp found himself battling du Pont for the support of economic conservatives and Robertson for the vote of moral conservatives. Meanwhile, Bush's money, strong organization, and links to President Reagan garnered him the support of the majority of conservative voters in the Republican ranks (Runkel 1989, 12-15). Disappointing fourth- and third-place showings in Iowa and New Hampshire left South Carolina as Kemp's last hope for a pre-Super Tuesday victory. Despite massive campaign spending in the state, Kemp trailed Bush, Dole, and Robertson in the South Carolina vote, leaving Kemp little realistic hope of success on Super Tuesday. Kemp officially ended his campaign two days later, on March 10, after spending $15 million and eleven months on the campaign trail (Warren, March 11, 1988).

Paul Simon:
Nice Guys Finish Second, Sometimes Third

Originally, Paul Simon did not want to run for the presidency. He wanted Senator Dale Bumpers of Arkansas to run, viewing Bumpers as a more reliable advocate of Hart's "new ideas" (Germond and Wicover 1989, 219). Bumpers's withdrawal from the race forced Simon to reverse himself and declare his candidacy in April 1987. Simon depicted himself as an old-fashioned Democrat in the style of Hubert Humphrey or Franklin Delano Roosevelt. Wearing his trademark bow tie, Simon believed his small-town, nice-guy image would play well in Iowa and New Hampshire, thus giving him momentum to ride into Super Tuesday.

In reality, the Simon campaign had five phases. Phase one entailed using Simon's regional appeal to win in Iowa. Coming from neighboring Illinois, Simon at times led the Iowa public opinion polls. But Dick Gephardt of Missouri also had next-door-neighbor appeal. Furthermore, Gephardt struck an emotional appeal in pro-labor Iowa with television commercials emphasizing trade sanctions against Korea and Japan. Simon finished three percentage points behind Gephardt in the Iowa caucuses, torpedoing phase one. In phase two, the Simon campaign aimed to finish second to Dukakis in New Hampshire, ahead of Gephardt. While not being geographically close to New Hampshire, Simon anticipated that his small-town roots would play well in New Hampshire. These roots did not play well enough; Simon finished third, trailing Gephardt once again. With no early victory, Simon's campaign treasury fell $500,000 in debt (Harvey and

Straus, February 25, 1988). In phase three, Simon asserted he would withdraw from the race if he did not win either South Dakota's primary or Minnesota's caucus on February 23. Phase three lasted twenty-four hours. Illinois politicians slated as Simon delegates could not be elected to the Democratic national convention if Simon withdrew from the race. So Simon's do-or-die strategy in South Dakota and Minnesota was dropped. If that strategy had continued, Simon would have exited the race sooner, as he lost to Gephardt in South Dakota and Dukakis in Minnesota.

In phase four of Simon's campaign, the candidate bypassed Super Tuesday with plans to restart his campaign in his home state of Illinois. Super Tuesday, Simon predicted, would end in a stalemate. The Democratic race for the presidency would begin anew in Illinois. Super Tuesday produced a three-way tie, not exactly a stalemate. Simon won the Illinois primary, but, as it was his home state, the victory was discounted. The last hope for the Simon campaign centered on Wisconsin. In this final phase, Simon played up his father's roots in that state and his own long-term progressive stands. Once again, Simon's hopes were dashed as he trailed Dukakis, Jackson, and Gore in the Wisconsin vote. Terry Michael, from Simon's campaign staff, concluded, "we [got] shot in Wisconsin, where we ran out of scenarios," (Runkel 1989, 17). Simon's momentum-seeking candidacy died on April 7.

Gary Hart:
The Candidate of the Future Burns Up on Reentry

The Hart campaign had two phases: pre- and post-Donna Rice. In the first phase, Hart claimed front-runner status based on his second-place finish to Walter Mondale in the 1984 race. In the pre-Donna Rice phase, Hart pursued a delegate acquisition strategy. Under this plan, Hart foresaw Super Tuesday as just another early contest that would narrow the field of candidates. Hart would use 1987 to pursue in the South the type of retail campaigning usually found only in New Hampshire and Iowa. Hart's front-runner status would force the national press to follow him as he ventured to Eclectic, Alabama, or Columbus, Georgia (Germond and Witcover 1989, 181). Nevertheless, Hart presumed the real battle in 1988 would begin after Super Tuesday among the four or five remaining candidates. Hart would be one of these candidates along with southern favorites Jackson and Gore plus one or two others. Financial resources would be kept back from Super Tuesday to be used for the Big State Showdowns to follow (Runkel 1989, 17-19). Hart's initial strategy ended in May 1987 when the *Miami Herald* printed a story alleging an adulterous liaison with model Donna Rice. The incident rekindled the character question that dogged Hart in the last half of the 1984 campaign and seemed to confirm persistent rumors of Hart's infidelities.

Under constant media criticism, Hart withdrew from the race on May 9, 1987.

Hart reentered the race on December 15, 1987, but questions abounded as to whether he could turn his notorious celebrity status into primary votes and delegates. In phase two, Hart echoed his 1984 theme of the candidate of the future, stressing new methods of dealing with foreign and domestic policies (Runkel 1989). While having a high public recognition factor, Hart found his campaign financially strapped after the seven-month hiatus, and he was unable to hire any experienced staffers, as they had already committed themselves to other candidates. Bypassing the Iowa caucus, which requires extensive organizational efforts, Hart planned to spend about half his time in early 1988 in New Hampshire and the other half in the South (Carroll, January 1, 1988). Neither effort paid off, with Hart's celebrity status failing to attract supporters in New England. Hart ran mostly a lonely campaign in the South, ignored by the media. Hart often turned to university audiences in search of supporters for his new ideas. Needless to say, Hart captured a mere 2 percent of the vote on Super Tuesday, forcing him from the race for a second time on March 10.

CONTENDERS AT THE MAIN EVENT: ON THE DEMOCRATIC SIDE . . .

Richard A. Gephardt: "The Campaign That Was Eaten by Iowa"

Bill Carrick, of the Gephardt campaign, described his boss's fate as a B movie—"The Campaign That Was Eaten by Iowa" (Runkel 1989, 3). After Hart dropped out of the race in 1987, Gephardt faced media expectations requiring him to win Iowa. These expectations caused Gephardt to pull his resources out of New Hampshire and the South to concentrate on Iowa. Fighting off challenges from Simon and even Dukakis, Gephardt won Iowa with a populist theme of blaming the establishment for the loss of jobs and farms, and with a television commercial claiming a $10,000 Chrysler K-car would cost $48,000 in South Korea because of tariffs and taxes. How many Americans, Gephardt asked, would be willing to buy a $48,000 Hyundai?

Gephardt hoped his Iowa victory would provide the momentum to help him do well in New Hampshire. He did finish second to the expected leader, Michael Dukakis, and then turned to the Lesser Antilles contests to keep his momentum building. Gephardt would continue to need primary victories to build his reputation and bring in more financial contributions. In a last-minute television advertisement blitz in South Dakota, Gephardt attacked Dukakis's 1987 proposal that financially strapped midwestern farmers grow blueberries, flowers, and Belgian endives. With this commercial, Gephardt gained thirty points in the public opinion polls in six days to win South Dakota's primary (Sack, March 2, 1988). With victories in Iowa and South Dakota, and a second-place finish in New Hampshire, Gephardt's momentum-driven candidacy was poised to take on Super Tuesday. However, Gephardt had spent so much time and money on these early contests, he had no resources left.

The 1988 election calendar made an Iowa-based momentum strategy less viable than in previous years. The seven events preceding Super Tuesday allowed other Democratic winners to grab a portion of the media's attention. The contentious battle between Bush and Dole on the Republican side and repeated questions about the true strength of Robertson's invisible army siphoned off more of the media coverage Gephardt expected to gain from his Iowa victory. Gephardt also received less coverage from the media because they expected him, as the leader in the Iowa polls, to win the caucuses. The media has a bias for surprises, and Gephardt's victory was not as surprising as those of Hart in 1984 or Carter in 1976. The attention Gephardt did receive from the media was "more cynical, more probing" than the lenient treatment of Gary Hart in the early phase of the 1984 campaign (Dionne, March 20, 1988, 26; see also Germond and Witcover 1989, 248, 268).

In addition to extra competition for media attention, the front-loaded 1988 election calendar made it more difficult for a candidate to reap a financial reward from an early campaign victory. Jimmy Carter in 1976 had seven weeks from his Iowa victory to the first southern primary. Gephardt had a mere four. Gephardt simply did not have enough time to replenish his diminished campaign war chest with new contributions spawned by his Iowa victory. Momentum-seeking candidates in 1988 found they could not capture the increased media attention and financial contributions they needed to convert early victories into a presidential nomination.

When Gephardt announced his candidacy in February 1987, he saw the South as the key to winning the nomination because of the large number of delegates available on Super Tuesday. Being from a border state, Gephardt felt he could win the support of the moderate-to-conservative white southern voter through frequent visits and by collecting endorsements from numerous southern congressmen (Straus, March 1, 1987). Yet by March 1988, Gephardt had abandoned the South for over six weeks and faced stiff competition from a true southerner in Al Gore (Straus, February 20, 1988). With little lead time, Gephardt ventured into Super Tuesday with skeletal state organizations and very little cash. In fact, Gephardt spent the first week of March outside the South trying to raise enough money to buy television time in Super Tuesday's 121 media markets (Risen, March 4, 1988).

For Super Tuesday, Gephardt reiterated his populist theme, proclaiming, "It's your fight, too" on television, in debates, and on the stump.

Targeting the unemployed and disgruntled, Gephardt campaigned intensely in the hard-hit textile and oil states of Texas, Louisiana, Oklahoma, Arkansas, North Carolina, and South Carolina. Gephardt replayed his $48,000 Hyundai advertisement. He once again attacked Dukakis with the Belgian endive commercial and with a second commercial that announced, "First the Dukakis campaign smeared Joe Biden with a negative attack video. Then the Dukakis campaign was caught spying on Paul Simon. Now Dukakis is trying to smear Dick Gephardt" (Sack, March 5, 1988, 6). Playing on southern sentiments, another Gephardt commercial featured Representative Marvin Leath (D-Tex.) proclaiming Gephardt "stood with us for lower taxes, for an oil import fee, to make America strong, for a tough trade bill to stand up for American workers. On all these issues, Gore and Dukakis were opposed to us" (Sack, March 1, 1988a, 4). With only $1 million for television time, Gephardt's commercials ran foremost in Texas and Florida and to a lesser extent in Alabama, Arkansas, Louisiana, and Oklahoma (Sack, March 5, 1988), while completely ignoring Tennessee, Virginia, and Maryland, where polls showed him trailing badly (Risen, March 4, 1988).

Gephardt's competitors, however, were not going to let this congressional insider portray himself as an anti-Washington populist. At the Williamsburg debate on February 29, Gore and Dukakis lashed out against Gephardt for supporting Reagan's 1981 tax bill. Throughout the South, Dukakis and Gore ran negative advertisements against Gephardt. One Dukakis commercial accused Gephardt of flip-flopping on the issues, while another criticized Gephardt for taking contributions from political action committees. In the states where Gephardt was the strongest, Gore featured commercials criticizing him for switching issue positions (Sack, March 5, 1988). Attacked by Dukakis, fighting with Gore for the same middle-of-the-road voters, and strapped for cash, the Gephardt campaign was unable to duplicate its previous successes in the South. On March 28, the Gephardt campaign folded.

Albert Gore, Jr.:
The Candidate from the South?

Al Gore revived his Tennessee drawl as he campaigned across the South in preparation for Super Tuesday. While Babbitt's, Gephardt's, and Simon's strategies focused on Iowa, Gore's strategy centered on Super Tuesday. Although Gore spent considerable money in Iowa and New Hampshire, he abandoned his campaign in those two states in late 1987 to concentrate on the South. By foregoing these initial contests, Gore undertook the risk of being ignored by the media during the crucial first weeks of the formal contest for the presidency. The numerous debates scheduled for 1988 helped Gore keep his name in the news. Moreover, Gore garnered local media attention by gathering up endorsements across the South, including Virginia Governor Charles Robb, former Attorney General Griffin Bell, and, at the last minute, Georgia Senator Sam Nunn. On the plus side, abandoning the northern contests preempted the press from classifying Gore's poor showings in Iowa and New Hampshire as losses and allowed the Tennessee senator to husband his resources for the southern campaign.

Unlike the other campaigns, which were financially strapped by Super Tuesday, Gore banked $3 million for the southern campaign (Runkel 1989, 21-23) and borrowed another $1 million. What the Gore campaign lacked was a message. Being the southern candidate might attract a few votes on Super Tuesday, but it would not propel Gore to the nomination as the campaign trail headed north to the Big State Showdowns. Gore established himself as the most conservative candidate on foreign policy, but his domestic themes of social justice, economic growth, and lowering the deficit through a bipartisan consensus were too vague to have much impact on voters (Sack, February 26, 1988; Alter and Clift, February 29, 1988). Finally, in late February of 1988, Gore adopted a populist theme similar to Gephardt's (Sack, March 1, 1988b).

The expanse of Super Tuesday necessitated that Gore visit at least three media markets a day (Sack and Straus, February 17, 1988). His opponents conceded to Gore his home state of Tennessee and the bordering state of Kentucky. Still, even Gore's budget would be stretched thin by Super Tuesday, leading him to concentrate on Alabama, Oklahoma, Arkansas, and Texas. Gore's support of oil import fees would help in the latter three oil states. In addition, Gore played up his southern connections. In Oklahoma, he told how a distant relative once served as its U.S. senator. In targeting North Carolina, Gore reminded voters that Tennessee and North Carolina were once the same state and that tobacco was grown on his family's farm (Harris, March 1, 1988). But Gore would eventually have to win outside the South in order to be taken seriously. Therefore, Gore spent time in Nevada before its Super Tuesday caucus and in Wyoming before its March 5 caucus.

Gore launched his media campaign for Super Tuesday the day after the Iowa caucus. With the size of Super Tuesday, Gore realized that a national advertising campaign on cable television might actually be cheaper than buying time in 121 separate media markets (Katz, February 17, 1988). Gore's early biographical commercials ran both on cable and local television (Sack, March 2, 1988). In a fight with Gephardt for the moderate to conservative southern voter, Gore blasted Gephardt in four separate advertisements. In his own version of Dukakis's "flip-flop" commercial, Gore rebroadcast portions of the Dallas debate in which he scolded Gephardt for having "voted against the minimum wage . . . now you say you're for it. You voted against the Department of Education . . . now you say you're for it" (Straus, March 4, 1988, 6).

Gephardt's victory in Iowa upset Gore's plan to win Super Tuesday via regional pride and endorsements. Gore had hoped to face two liberals on Super Tuesday, Simon and Dukakis, and walk away with the traditional Democratic vote in the South (Alter and Clift, February 29, 1988). Faced with competition for the moderate-to-conservative vote of white southerners, Gore vigorously attacked Gephardt. When late polls showed Gephardt's support rising in Texas, Gore purchased time to broadcast additional anti-Gephardt commercials. A similar strategy was employed in northern Florida (Sack, March 5, 1988). Gore preferred to face Dukakis in the remaining primaries, where he could proclaim the message that Dukakis as a northern liberal would be as unelectable as Mondale had been in 1984. With Dukakis's help, Gore defeated Gephardt in the South, but as he moved north to face Dukakis, Gore faced less friendly voters and found his campaign financially strapped. Gore would lose the Big State Showdowns to Dukakis and fade from the race after New York's April 19 primary.

Jesse Jackson:
The Rainbow Coalition over Fifty States

Jesse Jackson, with twenty years of stump speeches and the experience of running in 1984, planned to compete in every state and remain in the nomination race until the very end. Unlike other candidates, Jackson did not face a no-lose situation in Iowa and New Hampshire. Not expected to do well in these states with few black voters, Jackson could finish in third or fourth place and remain respectable. In actuality, Jackson placed fourth in both Iowa and New Hampshire with 11 percent and 8 percent of the vote, respectively. Jackson did considerably better in the Lesser Antilles contests in Minnesota, Maine, and Vermont, capturing the support of almost one out of four participants. Meanwhile, Jackson and his advisers relished the thought of Super Tuesday and the new southern electorate of blacks, Hispanics, and disgruntled farmers and factory workers. With his Rainbow Coalition, Jackson hoped to emerge a winner from Super Tuesday, but afterwards he would need at least two other candidates to remain in the race to prevent the Democratic contest from narrowing to a black versus a white candidate (Runkel 1989, 23-25).

Jackson conducted a more sophisticated, better-financed campaign in 1988 than in 1984. With a better understanding of how complicated rules turn votes into delegates, Jackson in 1988 made sure that he filed full delegate slates in each election district. Jackson's more sophisticated organization used computers and phones to locate and mobilize supporters (Painton, February 26, 1988), though he still had no money for polling (Morrison 1988, 161). Jackson's fund-raising operations were more sophisticated in 1988, incorporating both direct-mail and telephone solicitation. But this fund-raising effort started late, leaving the Jackson campaign with fewer monetary resources than other candidates at the start of 1988 (Berke, May 21, 1988). Jackson also was better off in 1988 because he had no competitor for the black vote as he did in 1984 from Mondale, whose long support of civil rights measures earned him the support of some black voters (Germond and Witcover 1989, 216).

The Jackson campaign did not neglect the South in the early days of 1988, as so many of the other candidates did. Still, Jackson continued to operate a limited media campaign. He was the last to initiate a media campaign in the South, and he broadcast all his commercials in the less expensive secondary media markets such as Roanoke, Virginia, and Midland, Texas (Morrison 1988, 160). Jackson's major advertisement, broadcast first on March 4, featured an endorsement by Bill Cosby. Jackson's only other advertisement stressed the theme that he could win the presidency.

Jackson continued to maintain his own unique style. Memorable phrases such as "Better to have Head Start and day care on the front side than jail care and welfare on the backside" enthralled audiences (Gillette, February 26, 1988, 30). Only Jackson consistently refused to criticize his opponents, even though Gephardt and Gore had stolen his populist theme. Jackson continued to reach black audiences through churches, but he also attempted to reach a broader audience with a message based on economic inequalities, not racial inequalities (Oreskes, March 2, 1988). For example, in the early midwestern caucuses and the South, Jackson related the story of two farmers. The first farmer's indication that he preferred Jackson led the second to respond that he agreed but he was uneasy because Jackson is black. The punch line comes when the first farmer counters, "But you don't seem to understand. . . . the guys that took our farms were white" (Painton, March 3, 1988, 8).

By Super Tuesday, Jackson established a national constituency that included liberal whites as well as blacks. The intensity of support from his core constituency allowed him to be competitive with a smaller campaign budget and to remain above the fray among Gephardt, Gore, and Dukakis. His success on Super Tuesday and in the early contests would bring Jackson more financial contributions than in 1984, and a victory in Michigan and second-place finishes in Illinois, Connecticut, and Wisconsin would drawn even more attention to Jackson. With the New York primary eliminating Gore from the competition, only Dukakis and Jackson remained in the race until the Democratic convention.

Michael Dukakis:
New Hampshire and Four Corners for Super Tuesday

Super Tuesday always played a dominant role in Massachusetts Governor Michael Dukakis's strategy. Being from a neighboring state to New

Hampshire, Dukakis felt confident he could win there, especially if he placed a respectable third or fourth in Iowa. Resources, however, would not be squandered on these two initial contests. With financial contributions from Massachusetts supporters and the Greek community, Dukakis had sufficient funds to establish state and local organizations across the South. His plan for Super Tuesday, however, concentrated on winning the four corners. In his own region of the Northeast, Dukakis would have no trouble winning the Massachusetts and Rhode Island primaries. A win in Maryland would complete a blitz of the eastern branch of Super Tuesday. In the West, Dukakis planned to win delegates in Washington's caucus. In the South, Dukakis aimed for the southeast corner in Florida, where numerous northerners retired, and the southwest corner in Texas, where his ability to speak Spanish would help him win the Latino vote (Runkel 1989, 8; Black and Oliphant 1989, 99).

Dukakis's liability for Super Tuesday was his reputation as a northern liberal with a Greek name. Concern over winning in the more conservative South led his southern coordinator, Marsha Hale, to test opinions in focus groups in Texas, Florida, Alabama, and North Carolina. Participants revealed they were insulted by the notion that southerners would not vote for a Greek American (Drogin, March 1, 1988). By Super Tuesday, Dukakis was proclaiming "I don't have a Southern strategy . . . I have an American strategy" (Silk, February 18, 1988, 8).

Dukakis's assets for Super Tuesday included his organizational and financial resources. For example, in Arkansas the Dukakis campaign had local chairmen in two out of every three counties plus scores of local endorsements. Besides Texas and Florida, Dukakis's ample funds stretched to target Arkansas, the northern Virginia suburbs, the Research Triangle area of North Carolina, and central Georgia (Silk, February 18, 1988). Coming out of New Hampshire with about $4 million on hand, Dukakis would be able to spend lavishly on the Super Tuesday campaign. With a $1.5 million advertising budget, Dukakis began his Super Tuesday media campaign by broadcasting a biographical advertisement in Florida, Texas, and Maryland, and Spanish language commercials in south Texas (Drogin, March 1, 1988). The number and frequency of advertisements increased as Super Tuesday approached. Dukakis's money allowed him to run both positive advertisements focusing on his qualities and positions in geographical areas where he had stronger support, such as south Florida, and negative commercials attacking his opponents in their areas of strength, such as anti-Gephardt commercials in central Florida.[3]

Dukakis attacked Gephardt's economic stands with the "flip-flop" advertisement. While a man dressed in a business suit and coiffed in a blond wig completed handsprings and jumped through a hoop, an announcer proclaimed, "You know where Mike Dukakis stands. But Congressman Gephardt? He's still up in the air" (Sack, March 5, 1988, 6). A second commercial criticized Gephardt for accepting political action committee contributions. Taking off from Gephardt's theme of "it's your fight, too," the Dukakis commercial listed twenty-four corporate PACs contributing to the Gephardt campaign, while asking, "Kinda makes you wonder. Is Dick Gephardt really fighting your fight . . . or theirs?" (Straus, March 4, 1988, 6).[4] Dukakis also made use of the *Atlanta Constitution* debate on February 27 to jab Gephardt for his support of Reagan's 1981 tax cut and Gore for his lack of executive experience (Sack, February 28, 1988).

A strong financial base coupled with a plan to chip away at the corners of the new South poised Dukakis to surprise those expecting southern conservatives to dictate the results of Super Tuesday. His four-corner strategy would provide Dukakis with a large number of Super Tuesday's delegates. Massachusetts and Rhode Island controlled 135 delegates, and Dukakis won 97. Florida had 146 delegates to offer; Texas, 198. Dukakis won 90 and 72, respectively. Even the Washington caucuses had 72 delegates, and Dukakis claimed 38.[5] (See table A.1 in the appendix for delegates won by each candidate on Super Tuesday.) Besides employing a strategy to win delegates on Super Tuesday, Dukakis emerged from Super Tuesday with ample resources. He had $2 million in his campaign chest, with another $1 million matching payment due soon (Berke, March 10, 1988). In contrast, Gore left Super Tuesday with very little money on hand (Sack, March 10, 1988). With superior resources and a narrowed field, Dukakis after Super Tuesday was poised to win large blocs of delegates in the upcoming series of large, northern industrial state primaries. As Tad Devine, Dukakis's delegate counter, had predicted, the 1988 nomination would be won through attrition, not momentum (Black and Oliphant 1989, 97).

AND ON THE REPUBLICAN SIDE . . .

Robert Dole:
The Alternative to Bush

While Kemp and du Pont hoped to be the alternative to the alternative to Bush, Dole planned to be *the* alternative to Bush. If only Dole could convince Republicans to switch from Bush to himself. But Dole found himself faced with a majority of Republican voters who thought "George Bush deserves to be the nominee in 1988" (Runkel 1989, 36-37). Dole also needed to change his public image as the sharp-tongued hatchet man of the 1976 campaign. Dole faced an uphill battle. Geography, however, could help Dole achieve a good start to his campaign. Dole's strongest support lay in the Midwest, where Reagan, and therefore Bush, was less popular. Results from Iowa, Dole hoped, would give his campaign a "bounce" before New

Hampshire, while Minnesota's caucuses and South Dakota's primary the week after New Hampshire could sustain his drive.

Dole attacked Bush throughout the early campaign period with two themes. In the first, Dole proclaimed he was "one of us," implying Bush's background of wealth and privilege left his opponent out of touch with the average American. Dole's second attack contrasted Bush's claim of the best résumé with Dole's claim of an actual record. According to Dole, while Bush stood by as Reagan's vice president, Dole produced a record of accomplishments as the Republican leader in the Senate. In the South, Dole ran a commercial showing a man walking through a snowy field without leaving any footprints, alluding to Bush's lack of a record (Rosenthal, March 1, 1988).

Numerous reports of bickering, attacks, and counterattacks between Bush and Dole dominated the media coverage of the pre-Super Tuesday Republican race, but each candidate won in his strong areas: Dole in the Midwest, Bush in the East. Dole, however, faced three disadvantages heading into Super Tuesday. First, Dole spent considerable time and money in the Lesser Antilles contests, whereas Bush bypassed Minnesota and South Dakota for South Carolina. Second, Dole on Super Tuesday would have to compete with Bush's popularity in the South, which rested on Reagan's vast popularity in the region. Third, Dole's retort to Bush that he "stop lying about my record" on national television at the close of the New Hampshire primary reminded voters of Dole's nasty side.

Dole continued to attack Bush in the South. He reiterated his own populist theme of "He's one of us," while attacking Bush on the Iran-Contra scandal. Dole implied that Bush was not tough enough to be president. With South Carolina Senator Strom Thurmond's endorsement, Dole stressed his conservative positions on defense, school prayer, and abortion, trying to capture the South's mainstream conservatives (Shepard and Christensen, February 25, 1988). Yet by the first week in March, Dole knew he could not overcome Bush's lead in the South. Dole's hopes turned to keeping the number of delegates won by Bush on Super Tuesday under five hundred, allowing Dole to catch up once the race moved on to the West and the Midwest (Feeney, March 2, 1988).

Scandal and disorganization continually plagued the Dole campaign, confirming Dole's image as a candidate who "couldn't organize a two-car funeral" (Germond and Witcover 1989, 147). In January, questions arose over whether Dole helped a former aide obtain a government contract and whether Dole's current campaign finance director personally profited from his role as director of the blind trust established for Elizabeth Dole's assets when she was secretary of transportation. In February, the Dole campaign suffered more negative publicity as two aides were curtly fired, their bags ordered off the campaign's chartered airplane. Even the day-to-day conduct of the campaign seemed disorganized. Campaigning across the South, Dole personally changed his schedule at the last minute. As a result, his advance men had little time to round up audiences for his public appearances. For a Florence, South Carolina, appearance, Dole's local chairman called on the members of his country club and his college political science class to assemble a crowd for Dole's airport appearance (Christensen, February 26, 1988). In Florida, Dole visited the construction site of Universal Studio's new theme park. Greeted by actors wearing Woody Woodpecker and Frankenstein costumes, Dole's three-sentence speech was drowned out by noise from bulldozers working in the background. Perhaps it was fortunate for Dole that no voters were there (Balzar, February 26, 1988). A few days later George Bush also campaigned at a Florida construction site, but he was cheered by construction workers as he donned a hard hat and climbed behind the wheel of a construction vehicle (McQuaid, March 6, 1988). Continuing the saga of a mismanaged campaign, in Tennessee the Dole campaign failed to file a full slate of delegates (Feeney, March 2, 1988). In the end, Dole was forced to shore up support in previous strongholds, such as Missouri and Oklahoma, (Secter and Decker, March 8, 1988) and to rely on the Robertson campaign to help slow Bush's march through the South. After Super Tuesday, Dole would struggle through the Illinois and Wisconsin primaries before money difficulties led him to quit the race.

Marion G. "Pat" Robertson:
The Man Who Would Be a Statesman

On February 8, 1988, Pat Robertson "blew up" at NBC anchorman Tom Brokaw for calling him a televangelist. The rancorous episode occurred because Robertson and his advisers wanted him to have the image "of a statesman with a religious background rather than a religious man with a statesman background" (Runkel 1989, 28). Robertson's religious background and lack of previous public office gave him high negatives in public opinion polls, even in the South. By casting a statesmanlike image, Robertson hoped to add economic conservatives to his initial support base among religious conservatives.

Robertson's Super Tuesday strategy entailed winning three small states (Alabama, Georgia, and Mississippi) and one large state (Texas). In an unusual move, Robertson's campaign targeted congressional districts with few traditional Republican voters. With fewer voters, Robertson's fervent followers could predominate, just as they had done in earlier caucus states— Michigan, Hawaii, Nevada, Alaska, Iowa, and Minnesota (Runkel 1989, 26-28). Robertson was the only candidate to test Bush in his home state of Texas, but Robertson targeted an atypical Republican constituency: charismatic Hispanics. Robertson never believed that Bush would fall from the race early. Instead, Robertson hoped to win in areas where Bush's broad-based traditional Republican vote was the weakest. Robertson planned to win in low turnout caucuses and in primaries in nontraditional Republican areas and to use the delegate-selection process to infiltrate local party organizations.

While Robertson lacked a political background, he possessed two necessary political skills: fund-raising abilities and familiarity with electronic communications. Robertson's background as a television evangelist taught him how to raise huge sums of money in small contributions from a large number of people. As the founder of the Christian Broadcasting Network, the third largest cable network, Robertson knew how to use the latest broadcast technology. He began his campaign with a live satellite broadcast to 218 locations across the country, capturing an audience between 200,000 and 300,000 and picking up 50,000 new contributors (Runkel 1989, 29). In South Carolina the Robertson campaign distributed thousands of audio tapes (Straus, March 1, 1988).

While possessing technical expertise, Robertson tended to be less careful about what he said. After finishing second in Iowa, Robertson boasted he would win in South Carolina and then sweep the South. Most candidates learn to downplay their chances, especially to the media, so that when they exceed these low expectations the media report a victory. Robertson also became embroiled in numerous controversies. In February, Robertson claimed Bush manipulated the timing of revelations that fellow Pentecostal preacher Jimmy Swaggart employed a prostitute. In a second claim, Robertson averred that his television network knew where U.S. hostages were held in Lebanon, only to be rebuked by the State Department. Similarly, Robertson's claim that the Soviet Union maintains nuclear missiles in Cuba was dismissed by the Reagan administration. Robertson alienated potential supporters among religiously conservative blacks by criticizing those opposing the South African government as playing into the hands of the communists. In a final attempt to negate bad publicity, Robertson dropped his libel suit against former California Representative Pete McCloskey a few days before Super Tuesday. McCloskey, who served with Robertson in Korea, vowed Robertson's father, a former U.S. Senator, had helped his son evade combat duty.

Despite the negative press, and polls of southern voters showing many unfavorable toward his candidacy, Robertson maintained the faith that his invisible army of religious conservatives would help him win in South Carolina and then march across the South. Bush, however, held other plans for South Carolina. Furthermore, as we shall see in subsequent chapters, the religious right is composed of many elements, not all of them favorable to Robertson's candidacy. Robertson would finish third on Super Tuesday but would use delegate-selection procedures to lay the groundwork for a future role in southern Republican politics. For instance, in Georgia the actual convention delegates were chosen in a caucus-convention process that followed the primary. Delegates chosen would be bound to vote for Bush, the primary winner, in the presidential balloting but would be free to vote as they pleased on platform and other issues (Baxter, March 13, 1988).[6] Robertson and his supporters continued to engage in a long-term strategy to gain influence in local and state Republican party organizations in Arizona, Georgia, Florida, Hawaii, Michigan, Nevada, Oregon, South Carolina, Virginia, and Washington (Hertzke 1989).

George Bush:
The Man Inside the Invisible Circle

Bob Teeter, a longtime Republican pollster and campaign strategist, authored the invisible circle theory of presidential candidacies. Inside the invisible circle reside candidates viewed by the public as realistic presidential material. Candidates that "if people woke up the next day and heard he was President, they would say, 'He's all right. He could do that'" (Runkel 1989, 32). Safely ensconced inside the invisible circle at the beginning of the 1988 campaign was George Bush.

Bush possessed more assets than most candidates: universal public recognition, a huge campaign war chest, the support of most Republican officials, experience with the national media and with running a national campaign, and knowledge of how to play the primary rules. The Bush campaign estimated that the "bounce"—the increased public approval— from a primary victory lasted seventy-two hours (Runkel 1989, 34). With this in mind, the Bush campaign felt they could win in New Hampshire regardless of what happened in Iowa. Furthermore, the seventy-two-hour bounce would help Bush right before Super Tuesday, as the friendly state of South Carolina held its primary the Saturday before March 8. Bush's South Carolina connections were both personal and political. As a child Bush stayed on a Barnwell county plantation, and his wife attended Ashly Hall, a private girls' school in Charleston (Baxter, February 21, 1988). More important, Bush's 1988 campaign strategist, Lee Atwater, hailed from South Carolina, and Atwater had connections to South Carolina's Governor Carroll A. Campbell, who eventually headed up Bush's southern campaign.

Besides the favorable 1988 calendar, Bush possessed the ability as the Republican front-runner to manipulate the nature of the race. He hoped to convince the other Republican candidates that the real contest for the party's presidential nomination would be over the support of the right wing of the Republican party. As early as 1985, Bush made overtures to more conservative Republicans. At this stage in the campaign Bush feared Kemp's popularity with the party's right wing the most. By moving to the right, Bush could capture a portion of the conservative faction while fooling other candidates to move to the right too. Du Pont, and to a lesser extent Dole, took the bait, forcing Kemp to vie with those competitors for his home base. After convincing the other candidates of the importance of the party's right wing, Bush would move to the center of the party, where he always believed the majority of Republican voters congregated (Germond and Witcover 1989, 70-72).

As the acknowledged front-runner with ample resources, Bush could withstand a few bumps on the road to Super Tuesday. He realized early his vulnerability in Iowa, where a prolonged agricultural recession made Ronald Reagan, and thus Bush, less popular. But Bush had strong support in New Hampshire, aided by Governor John Sununu's strong statewide organization. Besides, Iowa's bounce would be fading by the primary date. With South Carolina lined up directly before Super Tuesday, Bush abandoned the Lesser Antilles contests in Minnesota and South Dakota to Dole.

Bush's strengths in the South included both the obvious and less apparent. With the popularity of Reagan in the South, Bush would have clear sailing if he staved off challenges from the right. In addition, Bush possessed special strengths in the two largest states on Super Tuesday. Bush claimed Texas as his home state: he built an oil-drilling business there and served as a U.S. Representative from 1967 to 1970. In Florida, Bush earned the support of fervent anticommunist Cubans, partly as a result of his past directorship of the CIA. Bush's son also held the post of Florida's secretary of commerce. Finally, the Bush family maintained a vacation home in Florida.

Across the South, the Bush campaign ran like a well-oiled machine. His schedule listed not only precise times for events, but also what to wear, what the weather would be like, and what meals would be served on the campaign plane. As vice president, Bush's motorcade included local police, who sped ahead to seal off intersections and freeway on-ramps (McQuaid, March 6, 1988). The vice presidency and his acknowledged front-runner status allowed Bush to easily accumulate sufficient financial resources to campaign in even his weakest states: Missouri, Oklahoma, and Arkansas. As the eve of Super Tuesday approached, the Bush campaign conceded possible defeat only in North Carolina and Maryland (Eichel, March 8, 1988). On Super Tuesday he would even win these states, with victories in all states except Washington, where he lost the caucuses to Robertson. With the numerous winner-take-all victories, Bush accumulated nearly six hundred delegates and for all practical purposes wrapped up the Republican nomination.

GOALS AND STRATEGIES

Each of the major Super Tuesday candidates approached Super Tuesday with a goal in mind. Dukakis and Bush most clearly fit the category of candidates pursuing delegates. Assured of winning their own base of support, both forayed into their competitors' territories to capture a few more delegates. The key to Bush's and Dukakis's successes lay in their ample financial resources and numerous state and local organizations. Robertson also appeared to be employing a delegate-acquisition strategy. In a way, Robertson's strategy was similar to Dukakis's. Both sought delegates from atypical corners: Dukakis from the less traditional South, and Robertson from nontraditional Republicans. Jackson, too, may fit the delegate-acquisition category. With blacks comprising one-third of the southern Democratic electorate and the lowered 15 percent threshold for winning delegates, Jackson could expect to win nearly one-third of the delegates on Super Tuesday. Each of these delegate-seeking candidacies staked out a core constituency to win on Super Tuesday: Reagan supporters, the religious right, the four corners, or blacks. Each candidate also had sufficient resources for his tasks. Bush and Dukakis withheld campaign funds for their Super Tuesday campaigns. Robertson raised significant funds but perhaps spent them too quickly. What Jackson lacked in financial resources, he made up for in universal recognition and a charismatic personality. With these assets, each of these four candidates was poised to accumulate delegates on Super Tuesday.

Gore's and Dole's Super Tuesday strategies centered on defeating rivals. Gore needed to eliminate Gephardt as a threat to his core constituency: the traditional southern Democrat. If Gore split that vote with Gephardt, he would fall behind Dukakis and Jackson in the quest for Super Tuesday delegates. Gore needed to expend resources to stop Gephardt as much as to try to capture votes for himself. Similarly, Dole's strategy hinged on injuring the Bush campaign. However, Bush's strengths and Dole's mismanaged campaign left Dole in a defensive position as March 8 approached. The key element to both Dole and Gore adopting an attack strategy was a competitor for their core constituency.

The final possible strategy centers on seeking or maintaining momentum. Candidates striving for this goal are still searching for their core constituency but are hampered by limited resources. Kemp and Gephardt epitomize this strategy, but each lacked an essential ingredient to be successful. Kemp lacked victories in previous events. Even his last-ditch effort in South Carolina failed to produce a victory or even a second-place finish. Gephardt had a few victories under his belt but had little money to counter the attacks of Dukakis and Gore.

A candidate in planning strategy must first define his core constituency. Second, he must consider whether any other candidate is challenging him for this constituency, and third, the candidate must attain the resources needed to pursue his goals. A candidate who can define his constituency and who possesses ample resources will pursue a delegate-acquisition strategy, which, given the number of delegates at stake on Super Tuesday, should be the preferred strategy. A candidate who faces competition for his core constituency, however, must worry first about eliminating his rival. This strategy also requires ample resources in order to be successful. Finally, candidates with few resources must still seek recognition through momentum, at best a temporary strategy. Eventually all candidates must win large blocs of delegates to be nominated. The sooner a candidate can adopt a delegate-acquisition strategy, the more likely he will be to win the nomination. Having reviewed the individual strategies of the 1988 Democratic and Republican candidates, let us now turn to a more systematic investigation of the effects of Super Tuesday on candidate strategies.

EFFECTS OF SUPER TUESDAY ON CANDIDATE ALLOCATION OF RESOURCES

Southerners hoped that Super Tuesday would force candidates to pay more attention to the South. Two indicators of attention would be the number of campaign visits to southern states and the number of campaign funds allocated to the South. Table 3.1 lists campaign visits to the South, Iowa, and New Hampshire. Gore and Jackson on the Democratic side and Bush, Dole, and Robertson on the Republican side did spend more time in the South than in Iowa and New Hampshire. Yet all the Democratic and Republican candidates combined made 846 visits to Iowa, 655 trips to New Hampshire, and 837 trips to the South. In other words, for every trip the typical candidate made to a southern state he made one and three-fourths trips to either Iowa or New Hampshire. This disparity in attention becomes even clearer when one considers that only 235,000 individuals participated in Iowa's caucuses, which selected 2 percent of the delegates; 281,000 voted in the New Hampshire primary to select 1 percent of the delegates; while 14.6 million voted on Super Tuesday to select one-third of all delegates. Even in 1988, candidates continued to spend exorbitant amounts of time in the Big Two Opener events.

Campaign spending figures reveal the same pattern. Table 3.2 presents expenditure figures by Democratic candidates in the various states. Numbers given in this table represent money spent in each state as a percentage of Federal Election Commission (FEC) maximums.[7] Since FEC limits are based on state population figures, using these limits controls expenditure patterns for the varying sizes of the states. These percentages give us a better picture of candidate strategies, since a candidate cannot spend 100 percent in every state and still remain within national spending limits. Candidates could not even reasonably spend 25 percent of state spending limits in all the Super Tuesday states, since this would amount to $6 million. These percentage figures, however, do not tell the whole story. Although the percentage figures for Iowa and New Hampshire are quite high and those for Super Tuesday states are lower, candidates actually spent more on Super Tuesday

Table 3.1: Total Number of Visits to Iowa, New Hampshire, and the South by
1988 Presidential Candidate

	Iowa	New Hampshire	South
Democrats			
Babbitt	118	60	18
Dukakis	84	36	81
Gephardt	144	51	58
Gore	32	51	150
Hart	18	22	17
Jackson	62	19	85
Simon	88	49	32
Republicans			
Bush	38	25	102
Dole	48	56	116
du Pont	91	87	10
Haig	24	80	37
Kemp	69	83	51
Robertson	30	36	80

Sources: Hadley and Stanley 1989, 25, for Iowa; New Hampshire; and Gephardt, Jackson, du Pont and Haig in South. Rest of South figures from "Southern Days," March 9, 1988, *USA Today*, 7a.

than in Iowa or New Hampshire. For instance, Bush spent $774,696 in Iowa, $481,329 in New Hampshire, and $1,118,471 in Florida. (See tables A.3 and A.4 in the appendix for the actual spending figures.)

As the first row of numbers in table 3.2 demonstrates, Democratic candidates spent heavily in Iowa. Dukakis, Gephardt, and Simon spent over 90 percent of the maximum allowed, whereas Babbitt spent over 80 percent.[8] Gore, who claimed to have bypassed Iowa, spent only 34 percent of the FEC maximum, but this was a greater percentage than he spent in any of the southern states. New Hampshire, once again, received a great deal of attention from the Democratic candidates. Three spent over 90 percent of the maximum allowed and two more spent over 75 percent. On average, Democratic candidates paid slightly more attention to New Hampshire than Iowa. Combined, these two states represent the most extensive campaign allocation patterns. Even a low-spending candidate such as Jackson emphasized Iowa and New Hampshire more than he did any other state in his campaign strategy. Iowa and New Hampshire continued to draw excessive attention from the Democratic candidates in 1988. Expenditure patterns also indicate that the Lesser Antilles contests drew significant attention from four of the six candidates: Dukakis, Gephardt, Gore, and Simon. Iowa, New Hampshire, and the other early contests garnered the bulk of the candidates' attentions in 1988, despite, or perhaps because of, the presence of Super Tuesday. No candidate could afford to blanket fourteen southern states with advertisements or personal appearances. Many candidates hoped that victories in the more manageable smaller states holding early primaries or caucuses would generate national publicity and boost their fortunes on Super Tuesday.

Only Gore's average spending in the Super Tuesday states, at 12.2 percent, topped his overall campaign average of 9.0 percent. In nine of the fourteen Super Tuesday states, Gore spent above his national average. Gephardt placed second in relative attention to the South, exceeding his national average in half of the states. Dukakis surpassed his average in only five states. However, since Dukakis's average expenditure nationwide exceeded Gephardt's, Dukakis allocated more money to the South than did Gephardt. Jackson expended little money in the South. With his national reputation and strong support from the black community, Jackson had less need to advertise heavily to garner votes. He also had less money at this time to spend. Jackson's biggest gains in contributions came in March, such that he spent more heavily in the Showdown and Finale states. Gore also spent heavily in the Showdown states trying to demonstrate he could win outside the South, but to less avail. In general, table 3.2 confirms that Democratic candidates continued to allocate more campaign resources to Iowa and New Hampshire than they did to Super Tuesday or any of the later contests.

The spending that did occur in the Super Tuesday states reveals each candidate's strategy. Dukakis's spending patterns reflected his four-corner strategy. Dukakis spent more money than his competitors in Texas, Florida, Maryland, Massachusetts, and the caucus states. Meanwhile, Gore topped all other Democrats in nine of the southern states. Gephardt concentrated his money on Georgia, Florida, Alabama, and Oklahoma but only outspent his competitors in Louisiana, which most other Democratic candidates conceded to Jackson, and in his home state of Missouri. Jackson allocated his slim financial resources to the states with the largest black populations. These candidate allocation patterns did affect the election outcome. The Democratic candidate who spent the most in a Super Tuesday state won that state 75 percent of the time (Wilcox 1991).[9]

Republican spending patterns presented in table 3.3 replicate Democratic patterns. Candidates on average spent the highest proportion of FEC maximums in New Hampshire, an astonishing 98 percent for the five remaining candidates, as Haig had already dropped out of the race. The only difference between Democratic and Republican spending patterns is that on average Republican candidates spent 50 percent more money than Democrats in the first two contests.

Republican candidates spent a higher percentage of FEC limits in the Lesser Antilles states than they did on Super Tuesday. In South Carolina's

Table 3.2: Percent of Maximum State Spending Limits
by 1988 Democratic Candidates

	Babbitt	Dukakis	Gephart	Gore	Hart	Jackson	Simon	average
Iowa	84.0	97.6	96.9	33.8	26.7	25.2	102.1	52.2
New Hampshire	47.8	95.2	79.6	95.0	73.1	15.8	97.1	58.2
Lesser Antilles								
caucus	.0	31.7	7.6	8.3	.0	2.1	8.2	8.5
primary	.0	33.6	16.0	11.1	.1	2.7	3.5	10.4
Super Tuesday								
caucus	.0	3.4	.1	2.7	.1	.5	.1	1.7
North primary	.0	9.8	5.5	.0	.2	.4	1.9	2.8
South primary:								
Alabama	.0	6.4	11.0	20.8	.2	2.3	.6	7.0
Arkansas	.0	16.0	9.0	19.8	.8	2.3	3.0	8.2
Florida	.0	21.5	9.3	5.4	.0	.9	.7	6.4
Georgia	.0	8.2	9.2	14.6	.3	2.7	2.0	6.0
Kentucky	.0	6.0	.1	12.1	.0	3.9	.5	3.9
Louisiana	.0	2.4	7.1	6.5	.0	2.4	.4	3.2
Maryland	.0	19.5	.2	3.2	.0	1.5	1.0	4.2
Mississippi	.0	.8	1.1	13.5	.0	3.3	.6	3.3
Missouri	.0	.3	20.9	.0	.1	.3	.9	3.8
North Carolina	.0	19.6	1.4	20.3	.0	4.1	3.4	7.7
Oklahoma	.0	9.2	10.8	18.1	.3	.0	.7	6.6
Tennessee	.0	1.0	.1	2.1	.0	.9	.3	.9
Texas	.0	24.6	10.3	21.8	.9	1.7	1.3	10.1
Virginia	.0	5.4	.1	13.2	.0	1.3	1.4	3.5
S.S.T. average	.0	10.1	6.5	12.2	.2	2.0	1.2	5.3
Showdown States								
caucus	.1	4.8	3.4	2.0	.0	1.8	.3	2.9
primary	.4	14.4	.8	15.9	.1	7.3	4.0	11.1
Finale								
primary	.3	10.4	2.5	.5	.1	7.0	.6	8.7
Campaign average	2.7	14.7	7.7	9.0	2.1	4.0	5.5	8.1

Values are the percent of maximum spending allowed by FEC limits for individual states, or the average for grouped caucus or primary states.

average = average expenditure for active candidates only
Campaign average = each candidate's average for entire campaign
S.S.T. average = average for southern Super Tuesday states

Table 3.3: Percent of Maximum State Spending Limits by
1988 Republican Candidates

	Bush	Dole	du Pont	Haig	Kemp	Robertson	average
Iowa	99.9	102.3	79.3	5.1	98.7	100.8	81.0
New Hampshire	104.4	100.3	95.7	35.6	92.4	96.9	97.9
Lesser Antilles							
caucus	13.6	24.5	1.0	.0	2.7	12.1	11.2
primary	33.4	53.4	1.8	.1	6.6	22.5	25.1
South Carolina	63.4	37.1	.0	.3	49.7	42.0	48.0
Super Tuesday							
caucus	7.6	27.6	.0	.0	.4	8.2	11.0
North primary	34.4	38.5	6.7	.0	21.8	7.6	25.6
South primary:							
Alabama	8.0	19.8	.0	.0	1.6	18.0	11.9
Arkansas	13.4	12.3	.0	.0	3.5	10.5	9.9
Florida	32.5	8.9	.0	.1	.4	20.6	15.6
Georgia	15.3	17.7	.0	.6	1.3	14.1	12.1
Kentucky	11.4	8.8	.0	.1	.1	9.0	7.3
Louisiana	13.6	16.8	.0	.0	.4	20.8	12.9
Maryland	9.2	21.8	.0	.0	.1	3.0	8.5
Mississippi	27.8	12.2	.0	.0	.6	19.6	15.1
Missouri	22.8	30.8	.0	.1	.4	6.8	15.2
North Carolina	11.6	40.2	.0	.0	.4	9.4	15.4
Oklahoma	20.6	34.9	.0	.3	.6	16.1	18.1
Tennessee	8.7	20.2	.0	1.3	.0	12.7	10.4
Texas	9.7	3.6	.0	.3	.4	22.5	9.1
Virginia	3.4	4.6	.0	.0	.3	19.0	5.6
S.S.T. average	14.9	18.0	.0	.2	.7	14.4	11.9
Showdown States							
caucus	2.9	2.6	.0	.0	.3	5.4	4.2
primary	13.2	11.5	2.0	.0	.6	3.1	9.4
Finale							
primary	1.6	8.1	.8	.0	.5	3.5	2.4
Campaign average	16.2	20.8	4.3	.9	6.7	13.5	13.5

Values are the percent of maximum spending allowed by FEC limits for individual states, or the average for grouped caucus or primary states.

average = average expenditure for active candidates only
Campaign average = each candidate's average for entire campaign
S.S.T. average = average for southern Super Tuesday states

early primary, the four remaining candidates spent 38 to 63 percent of the maximum allowed. Kemp's bleak financial picture begins to emerge at this stage; he funneled his few remaining resources into a last-ditch effort in South Carolina. In the other Lesser Antilles primaries, candidates allocated 25 percent of the maximum. Only in the early caucus states did Republican candidates spend less on average than they did in the South. Even in those there were some exceptions. Dole exceeded his Super Tuesday average in the Lesser Antilles caucuses.

Only Robertson allocated more money to Super Tuesday states (14.4 percent) than he did in his campaign as a whole (13.5 percent). Dole, however, spent the largest proportion of the FEC maximum in the Super Tuesday states at 18 percent. Additionally, Bush spent slightly more than Robertson, but again this was less than his campaign average.

As for individual states, Bush spent more than his competitors in Arkansas, Florida, Kentucky, and Mississippi. Robertson was the top spender in three states: Louisiana, Texas, and Virginia. Dole led the Republican pack in spending in six states. Maisel (1988) asserts that Dole could have won more delegates on Super Tuesday by focusing his spending and campaigning on fewer states. As it was, Republican spending on Super Tuesday was unrelated to election victories. Bush won despite being outspent in twelve states (Wilcox 1991).

Besides the southern states on Super Tuesday, two northern states held primaries. Spending figures in table 3.3 might suggest that these two states received extraordinary attention from the Republican candidates. These figures, however, are misleading. The high levels of spending are attributable to Massachusetts, yet no candidate targeted this state. Rather, candidates used Massachusetts to circumvent FEC limits for New Hampshire. Cars rented in Boston but driven in New Hampshire counted against Massachusetts's limits, not New Hampshire's. Staffers and candidates stayed the night in Massachusetts hotels. Even commercials for the New Hampshire campaign could be broadcast on Boston television stations and still reach the bulk of New Hampshire voters.

Republican spending began to taper off by the Showdown states. Dole attempted to revive his campaign in Illinois, but Bush continued to trounce him at the polls. Furthermore, Dole was running out of money by this time. Rather than borrowing more funds from his Senate campaign committee, Dole withdrew from the race at the end of March. Robertson remained in the race until the middle of May but greatly scaled back his campaigning. Republican candidates had one additional concern by the time of the Showdown states. The heavy spending by Bush, Dole, and especially Robertson in early primaries and caucuses placed their campaigns up against the overall FEC spending limits for the entire nomination season.

We have seen that Republican and Democratic patterns of allocating financial assets and candidate time in 1988 continued to stress Iowa and New Hampshire. Yet the Super Tuesday states may have received more attention than expected based on previous campaign expenditure patterns. Gurian (1989) found that candidates' expenditures in a state depended on the number of delegates at stake in a primary or caucus, the amount of media attention to the state, whether a state held a primary or caucus, the date of the event, and the number of other events on the same day. Iowa and New Hampshire also had a special status, with all candidates spending more resources in these states.

To apply most of Gurian's (1989) findings to 1988 expenditure patterns, two regression analyses were performed. Separate analyses were conducted for Republican versus Democratic candidates, as the former spent considerably more funds than the latter. Furthermore, the Republican race essentially came to an end shortly after Super Tuesday when Dole withdrew from the race. Therefore, the Republican analysis only includes those states in which Dole remained an active candidate. The dependent variable in each equation is the average expenditure for candidates from one party in each state. These are the same figures as found in the final columns of tables 3.2 and 3.3. For the independent variables, five dummy variables were constructed with a value of one used to designate Iowa, New Hampshire, a Super Tuesday state, a primary (versus a caucus), and a home state of one of the presidential candidates. The latter was included because of Aldrich's (1980) assumption that candidates concede to their opponents states in which their opponents have a strong advantage in order to save precious campaign resources for states in which they have a better chance of winning. The dummy variable indicating a southern Super Tuesday state will inform us whether candidates allocated more money than expected to these contests by producing a positive coefficient, less money than expected with a negative coefficient, or allocated money to these states in the same pattern as for all other states by a nonsignificant coefficient. The number of delegates available in a state, the sixth independent variable, represents one aspect of a state's importance to winning the nomination. The date of the primary (measured as the number of days since January 1) indicates another aspect of a state's importance, as an early win is necessary to capture momentum or to avoid being winnowed from the field. Finally, the number of other states holding primaries or caucuses dictates whether resources will be stretched thin on a particular date.

Table 3.4 presents the results of the two regression equations. Once again, the extraordinary levels of spending in Iowa and New Hampshire are confirmed. Meanwhile, the presence of Super Tuesday had no effect on Democratic spending. Democratic allocations to southern states can adequately be explained by the number of delegates available in each state, the fact that primaries rather than caucuses were held, the number of events on

Table 3.4: Multiple Regression Analyses Explaining Average Level
of Campaign Spending by Democratic and Republican Candidates in the
1988 Primaries and Caucuses

	Democrats	Republicans
Iowa	.59**	.59**
New Hampshire	.61**	.52**
Super Tuesday	− .05	− .38*
Number of delegates	.10^z	− .03
Date	− .10	.01
Primary versus caucus	.23**	.52**
Number events on date	− .20*	− .15
Home state	− .10^z	.03
R	.94	.94
R^2	.89	.89
Number of cases	(51)	(29)

Entries are standardized regression coefficients.

^{z} = statistically significant at the .10 level
 * = statistically significant at the .05 level
** = statistically significant at the .01 level

the date, and the presence of home-state candidates. On the Republican side, Super Tuesday states received lower than expected levels of spending. Republican candidates concentrated their spending on Iowa, New Hampshire, and the primary states.[10] The eight factors presented in table 3.4 explain 89 percent of the variance in state campaign expenditures for candidates of both parties.

Super Tuesday did not have the desired effect of causing 1988 candidates to allocate more resources to the southern states. Some increase in attention may have occurred, but this was more likely the result of a state switching from a caucus to a primary or moving its delegate selection to an early date. Other states may have experienced a loss as the clustering of primaries on one date stretched candidate resources thin. Table 3.4 even suggests that, for Republican candidates, Super Tuesday had the negative effect of reducing the amount of attention to individual states.

CHANGING PATTERNS OF CAMPAIGN RESOURCE ALLOCATION

While Super Tuesday did not cause candidates in 1988 to expend extraordinary time or money in the southern states, perhaps Super Tuesday provided the South with its fair share of attention, unlike in previous years when the region was neglected. Only comparisons with earlier years will reveal whether Super Tuesday helped the South capture additional attention from candidates.

Table 3.5 lists the number of trips made by Democratic and Republican candidates to the various states in 1976 and 1988. John Aldrich (1980) provides the list of visits made during the campaign year by six major Democratic and two Republican candidates in 1976. A similar compilation of candidate visits in 1988 was combed from *USA Today's* daily listing of candidate itineraries and was supplemented by other newspaper accounts of the campaign. Following Aldrich's lead, each day, or portion of a day, a candidate spent in a state counted as one visit. Only visits after mid-January in both years were included.

According to figures in table 3.5, the South did not see any more of the candidates in 1988 than they did in 1976. Democratic candidates made 145 election year visits to the South in 1976 and 149 in 1988, with each southern state receiving on average 14.8 visits in 1976 and 10.6 in 1988. T-tests presented in table 3.5 indicate no significant differences in the average number of trips to the southern states between 1976 and 1988. On the Republican side, eleven more candidate visits occurred in 1988 than in 1976, but once again the average number of visits was statistically about the same for both years (7.8 in 1976 and 6.7 in 1988). Therefore, the South did not gain in candidate attention by moving to Super Tuesday.

Several states actually received considerably more attention in 1976 than in 1988. The foremost example is Florida, where a heated contest between Ford and Reagan brought both candidates to the state for twenty-five days in 1976. Meanwhile, Carter's battle with Wallace to survive as the southern candidate brought them, along with "Scoop" Jackson, to Florida for fifty-seven visits. In 1988, Florida received less than half as much attention. Similarly, Maryland and Tennessee saw more of the Democratic candidates in 1976 than in 1988, while North Carolina followed the same pattern on the Republican side. A few southern states did receive more attention in 1988, most notably Georgia, perhaps because it is the major air transportation center in the South. Alabama, Texas, and Virginia on the Democratic side and Oklahoma on the Republican side also gained more attention in 1988 than in 1976. Overall, however, Super Tuesday did not increase candidate attention to the South during the campaign year. South Carolina, however, by holding a separate Republican primary three days before Super Tuesday, greatly increased the number of campaign visits, catching up to Iowa but still lagging behind New Hampshire.

Iowa and New Hampshire continued to gain ground in attention between 1976 and 1988. Candidates spent more time in these two states in 1988 than in 1976. Some of this increased attention on the Republican side may be owing to the fact that there were more candidates in 1988 (six) than in 1976

Table 3.5: Number of Visits to States by Candidates, 1976 and 1988.

	Democrats		Republicans	
	1976	1988	1976	1988
Iowa	20	80	2	37
New Hampshire	37	60	24	85
South Carolina[a]	—	—	0	32
Super Tuesday states				
Alabama	1	7	4	4
Arkansas	6	6	1	1
Florida	57	17	25	12
Georgia	3	25	6	17
Kentucky	9	7	2	5
Louisiana	4[b]	5	3[b]	8
Maryland	22	6	1	1
Mississippi	3[b]	4	2[b]	3
Missouri	2[b]	1	5[b]	8
North Carolina	14	15	14	8
Oklahoma	1[b]	5	1[b]	8
Tennessee	8	1	3	7
Texas	13	37	14	11
Virginia	2[b]	13	2[b]	1
primary average	14.8	10.6	7.8	6.7
t-test with 1988	.70		.38	
caucus average	2.4		2.6	
total visits	145	149	83	94
All other primaries[c]				
average visits	22.1	16.0	5.0	8.0
total visits	441	319	100	167
number of states	(20)	(20)	(20)	(21)
t-test with 1988	.87		− .75	
t-test with S.T.	.80	.99	− .80	.30
All other caucuses				
average visits	1.5	6.0	1.2	1.6
total visits	23	90	17	21
number of states	(15)	(15)	(14)	(13)
t-test with 1988	− 1.61		− .64	
t-test with S.T.	− .80		− 2.17*	

* = statistically significant at .05 level

[a]South Carolina Democratic caucuses included with all other caucuses
[b]caucus state
[c]includes beauty contest primaries

S.T. = Super Tuesday states

Source for 1976 visits: Aldrich 1980, 232-33.

(two), but similar increases occurred on the Democratic side, in which the number of candidates remained approximately the same (six in 1976, seven in 1988). While Iowa and New Hampshire gained attention from candidates of both parties, Democratic candidates grew to spend more time in Iowa, and Republicans continued to pay more attention to New Hampshire. The greater attention by Democratic candidates to the Iowa caucuses may be owing to the historical precedent of Carter's 1976 victory. In addition, Democratic caucus rules make caucuses more attractive to the candidates by binding delegates selected to specific candidates. Republican rules allow for the selection of more uncommitted delegates.

Spending patterns by the candidates over recent election years tell the same story as the visitation data. As demonstrated in table 3.6, average expenditures per active candidate, controlled for state population sizes through the use of FEC maximums, signal that Super Tuesday did not have the desired effect of increasing candidate attention to the South. On the Democratic side, candidates spent more money in southern states in 1976 and 1984 than in 1988, with t-tests confirming that these differences are statistically significant. Only in the contest between Carter and Kennedy in 1980 did expenditure levels in the South fall below 1988 levels. Rather, in 1980, Carter and Kennedy both concentrated on the two early contests of Iowa and New Hampshire. Of course, in 1976 and 1984, as well as 1988, expenditure levels in Iowa and New Hampshire topped those in other regions of the country. Individual states tell the same story as the southern averages. Each state received more attention from candidates in at least one previous year than they did in 1988. Iowa, in contrast, continued to gain attention with each year, an astonishing 311 percent increase in expenditures from 1976 to 1988. Expenditure levels in New Hampshire remained relatively stable but high. Meanwhile, total expenditures in the South dropped 64 percent between 1976 and 1988, which matched the drop for other primary (-61 percent) and caucus (-62 percent) states. Super Tuesday made Iowa more important to candidates' strategies, not less. Or, at least, Super Tuesday did not disrupt the pattern of increasing attention to Iowa with each subsequent election.

The figures for Republican candidates presented in table 3.7 once again tell the same story. Spending in southern states fell 52 percent between 1976 and 1988 and 21 percent between 1980 and 1988. Meanwhile, spending levels in Iowa rose 397 percent between 1976 and 1988. New Hampshire continued to receive astonishingly high levels of candidate expenditures, topping 90 percent in 1976 and 1988 and falling to 73 percent of FEC maximums in 1980, when a larger number of minor candidates with fewer resources brought the Republican average down. Besides declines in spending in southern states, expenditures for Republican candidates fell for other primary states (-61 percent between 1976 and 1988). Besides Iowa, the

Table 3.6: Percent of State Spending Limits by Democratic Candidates, 1976-1988

	1976	1980	1976	1988
Iowa	12.7	95.6	33.9	52.2
New Hampshire	57.2	75.3	57.4	58.2
Super Tuesday states				
Alabama	13.9	6.7	22.4	7.0
Arkansas	21.1	1.7	13.3[a]	8.2
Florida	22.3	17.2	10.7	6.4
Georgia	8.0	2.4	17.7	6.0
Kentucky	14.7	.3	2.1[a]	3.9
Louisiana	12.1[a]	2.5	4.4	3.2
Maryland	26.6	9.0	8.0	4.2
Mississippi	22.9[a]	1.3[a]	9.1[a]	3.3
Missouri	7.1[a]	5.4[a]	10.0[a]	3.8
North Carolina	16.2	1.3	5.0	7.7
Oklahoma	14.8[a]	6.6[a]	10.9[a]	6.6
Tennessee	8.5	1.6	9.0	.9
Texas	11.4	5.7[b]	6.0[a]	10.1
Virginia	4.7[a]	5.0[a]	6.1[a]	3.5
average primaries	15.9	4.8	11.0	5.3
t-test with 1988	5.33**	−.30	2.69*	
average caucuses	12.3	4.5	8.2	
total	204.4	66.4	134.7	74.5
All other primaries[c]				
average spending	22.3	12.4	9.9	8.6
total spending	445.9	286.3	208.0	171.7
number of states	(20)	(23)	(21)	(20)
t-test with 1988	4.09**	1.54	.61	
t-test with S.T.	1.36	2.37*	−.35	1.96[z]
All other caucuses				
average spending	9.8	8.8	5.7	3.7
total spending	146.9	105.9	80.0	55.4
number of states	(15)	(12)	(14)	(15)
t-test with 1988	3.46**	1.10	.88	
t-test with S.T.	−.82	.49	−.80	

Values are percent of maximum FEC limits. Values may not sum to totals given due to rounding.

[z] = statistically significant at .10 level
* = statistically significant at .05 level
** = statistically significant at .01 level

[a]caucus
[b]beauty contest primary, included with primary average
[c]includes beauty contest primaries

S.T. = Super Tuesday states

Table 3.7: Percent of State Spending Limits by Republican Candidates, 1976-1988

	1976	1980	1988
Iowa	16.3	59.3	81.0
New Hampshire	96.0	73.3	97.9
South Carolina	8.0	69.5	48.1
Super Tuesday states			
Alabama	17.7	38.2	11.9
Arkansas	18.1	8.6[a]	9.9
Florida	77.8	41.5	15.6
Georgia	18.8	10.2	12.1
Kentucky	23.2	9.2	7.3
Louisiana	3.0[a]	4.8	12.9
Maryland	13.5	14.5	8.5
Mississippi	6.4[a]	28.0	15.1
Missouri	13.0[a]	3.7[a]	15.2
North Carolina	67.6	7.6	15.4
Oklahoma	8.5[a]	4.5[a]	18.1
Tennessee	23.0	7.9	10.4
Texas	52.9	20.9	9.1
Virginia	4.1[a]	12.4[a]	5.6[b]
primary average	34.7	18.3	11.9
t-test with 1988	3.27**	1.62	
caucus average	7.0	7.3	
total spending	347.2	211.8	167.0
All other primaries[c]			
average spending	22.9	17.1	8.4
total spending	458.1	392.3	176.5
number of states	(20)	(23)	(21)
t-test with 1988	3.03**	2.26*	
t-test with S.T.	−1.49	−.25	−1.03
All other caucuses			
average spending	7.7	5.8	9.2
total spending	107.9	64.3	120.1
number of states	(14)	(11)	(13)
t-test with 1988	−.64	−1.40	
t-test with S.T.	.30	−.67	

Values are percent of maximum FEC limits. Values may not sum to totals given due to rounding.

* = statistically significant at .05 level
** = statistically significant at .01 level

[a]caucus
[b]beauty contest primary, included with primary average
[c]includes beauty contest primaries

S.T. = Super Tuesday states

only contests receiving a greater share of candidates' campaign funds in
1988 were the caucus states, although these increases were not statistically
significant. The final state to consider is South Carolina, which, as table 3.5
indicates, saw more candidate visits in 1988 than 1976. The expenditure
patterns tell a slightly different story. Whereas candidate attention to South
Carolina, in terms of overall expenditures, was higher in 1988 than in 1976,
the value for 1980 was even higher. In 1980, John Connally spent considerable sums in South Carolina, attempting to rescue his failing campaign.[11]
Reagan responded with extensive campaigning to protect his lead, while
Bush, buoyed by earlier successes, made a late effort in South Carolina,
hoping to finish ahead of Connally. Bush finished third in the vote behind
Reagan, the winner, and Connally.

SUMMARY

The hopes of Super Tuesday's creators that a regional primary would force
candidates to pay more attention to the South were dashed by the reality of a
three-week campaign. Candidates did not forgo Iowa's caucus or New
Hampshire's primary for the lure of hundreds of delegates on Super Tuesday.
Rather, candidates paid more attention to these two initial events in hopes of
catching momentum or maintaining credibility. As usual, several candidates
spent the bulk of their resources in these two contests, only to have meager
results force them from the race. Only after surviving Iowa and New
Hampshire did most candidates turn their attention toward the South. Along
the way, however, a few candidates detoured through the Midwest (i.e.,
South Dakota and Minnesota), while others found it necessary to make trips
to the east and west coasts to raise funds. By the time candidates came south
to campaign, they had few days left with thousands of miles to cover.
Candidates resorted to airwaves and airplanes to maximize their exposure.
Left behind was the intensive retail politics of Iowa and New Hampshire.
     The plans for a huge regional primary poised a few weeks after the start
of the nomination campaign failed to take account of the realities of
candidate strategies. Open races for the presidency lead to numerous candidates competing, and a significant portion of these candidates start out as
unknowns. These candidates must seek momentum to gain national recognition. Momentum requires that candidates allocate all of their meager resources to the two big opening events, in hopes that a victory or a better than
expected finish will garner media attention. These momentum-seeking
candidates could not even consider campaigning in the Super Tuesday states
until they conquered either Iowa or New Hampshire. However, the early date
of Super Tuesday made such a momentum-seeking strategy less likely to
succeed. With only four short weeks from the start of the campaign until

Super Tuesday, early victories could not be translated into increased financial contributions in time to be of use in the Super Tuesday states.

The Super Tuesday plan at first might seem better suited for the better-financed or better-known candidates seeking to gather delegates. After all, with more than one-third of all convention delegates being chosen on Super Tuesday, the South might be poised for increased attention from these candidates. But with fourteen southern primaries, two northern primaries, and western caucuses scheduled for March 8, even wealthy candidates could not allocate large sums of money to all the Super Tuesday states. No candidate, however well financed, would have enough money to blanket all the states. Furthermore, candidates expecting a continuation of the nomination battle after Super Tuesday needed to retain a portion of their campaign treasury for subsequent primary battles, as Dukakis did. Each of the well-financed candidates in 1988 also had a reason to spend funds early. Dukakis needed to earn votes outside of New Hampshire to support his claim of being a national candidate before descending to the South, Dole had to unseat Bush early to have a chance at the nomination, and Robertson needed to outmaneuver Kemp and Haig for the right wing of the Republican party. The immediate goal of unseating a rival caused Robertson and Dole, as well as Gephardt and Simon, to concentrate on the earlier contests. Bush and Dukakis, with their goals of gathering delegates, needed to seek supporters in all areas of the country, not just in the South. Thus, the plans of Super Tuesday's architects gave way to the more immediate goals of the 1988 candidates.

The premise behind the South's plan to capture more attention also proved false. The South was not ignored by candidates in previous campaigns. Super Tuesday states received the same attention, in terms of candidate visits and campaign expenditures, as other primary and caucus states in 1976, 1980, and 1984. Some southern states even received extraordinary attention in specific years, such as Florida in 1976 and 1980, Alabama in 1980 (Republican) and 1984 (Democrat), and North Carolina and Texas in 1976. Starting with a false premise of neglect, the Super Tuesday plan did not work. Candidates increased their attention to Iowa while continuing to spend extraordinary time and money in New Hampshire. Perhaps the size of Super Tuesday made candidates relish the relatively inexpensive scale of the Iowa and New Hampshire campaigns. More likely, candidates, as generals, started with the plans from the previous war. The 1988 candidates simply did what the 1980 and 1984 candidates did, but even more so. They headed first and foremost to Iowa and New Hampshire.

4

Participation in Presidential Primaries

As we saw in Chapter 1, the Southern Legislative Conference avowed that one of the goals for Super Tuesday was "to encourage greater participation by southern voters." Participation would increase as a regional primary simplified the process and anticipated media coverage generated greater citizen interest. The goal of increasing primary turnout is not unique to Super Tuesday but characterized all the major reform movements. Progressives in the early 1900s advocated presidential primaries in order that the average person would have a greater say in presidential nominations. The McGovern-Fraser reforms of the early 1970s required that each state's procedures for selecting convention delegates be open to any Democrat who wished to participate.

Advocates of a nationwide regional primary system also averred that the switch would result in increased participation. By rationalizing the primary schedule, these reformers believed that more people would understand the presidential nomination process and participate in it. Further, regional primary advocates expected that an enlarged primary electorate would be more representative. That is, primary voters would have the same demographic characteristics, issue positions, and candidate preferences as those who did not vote. With a more representative electorate, presidential candidates winning nominations through primary victories would be more acceptable to the party's rank-and-file voter in the fall election. Advocates of regional primaries in other areas of the country also proclaimed the desire for increased participation. For example, when the Maine legislature debated adopting a presidential primary and joining a New England regional primary, State Representative Judy C. Kany remarked, "This is a superb way to get grassroots support into our delegate selection system." State Senator Esther H. Sorrell echoed the same theme in the debate in Vermont: "One of the key things we have to do is encourage participation of a turned-off electorate in the selection of government" (Doyle 1975, 142).

More participation signifies more democracy and fairer results. Yet less pristine goals often lurked behind these lofty principles. Turn-of-the-century Progressives felt control of nominations by party bosses advantaged conservative candidates. Opening the nomination process to grass-roots participation through presidential primaries would result in more progressive candidates winning. The mid-1970s reform movement arose when liberal Democrats found themselves locked out of the delegate selection process in many states during the 1968 campaign. To them, more openness would mean more liberals being able to participate. Similarly pragmatic goals underlay the pristine goal of increasing participation with Super Tuesday. Democratic and Republican leaders, as well as some candidates, hoped to mold the Super Tuesday electorate to their specific needs.

Southern Democratic leaders wanted to increase participation by one type of voter—the traditionally conservative southern white Democrat. In recent years, these Democrats earned the name of Reagan Democrats as they deserted the Democratic party in the 1980 and 1984 presidential elections. Drawing Reagan Democrats back into the Democratic primary electorate would help a more conservative candidate win the nomination, guaranteeing southern support for the Democratic nominee in the fall election. Neglected in these Democratic leaders' pragmatic goals were other elements of the Democratic party in the South, most notably blacks, liberals, and non-native southerners. What type of candidate would be advantaged by a truly representative southern Democratic primary electorate?

Southern Republicans, meanwhile, worked to insure that any increases in participation would advantage Republicans, not Democrats. To encourage southerners to vote in Republican primaries, the Southern Republican Primary Project was created with Haley Barbour of Mississippi as its head. This organization strived to convince southern voters that the Democratic primary was a liberal primary and the Republican primary was a conservative primary (Kirschten, February 2, 1988). Even Ronald Reagan helped. In a speech before the Southern Republican Leadership Conference, he averred: " 'Super Tuesday' presents our party with a tremendous opportunity—to convince those who share our values to vote for the Republican candidate of their choice in the Republican primary. Now, in my humble opinion, it shouldn't be too hard. . . . Any one of our Republican candidates stands head and shoulders above those running in the other party. And Republican candidates all agree with the people of the South. . . . Yes, the values of Southern voters are best represented by our Republican candidates for President" (Hadley and Stanley 1989, 20-21).

Republican leaders speculated that their party would benefit most on Super Tuesday in the eight open primary states, where any voter could participate in either the Democratic or Republican primary. The attractiveness of Republican presidential candidates would draw wavering Democrats into Republican primaries. In closed primary states, where participation is limited to those legally registered with a party, the Southern Republican Primary Project sent out mailings encouraging voters to switch their registration to the Republican party. If Republicans were successful at expanding their electorate, they foresaw a Democratic electorate composed solely of blacks and liberal whites. Such an electorate would continue to nominate presidential candidates too liberal to carry the South in the subsequent presidential election.

Presidential aspirants comprised the third force trying to manipulate the composition of the Super Tuesday electorate. Pat Robertson expected an "invisible army" of devoutly religious conservatives to turn out in the Republican primaries. Robertson even predicted massive defections from religiously conservative Democrats in open primary states (Martz, March 7, 1988). In closed primary states, Robertson's staff used his phone banks to urge voters to register as Republicans (Kirschten, February 2, 1988). While Republican and Democratic leaders wanted a larger voting electorate, Robertson could benefit from a small turnout. His fervent followers would vote while others stayed home, magnifying his support and winning Robertson more convention delegates. Similarly, Jesse Jackson's fate rested on a large turnout by southern blacks.

While Republican and Democratic leaders and politicians expected Super Tuesday to change the size and composition of the southern primary electorate, not all political scientists believed regional primaries would significantly affect turnout. Austin Ranney, a leading student of presidential primaries and a member of the McGovern-Fraser Commission, previously dismissed claims of increased participation made by advocates of regional primary legislation. Ranney asserted that even a national primary would increase participation by only a few percentage points and that participation would continue to be much lower in primaries than in general elections (Ranney 1978, 29). Other political scientists have noted that, although turnout in presidential primaries is low, those who do participate generally reflect the characteristics and concerns of fellow partisans who do not participate (Geer 1989; Hagen 1989; Keeter and Zukin 1983; Kritzer 1980; Norrander 1986a).

Nevertheless, politicians and candidates felt Super Tuesday presented them with an excellent opportunity to manipulate the composition of the electorate. The larger electorate many southern Democratic leaders desired would contain more traditional white Democratic voters. This "more representative" electorate would support more moderate candidates. Republican leaders meanwhile planned to once again steal away Reagan Democrats—this time perhaps for good. Robertson knew he could convince religious conservatives to turn out in disproportionate numbers, and Jesse Jackson continued his registration of southern blacks. This chapter will explore the results of these attempts to manipulate the electorate. First, we will examine the level of turnout in the southern states in 1988. Second, we will test whether Super Tuesday increased turnout in southern primaries. Finally, we will investigate the composition of the Super Tuesday primary electorates.

TURNOUT IN PRESIDENTIAL PRIMARIES

How many people should be expected to vote in presidential primaries has been the subject of a heated debate since primaries were first introduced in the early 1900s. Early presidential primary advocates expected rank-and-file voters to flock to the polls (Allin 1912). Yet the first scholarly examination of presidential primary turnout by Louise Overacker (1926) found turnout levels to be very low: only one-third to one-half the number voting in the subsequent presidential election. Austin Ranney (1972) calculated turnout in presidential primaries between 1948 and 1968 averaged 27 percent of the voting age population. He noted, however, that many of these primaries were uncontested: either no serious national candidate contested the primary or only one candidate's name appeared on the ballot. Only eleven times between 1948 and 1968 did a state have contested elections for both parties' primaries. Turnout in these primaries averaged 39 percent. (See Davis 1980 for a similar analysis.)

Part of the problem with discussing turnout in presidential primaries is as simple, and as complicated, as finding the proper measure. There are no preexisting figures on the number of potential voters in each party's primary, since not all states require residents to register as partisans. The best method for calculating turnout in presidential primaries, therefore, is to divide the number of votes cast in a party's primary by the normal partisan proportion of the voting age population (Norrander 1986c). This method has fewer biases than alternative measures, such as combining both parties' primary votes into one figure. Normal partisan support is calculated from five election averages for presidents, governors, senators, and U.S. representatives. Added to this is the partisan division of the state legislature.[1] Resulting averages are multiplied by a state's total voting age population to derive partisan voting age populations. This method was used to calculate turnout for all cases expect Washington, D.C. As equivalent election returns are not available for the nation's capital, the percent of residents registered with each party was substituted for partisan voting patterns when multiplying by the city's voting age population. The number of votes cast in a state's Democratic or Republican primary is then divided by the appropriate normal

Table 4.1: Turnout Rates in Democratic Primaries, 1960-1988, as a Percentage of the Normal Democratic Proportion of Voting Age Population

	1960	1964	1968	1972	1976	1980	1984	1988
Southern Super Tuesday states								
Alabama	—	—	—	—	—	12	21	21
Arkansas					50	41		44
Florida	13	15	19	42	37	26	24	24
Georgia					21	14	22	20
Kentucky					22	15		19
Louisiana						17	14	27
Maryland	28	43		37	35	25	23	23
Mississippi								29
Missouri								26
North Carolina				39	24	27	34	24
Oklahoma								28
Tennessee				34	21	17	17	29
Texas					—	22[a]		25
Virginia								15
average	21	29	19	38	30	22	22	25
All other primary states								
California	42	41	51	51	42	36	30	29
Connecticut						17	18	29
Idaho					31	19[a]	21[a]	19[a]
Illinois	2	3	0	34	33	30	40	35
Indiana	35	41	53	46	36	33	40	35
Kansas						27		
Massachusetts	6	4	13	27	29	33	22	23
Michigan				53	22	2[a]		

partisan proportion of the voting age population to calculate turnout in each party's primary.

Using this normal-vote-based measure of presidential primary turnout for 1988 reveals a large amount of variation in participation across the states. The lowest turnout rate of only 5 percent occurred in Rhode Island's Republican primary. In contrast, Wisconsin's Democratic primary experienced a participation rate of 55 percent. Participation rates averaged 29 percent in Democratic primaries and 20 percent in Republican primaries. Tables 4.1 and 4.2 provide complete lists of turnout figures for presidential primaries since 1960.

Turnout rates for presidential primaries held in the South on Super Tuesday varied on the Republican side from a low of 11 percent in Arkansas to a high of 28 percent in Georgia and Mississippi. Turnout in Democratic primaries ranged from 15 percent in Virginia to 44 percent in Arkansas. On average, turnout remained higher in southern Democratic primaries, averag-

Table 4.1, continued

	1960	1964	1968	1972	1976	1980	1984	1988
Montana					39	45	11[a]	42
Nebraska	26	16	43	45	38	33	32	37
Nevada					28	19		
New Hampshire	35	18	29	39	33	37	33	38
New Jersey	12	0	1	3	13	19	23	23
New Mexico				42		34	38	35
New York	—	—	—	—	—	16	20	23
North Dakota							15[a]	
Ohio	12	17	20	38	31	30	36	33
Oregon	56	44	60	54	49	35	38	36
Pennsylvania	7	7	17	34	32	37	38	35
Rhode Island				9	13	8	10	11
South Dakota	14	16	38	14	28	33	29	33[a]
Vermont					29[a]	28[a]	50[a]	31[a]
West Virginia	62	20	23	49	43	34	39	35
Wisconsin	80	68	60	74	42	34	33[a]	55
Washington, DC	—	—	—	—	8	17	26	22
average	30	23	31	38	31	27	29	31
national average	29	24	31	38	31	26	28	29

[a]beauty contest

— = primary held but no turnout figures available
blank = no primary held

Source: Compiled by author from number of votes cast published in Scammon (1962, 1966), Scammon and McGillivray (1989).

ing 25 percent, than in Republican primaries in the area, averaging 19 percent (t = −2.82, sign. = .01). But in comparison to national averages, southern Republican primaries fared better than southern Democratic primaries. Turnout in southern Democratic primaries lagged behind Democratic primaries in other regions of the country by seven percentage points (t = 2.18, sign. = .04). Participation rates in southern Republican primaries, however, did not fall significantly below the national average (t = .84, sign. = .41). Comparisons of Super Tuesday turnout levels to national averages, however, may be somewhat misleading. Turnout is often lower in the South for most types of elections.

Differences across the fifty states in terms of political traditions and the demographic composition of the electorate produce vast variations in turnout rates, even for presidential elections. Some states, such as Utah, North and South Dakota, and Minnesota, consistently have the highest turnout rates, averaging over 60 percent of the voting age population. Other states,

Table 4.2: Turnout Rates in Republican Primaries, 1960-1988, as a Percentage of the Normal Republican Proportion of Voting Age Population

	1960	1964	1968	1972	1976	1980	1984[a]	1988
Southern Super Tuesday states								
Alabama	—	—	—	—	—	32		21
Arkansas					7			11
Florida	7	10	4	19	22	19	10	21
Georgia					20	19	5	28
Kentucky					14	10		12
Louisiana						6	2	17
Maryland		12		11	15	15	7	17
Mississippi						5		28
Missouri								23
North Carolina				13	14	11		14
Oklahoma								21
Tennessee				9	16	12	5	16
Texas		11[b]			—	15	7	20
Virginia								12[c]
average				13	15	14	6	19
All other primary states								
California	31	45	27	34	34	34	22	22
Connecticut						18		9
Idaho					29	36	25	16
Illinois	24	26	0	1	20	28	14	21
Indiana	29	29	33	23	32	28	20	20
Kansas						30		
Massachusetts	4	7	8	8	13	28	5	18
Michigan				12	37	20		
Montana					39[c]	31[c]	26[c]	30[c]
Nebraska	16	30	40	33	35	32	22	29

such as South Carolina, Texas, Alabama, and Georgia, consistently have the lowest turnout rates, averaging only 35 percent of the voting age population (Bibby, Cotter, Gibson, and Huckshorn 1983). Some variation in turnout rests on differences among states in terms of the race, educational attainment, income level, and age of their citizens (Kim, Petrocik, and Enokson 1975). Variation in turnout also results from diverse political traditions. More competitive elections and easier registration laws produce higher turnout rates (Bibby, Cotter, Gibson, and Huckshorn 1983). Southern states historically have had less competitive elections and more stringent registration laws. Political culture also seems to matter. The traditionalistic political culture of southern states discourages widespread participation, as political decisions would be the responsibility of the social and economic elite, not the masses (Elazar 1984, 118-19). In contrast, a moralistic political culture, found mainly in states along the northern tier of the U.S., demands greater

Table 4.2, continued

	1960	1964	1968	1972	1976	1980	1984[a]	1988
Nevada					28	20		
New Hampshire	32	42	45	41	34	42	19	32
New Jersey	15	1	4		10	12	9	8
New Mexico				18		14	9	16
New York	—	—	—	—	—	—	—	—
North Dakota							17	17
Ohio	16	20	18	18	25	23	18	21
Oregon	42	56	56	38	39	38	28	29
Pennsylvania	27	13	8	5	19	29	14	19
Rhode Island				2	6	2	1	5
South Carolina						18		20
South Dakota	23	41	29	21	33	30		32
Vermont					16[c]	31[c]	15[c]	21[c]
West Virginia	28	29	20		36	29	28	27
Wisconsin	26	24	37	20	43	62	19	22
Washington, D.C.	—		—			17	15	16
average	24	29	25	20	28	27	17	21
national average	23	25	24	18	25	23	15	20

[a]many states did not hold Republican primaries in 1984, since Ronald Reagan was the sole candidate
[b]unofficial primary
[c]beauty contest

— = primary held but no turnout figures available
blank = no primary held

Source: Compiled by author from number of votes cast published in Scammon (1962, 1966), Scammon and McGillivray (1989).

citizen involvement in politics as part of their civic duty. Individualistic political culture produces moderate turnout rates as people become involved in politics only "for the sake of improving [their] own position" (Sharkansky 1969, 69).

Table 4.3 presents turnout rates for the 1988 Super Tuesday primaries, which somewhat compensate for general patterns of participation by measuring the drop-off in participation between the 1988 presidential primaries and the subsequent general election. With this control for more normal participation patterns, turnout is shown to be unusually low in Virginia, falling 34 percentage points below normal for Democrats and 36 percentage points below normal for Republicans. Virginia held its first presidential primary in 1988. Even more unusual, Virginia does not use primaries to select nominees for statewide offices. Furthermore, Virginia's Republican primary was solely a beauty contest, unconnected to the selection of convention delegates. Given these circumstances, it is easy to see why few Virginians participated in these unfamiliar primaries. In contrast, turnout in Arkansas's Democratic primary fell only 3 percentage points lower than in the fall presidential election. Arkansas held state, local, and congressional primaries at the same time as the presidential primary. As Democrats control almost all these offices in Arkansas, these jointly held primaries are some of the most important elections in the state. More important than these individual cases is that the average turnout drop of 22 percentage points for Democratic Super Tuesday primaries is no longer significantly different from the national average of 25 percentage points. As was true before, participation in southern Republican primaries matched turnout rates for other Republican primaries. Thus turnout in the Super Tuesday states was neither unusually low nor unusually high, given normal patterns of participation across the South. Still, this does not explain why turnout varied among the Super Tuesday states. We will now look to the effects of rules and candidate strategies to explain these differences.

Effects of Rules and Scheduling on Turnout

Presidential primary rules superimpose a potential set of constraints or encouragements on general participation patterns. Open primaries supposedly lead to higher turnout rates, since people are free to vote in either party's primary. Previous research, however, found open primary rules did not increase primary turnout. In fact, some evidence pointed to higher participation rates in closed primaries (Norrander and Smith 1985; Ranney 1977). Although Jewell (1984) found turnout higher in open Republican gubernatorial primaries. Southern Republican leaders did expect to benefit from open primary rules in eight Super Tuesday states. Average turnout rates for open and closed primaries, listed in table 4.4, part A, however, reveal that their expectations were incorrect. No significant difference in turnout rates occurred for either Democratic or Republican primaries in the open versus closed primaries.[2]

Republican party leaders' hopes of increased participation may have been dashed by another aspect of the presidential primary environment. Some states hold congressional or gubernatorial primaries on the same date as their presidential primary because it is cheaper to hold one joint election rather than two separate elections. Interest in these nonpresidential contests draw out more people to vote, as past research has demonstrated (Norrander 1986a; Norrander and Smith 1985). In 1988, many of the most interesting nonpresidential primary races fell on the Democratic side. Arkansas and Texas held primaries for Congress, plus state and local offices. As the Democratic party continues to dominate state and local offices in the South,

Table 4.3: Percentage Point Decrease in Turnout Rates for 1988 Presidential Primaries Compared to 1988 General Election

	Democrat	Republican
Alabama	−25	−25
Arkansas	−3	−36
Florida	−21	−24
Georgia	−19	−11
Kentucky	−29	−37
Louisiana	−24	−34
Maryland	−26	−32
Mississippi	−21	−22
Missouri	−29	−32
North Carolina	−20	−30
Oklahoma	−21	−28
Tennessee	−16	−29
Texas	−19	−24
Virginia	−34	−36
average Super Tuesday	−22	−29
average for other states	−25	−27
$t =$	−.74	.28
sign. $=$	.46	.78

the Democratic primary retains some of its historical significance. In Mississippi, John Stennis vacated the U.S. Senate seat he held for forty years, but the Republican primary was uncontested with Trent Lott, U.S. House minority whip, the assured candidate. Meanwhile, on the Democratic side a heated contest developed between Representative Wayne Dowdy and Secretary of State Dick Molpus. Louisiana held a nonpartisan race to fill a vacated U.S. House seat, but the field contained nine Democrats and only one Republican.

With the most interesting 1988 contests on the Democratic side, coupled with a tradition of important state and local Democratic primary battles, turnout in Democratic primaries held jointly with nonpresidential contests exceeded that in the solely presidential contests. (See table 4.4, part B.) Nonpresidential contests, however, did not stimulate participation on the Republican side. Perhaps there were too many situations like the Republican senatorial primary in Maryland. With only nine unknown candidates competing, 50,000 fewer Republicans voted in the senatorial primary than in the presidential primary (Benenson, March 12, 1988).

The legal purpose of most presidential primaries is to select delegates to the Democratic or Republican national party convention. A few presidential primaries, called beauty contests, are unconnected with the delegate selection process. The 1988 Republican presidential primary in Virginia was a

Table 4.4: Average Turnout Rates in Super Tuesday Primaries Held under Different Sets of Rules

Part A: Open Versus Closed Primaries			
	All	Democrat	Republican
% Open	22.9 (16)	26.0 (8)	19.8 (8)
% Closed	20.5 (12)	24.1 (6)	17.0 (6)
t =	.87	.49	.94
sign. =	.39	.63	.37

Part B: Presence of Other Elections Along with Presidential Primaries			
	All	Democrat	Republican
% None	20.6 (18)	22.7 (9)	18.5 (9)
% Other	24.2 (10)	29.7 (5)	18.6 (5)
t =	− 1.32	− 2.04	− .05
sign. =	.20	.06	.96

Part C: Effects of Delegate Distribution Rules			
	All	Democrat	Republican
% PR	22.3 (14)	26.3 (9)	15.0 (5)
% Bonus PR	23.3 (4)	23.3 (4)	
% WTA	21.6 (8)		21.6 (8)
% Loophole	22.9 (1)	22.9 (1)	
% Beauty	11.8 (1)		11.8 (1)
F =	.54	.29	4.81
sign. =	.71	.76	.03

Part D: Past Use of Presidential Primaries			
	All	Democrat	Republican
% Yes	21.9 (7)	24.5 (4)	18.5 (3)
% No	21.8 (21)	25.5 (10)	18.5 (11)
t =	.03	− .23	.00
sign. =	.98	.82	.99

Figures in parentheses are number of cases.

Bonus PR = bonus proportional representation
PR = proportional representation
WTA = winner-take-all

beauty contest, with actual delegates selected through a caucus-convention process instead. The remaining Super Tuesday primaries determined the selection of convention delegates, but a variety of rules were used to distribute convention delegates among the presidential candidates. A majority of the Republican primaries were winner-take-all: the presidential candidate who received the most votes in the preference vote was awarded all the state's convention delegates. The predominance of winner-take-all rules augmented Bush's Super Tuesday victories. While Bush won 57 percent of the vote, he captured 82 percent of the delegates.

Democratic rules forbid winner-take-all primaries. Instead, national Democratic rules since the reforms of the 1970s have encouraged states to use proportional representations, although in recent years more "loophole" primaries have been allowed. In these latter primaries, participants vote directly for convention delegates. Since each voter tends to select delegates supporting the same candidate, results similar to winner-take-all may occur. In contrast, under proportional representation, if the winning candidate in a five-candidate field wins 40 percent of the votes, he receives approximately 40 percent of the delegates. (See Lengle 1987 for a recapitulation of rule changes on the Democratic side.)

Proponents of proportional representation argued that turnout would rise in primaries using this rule as people come to view the resulting distribution of delegates as fairer. Additionally, voters would not feel they wasted their votes by supporting a candidate who could not win. Instead, each additional vote would help their candidate win more delegate slots (Ranney 1977). Proportional representation rules, however, have been shown to have negligible or even negative effects on turnout (Morris and Davis 1975; Norrander and Smith 1985; Ranney 1977). Such rules are too esoteric for the general public to be aware of them. If rules do affect turnout, they do so indirectly by affecting candidate strategies (Norrander and Smith 1985). Because the stakes are so high in winner-take-all or loophole primaries, candidates may spend more money in these states to ensure a first-place victory. Higher candidate expenditures may increase awareness and stimulate turnout.

Delegate distribution rules did influence turnout rates in the 1988 Super Tuesday. As shown in table 4.4, part C, the beauty contest in Virginia had an unusually low turnout rate. Meanwhile, southern states that employed winner-take-all rules had the highest Republican turnout rates. On the Democratic side, delegate distribution rules did not influence turnout rates. The uniformity of rules on the Democratic side—with nine states using proportional representation and four using the only slightly different proportional representation with an extra bonus delegate awarded to the winner—leaves very little variation to match up with turnout rates.

A final aspect of the structure of Super Tuesday primaries entails the history of presidential primaries in the various states. Alabama's and Florida's primaries date back to the 1920s. In contrast, Missouri, Oklahoma, and Virginia held their first presidential primaries in 1988. The longer a state holds any type of election, the more likely people will be familiar with the process and develop a personal history of voting. While turnout previously has been demonstrated to be higher in states that have held presidential primaries for a longer period of time (Rothenberg and Brody 1988), in Super Tuesday this does not appear to be the case. Turnout rates were not lower in the first-time primary states, as shown in table 4.4, part D. Perhaps the hoopla surrounding Super Tuesday allowed residents of new presidential primary states to become sufficiently aware of and interested in these elections to participate at the same rate as residents of older primary states. Alternatively, the historical importance and relatively high participation rates in southern Democratic primaries (Jewell 1984) may have added to the turnout rates in states holding their first or second presidential primary on Super Tuesday.

Potential Effects of Candidate Strategies on Turnout

The nature of the presidential nomination race—that is, how many candidates are competing and what strategies they employ—should affect participation rates. If a large number of candidates compete, more citizens should have a preferred candidate and want to vote. Past studies provide evidence supporting this point (Moran and Fenster 1982; Morris and Davis 1975; Norrander 1986a; Zeidenstein 1970). The number of candidates contesting the Super Tuesday primaries, however, did not vary, since all primaries were held on the same date. Nevertheless, by selecting the March 8 date, Super Tuesday's planners insured a large candidate field, and this may have played a role in increasing turnout through the South. We will check out this possibility in the next section.

In a vein similar to the number of candidates, the closeness of the nomination race should also influence primary turnout rates. If one candidate has accumulated sufficient delegates that he is assured of winning the nomination, few people may see a need to vote. In a wide-open race, supporters will turn out in higher numbers to insure their candidates' victory. Such appears to be the case in recent presidential nominations (Moran and Fenster 1982; Norrander 1986a; Rothenberg and Brody 1988), or at least for Democratic voters (Morris and Davis 1975; Davis 1980). Ranney (1977), however, reports no effects. Once again, the closeness of the national race did not vary for the Super Tuesday states, but the early March date provided a close race in both parties.

What does vary for Super Tuesday primaries is how extensively candidates campaign in each state. In some states, such as the earliest primary in New Hampshire, almost every candidate spends the legal limit. In other states, those later in the primary season or with fewer delegates at stake, candidates spend less. The more candidates spend, the more campaign stops, television appearances, and campaign commercials they make. These campaign events increase public awareness, which in turn increases turnout

(Norrander and Smith 1985; Ranney 1977; but for a negative finding see Kenney and Rice 1985).

In the 1988 Super Tuesday primaries, high levels of campaign expenditures were related to higher turnout rates in Republican primaries (r = .55, sign. = .02). On the Democratic side, however, campaign expenditures were unrelated to turnout (r = .20, nonsignificant). Two possible explanations exist for these interparty differences. First, rates of campaign expenditures were considerably higher on the Republican side. Whereas each Republican candidate spent on average 12.1 percent of the FEC limit in each state, Democratic candidates spent only 5.4 percent (t = 5.80, sign. = .00). The higher level of spending found on the Republican side may be needed to stimulate interest and increase turnout. A second possibility is that campaign expenditures have a greater effect on turnout rates for the minority party in a region. Republican primaries historically have not been very important in southern politics. Few people have habits of voting in them. High levels of campaign expenditures may be necessary to draw out new voters.[3]

Home-state pride in a candidate might draw out more voters. Four candidates laid claim to southern roots. Robertson's ministry emanated from Virginia Beach, while Bush once represented Texas in Congress. Tennesseans sent both Gore and his father to the U.S. Senate, while Gephardt hailed from Missouri. Nevertheless, turnout was not affected by these home-state candidates (partial r = $-$.02, sign. = .46, when controlling for party).

We have seen that turnout rates varied across the Super Tuesday primary states. Turnout was higher in Democratic primaries if the ballot contained additional nonpresidential contests. Delegate distribution rules affected Republican participation rates. Turnout was unusually low in Virginia's beauty contest primary, while Republican participation rates were highest in the winner-take-all contests. Finally, high levels of campaign spending increased turnout in the Republican, but not Democratic, primaries.

CHANGES IN TURNOUT RATES

Turnout did increase in southern primaries with the advent of Super Tuesday. As figures in table 4.5 demonstrate, 8.2 million more southerners voted in presidential primaries in 1988 than in 1984, and 5.6 million more votes were cast in 1988 than in 1980. Of course, some of these increases in numbers of voters is solely the result of more primaries being held in 1988. Using only states holding primaries in both years still reveals an increase of 3.1 million voters from 1980 to 1988 (1.6 million Democrats and 1.4 million Republicans) and 2.3 million from 1984 to 1988 (310,000 Democrats and 2 million Republicans). Similarly, figures in tables 4.1 and 4.2 reveal the average turnout rate for Democratic primaries in the South was 22 percent in 1980

Table 4.5: Number of Votes Cast in Southern Primaries, 1980-1988

	Democrat			Republican		
	1980	1984	1988	1980	1984	1988
Alabama	237,464	428,283	405,642	211,353	---------	213,561
Arkansas	448,290	---------	497,544	---------	---------	68,305
Florida	1,098,003	1,182,190	1,273,298	614,995	344,150	901,222
Georgia	384,780	684,541	622,752	200,171	50,793	400,928
Kentucky	240,331	---------	318,721	94,795	---------	121,402
Louisiana	358,741	318,810	624,450	41,683	16,687	144,781
Maryland	477,090	506,886	531,335	167,303	73,663	200,754
Mississippi	---------	---------	359,417	25,751	---------	158,526
Missouri	---------	---------	527,805	---------	---------	400,300
N. Carolina	737,262	960,857	679,958	168,391	---------	273,801
Oklahoma	---------	---------	392,727	---------	---------	208,938
Tennessee	294,680	322,063	576,314	195,210	85,924	254,252
Texas	1,377,354	---------	1,767,145	526,769	319,839	1,014,956
Virginia	---------	---------	364,899	---------	---------	234,142
Total	5,653,995	4,406,630	8,941,907	2,246,421	888,053	4,595,868

Source: Scammon and McGillivray 1989, 48-53.

and 1984; by 1988 the rate rose to 25 percent. On the Republican side, turnout jumped from 14 percent in 1980 to 19 percent in 1988 for a five-percentage-point increase. Turnout was unusually low in the 1984 Republican primaries, and several states canceled their primaries because President Ronald Reagan was the sole contender. For this reason, measures of increasing participation will be based on 1980 figures for the rest of this chapter.

Both parties in Arkansas, Kentucky, Missouri, Oklahoma, and Virginia, and the Democratic party in Mississippi and Texas, switched from caucuses in 1984 to primaries in 1988. To judge how much influence this switch had, we need first to examine general patterns of participation in caucuses. A caucus requires individuals to spend several hours in a meeting selecting delegates to attend an intermediate level convention, from which delegates are selected to attend state and national conventions. The complexity of the process and the long hours involved leave few people willing to participate in presidential caucuses. Those who do participate, however, play a greater role in delegate selection, have a chance of becoming delegates themselves, and often have the opportunity to vote on issue resolutions and other party matters. Nevertheless, few people participate. Table 4.6 lists participation rates for Democratic and Republican caucuses from 1976 to 1988.[4] (Once again, because Reagan was unopposed in 1984, no figures are available for Republican caucus participation in that year.) Caucus turnout rates presented

Table 4.6: Percentage Participation Rates in Presidential Caucuses

	Democrat				Republican		
	1976	1980	1984	1988	1976	1980	1988
Alaska	1	—	2	2	—	2	2
Arizona	4	2	4	4	—	—	—
Arkansas			2		—		
Colorado	4	—	5	3	—	—	1
Connecticut	9						
Delaware	—	1	1	2	—	—	—
Hawaii	1	1	1	1	—	—	2
Idaho		—a	—a	2a			
Iowa	5	10	8	12	2	9	11
Kansas	1		2	1	—		2
Kentucky		—					
Louisiana	6				—		
Maine	2	9	4	3	—	—	2
Michigan		—a	4	6			—
Minnesota	4	5	4	6	5	4	4
Mississippi	5	—	—		—		
Missouri	1	—	2		—	—	
Montana			4a		—a	—a	—a
Nevada			1	1			1
New Mexico	2				—		
North Dakota	3	—	2a	1	—	—	
Oklahoma	6	4	3		—	—	
South Carolina	5	5	3	3	—		
South Dakota				—a			
Texas		—a	—				
Utah	4	2	3	3	—	—	—
Vermont	2a	—a	1a	4a	—a	—a	—a
Virginia	1	1	1		—	—	—a
Washington	4	—	4	6	—	—	1
Wisconsin			2a				
Wyoming	1	—	2	2	—	—	0
national average	3	4	3	3	4	5	3

aaccompanied by a beauty contest primary

— = figures not available
blank = presidential primary used to select delegates, no caucus held

Source: *Congressional Quarterly Weekly Reports.*

in table 4.6 need to be taken with caution. The number of caucus participants often represents a "best guess" by state party officials. In many cases, no estimates of the number of participants are available, so turnout rates presented are from a nonrandom sample of all caucuses. Given these caveats, it is obvious that participation in caucuses is extremely low, averaging less than 5 percent. Past southern caucuses do not stand out as having either unusually high or low turnout rates.

How much Super Tuesday affected participation rates in each of the southern states is illustrated in table 4.7. For states that held primaries in previous years, turnout rose most for Mississippi Republicans, while turnout rates fell for North Carolina Democrats and Alabama Republicans. Still, on average, Democratic participation rates rose 3.9 percentage points from 1980 to 1988 and 1.7 percentage points from 1984 to 1988. These increases are not significantly steeper than the national averages of 2.5 percentage points (1980-1988, $t = -.59$, sign. $= .56$) and 1.6 percentage points (1984-1988, $t = -.02$, sign. $= .99$). In marked contrast, Republican turnout rates rose an average of 4.9 percentage points in the South between 1980 and 1988, while falling 7.1 percentage points in other regions of the country ($t = -3.35$, sign. $= .00$).

Increases in participation rates as states switched from caucuses to primaries are measurable on the Democratic side. Arkansas, Missouri, Oklahoma, and Virginia Democrats held primaries in 1988 while holding caucuses in 1984.[5] Turnout increased 26.2 percentage points in these states. Whether this is an unusually large increase in participation can be judged by comparing it to increases in participation for other states switching from caucuses to primaries. Two northern states held caucuses in 1984 to select Democratic delegates but employed primaries in 1988. Turnout in the 1988 primaries increased 45.2 percentage points over that in the 1984 caucuses. This figure, however, is somewhat misleading in that both northern states, Montana and Wisconsin, normally chose convention delegates through primaries. In 1984 they were forced to select delegates through caucuses because their open primary laws violated national Democratic party rules. Both states continued to hold beauty contest primaries in 1984. With a one-time use of caucuses and a history of holding presidential primaries, an unusually large difference in turnout rates between the 1984 caucuses and the 1988 presidential primaries should be expected.

Perhaps a better estimate of the effects of switching from a caucus to a primary can be made by comparing average turnout rates for caucuses, under 5 percent, with average turnout rates for primaries, approximately 25 percent. These averages indicate a 20-percentage-point increase in turnout might be expected when switching from a caucus to a primary. If this is an accurate estimate, the increase for the southern states of 26.2 percentage points may be slightly larger than average. Once again, the hoopla surround-

Table 4.7: Percentage Point Increase in Participation Rates for Southern Super Tuesday Primary States of 1988 over 1980 and 1984

| | Democrat | | Republican |
	1980-1988	1984-1988	1980-1988
Alabama	8.8	− .2	− 11.1
Arkansas	3.1	(42.1)	—
Florida	− 1.8	.2	1.9
Georgia	5.5	− 2.5	8.6
Kentucky	3.8	—	1.5
Louisiana	10.1	13.1	11.0
Maryland	− 2.1	− .1	2.4
Mississippi	—	—	23.0
Missouri	—	(23.9)	—
North Carolina	− 3.5	− 10.5	2.7
Oklahoma	(24.1)	(25.1)	—
Tennessee	11.7	11.7	4.2
Texas	3.0	—	4.8
Virginia	(13.5)	(13.5)	—
Average change for:			
South Super Tuesday	3.9 (18.8)	1.7 (26.2)	4.9
Other states	2.5	1.6 (45.2)	− 7.1
All states	2.9 (18.8)	1.6 (32.5)	− 3.2

Numbers in parentheses represent changes from caucuses to primaries.

ing Super Tuesday may have generated more awareness of the novel presidential primaries in these traditional caucus states.

In summary, turnout rates in southern primaries did increase with the creation of Super Tuesday. However, for Democratic primaries this increase was minimal from 1984 to 1988, with only a 4-percentage-point increase from 1980 to 1988, and these changes in participation did not significantly deviate from national averages. The Republican party may have gotten a bigger bang from Super Tuesday. While turnout in Republican primaries declined in other regions of the country between 1980 and 1988, turnout rose in the southern primaries. Not to be overlooked, however, is the fact that after Super Tuesday the Republican race soon ended. To obtain a truer picture of whether Super Tuesday created unique patterns of participation, we need to examine the causes of changing participation rates in all primary states.

Causes of Turnout Change

Super Tuesday's early primary date promised a contest in which more candidates would be competing, the level of campaign spending would be higher, and the national race would be closer. All these factors have been demonstrated to affect primary turnout rates (Morris and Davis 1975; Moran and Fenster 1982; Norrander and Smith 1985; Norrander 1986a; Ranney 1977; Rothenberg and Brody 1988). Therefore, we might expect any increases in turnout to be accounted for by changes in these factors. Regional primary advocates, however, often suggest that a regional primary system alone would increase participation by making the process more rational. If such is the case, turnout in the Super Tuesday states will have increased more than can be accounted for by changes in candidates, strategies, and the closeness of the national race.

To discover the reasons turnout increased for the southern Super Tuesday states, a multivariate analysis of change in turnout rates for all states between 1980 and 1988 was conducted. Ten variables were entered into a regression equation explaining turnout levels in the 1988 presidential primaries.[6] The first of these variables is turnout in 1980. The inclusion of this variable controls for previous turnout rates in presidential primaries in each state. Four variables measured changes in the campaign. One compared the number of candidates contesting a state's primary in 1980 with the number in 1988. A second variable measured changes in candidate expenditures. Changes in the closeness of the race at the national level and whether a state was home to one of the presidential contenders in either year rounded out the campaign variables.

Three variables measured changes in rules or scheduling. The first indicated whether congressional primaries were held on the same date as the presidential primary in 1980 or 1988. A second variable indicated whether a state changed its use of a beauty contest primary, and the third measured changes in delegate distribution rules.

Two additional variables will test whether divergent patterns of change prevailed between Democratic and Republican primaries, or between Super Tuesday primaries and those held in other states. Coding for the party variable results in a positive coefficient if greater increases in turnout occurred for Democratic primaries than for Republican primaries. The second variable, indicating whether a primary is a southern Super Tuesday state, produces a strong positive coefficient if turnout in the South increased at a greater rate than expected, given changes in the nature of the race, primary rules, and scheduling. If this occurs, Super Tuesday as a regional primary had an independent impact on turnout rates. A strong negative coefficient will indicate turnout continued to lag in the South despite the creation of Super Tuesday. A coefficient that is neither strongly negative nor strongly positive will indicate Super Tuesday had no independent influence on participation rates. In this case, turnout increases in the southern primaries could be explained by the same factors as turnout changes in other areas of the country.

Table 4.8: Explaining Changes in Turnout Rates between the 1980 and 1988
Presidential Primaries

Change in number of candidates	2.69*
Change in expenditures	5.50^z
Change in other races	.26^z
Change in closeness	−.81
Change in rules	.41
Change in home states	.14
Change in beauty contest	.41
Party	.27*
Super Tuesday	.03
Turnout in 1980	.59**
R	.83
R^2	.69
Adjusted R^2	.63
Number of cases	(60)

Coefficients are unstandardized regression coefficients for variables expressed in base 10
logs.

^{z} = statistically significant at the .10 level
* = statistically significant at the .05 level
** = statistically significant at the .01 level

Table 4.8 presents results from the multiple regression analysis of
turnout in the 1988 presidential primaries. Previous turnout rates in each
state played a significant role. A state that had a turnout rate 1 percent higher
than a second state in 1980 would have a turnout rate in 1988 that was an
additional .59 percent higher. Turnout rates in 1980 alone account for 47
percent of the variation in 1988 turnout rates.[7]

The small and insignificant coefficient for the Super Tuesday variable
indicates the nation's first regional primary had no independent effect on
turnout. Instead, factors associated with the early March 8 date accounted
for increased participation in southern primaries. In the nation as a whole,
turnout rose more in Democratic primaries, primaries contested by more
candidates, and states where candidates campaigned more intensely. Turnout fell if a state separated its congressional primary from its presidential
primary. Therefore, turnout rose in southern Super Tuesday primaries because the March 8 date insured that more candidates contested those
primaries and campaigned more vigorously in those states. Turnout rates did
not climb as high in Kentucky and North Carolina, as they separated their
congressional primaries from their presidential primaries. Turnout also
increased in the South because six states switched from using caucuses to
primaries. As caucuses usually have turnout rates of less than 5 percent,
turnout increased significantly in these states.

Super Tuesday's planners correctly hypothesized that Super Tuesday's early date would lead to higher participation rates. If the southern regional primary had been scheduled later in the primary season, fewer candidates would have contested these primaries and the national race would have been more lopsided. As a result, turnout would not have increased by 5 percent. Instead, turnout may have remained stable or even decreased, depending on the date chosen and the nature of the race at that time. Nevertheless, one element of the Super Tuesday plan worked, more Southerners participated in the presidential primaries. But who were these people? Did they create a primary electorate representative of all their fellow partisans, did the Democratic primary include the traditionally conservative southern white Democrat or did the Republican party steal away the Reagan Democrats, and what became of Robertson's invisible army?

COMPOSITION OF THE ELECTORATE

Democratic and Republican leaders, along with some of the presidential candidates, hoped to manipulate the composition and representativeness of the Super Tuesday electorate. As mentioned earlier in this chapter, Democratic leaders wanted to recapture the support of the moderate to conservative Democratic voter who had supported Reagan in 1980 and 1984. Meanwhile, Republican leaders tried to draw moderate and conservative voters into their primaries. Robertson counted on the support of his invisible army of religious conservatives, while Jackson's success depended on high levels of participation by southern blacks.

Political scientists are often concerned with the composition of primary electorates in order to tell whether the few people who vote are representative of the larger group that does not participate. Austin Ranney (1972) in his study of 1968 New Hampshire and Wisconsin presidential primary voters found them to be "older, of higher status in income and occupation, and more active in a variety of civic, religious, and political organizations" (27). More important, Ranney found voters to have slightly different views on issues than nonvoters. Ranney also uncovered some differences in candidate preferences between voters and nonvoters. Since Ranney's study, a number of political scientists continue to debate the representativeness of the presidential primary electorate. Some (e.g., Ladd 1978; Lengle 1981; Polsby 1983) continue to argue that the electorate is unrepresentative. Others, however, find that presidential primary voters closely resemble presidential election voters (e.g., Geer 1989; Hagen 1989; Keeter and Zukin 1983; Kritzer 1980; Norrander 1986a). Primary voters even match general election voters on ideological positions (Norrander 1989).[8]

To study the composition of the electorate, we will use the 1988 National Election Studies (NES) public opinion poll of Super Tuesday states. In this survey a pre-election poll was conducted, followed by a post-election reinterview, allowing us to know who voted in the primaries. NES surveyed residents of all Super Tuesday states, but since the planners' goals referred only to southern states, Massachusetts and Rhode Island residents were excluded from the analysis. Additionally, since people who are not registered cannot vote in any election, they have also been eliminated from the analysis.[9]

To judge the representativeness of Super Tuesday voters, we will compare voters in Democratic primaries to Democratic identifiers who were registered but who did not vote, and voters in Republican primaries to Republicans who did not vote.[10] Besides questioning representativeness between voters and nonvoters, we will want to know how much alike Democrats and Republicans are. If vast differences exist between the two partisan groups, a representative Democratic electorate may choose a presidential candidate that Democrats can support but that Republicans find unpalatable. Thus we will compare those who voted in the Republican primaries to those who voted in the Democratic primaries, and Republican nonvoters with Democratic nonvoters.

Demographic Composition

In general, people who are better educated, have higher incomes, and are older tend to vote more in presidential elections (Wolfinger and Rosenstone 1980). In lower turnout elections, some of these factors, especially age, have even greater effects (Hamilton 1971; Wolfinger, Rosenstone, and McIntosh 1981). Therefore, we might suspect that Super Tuesday primary voters would be older, better educated, and have higher incomes than those who did not vote. Figures in table 4.9 show this to be true. The average voter in the Democratic primaries on Super Tuesday was 48.6 years old, significantly older than nonvoting Democrats who averaged 44.3 years old. Similarly, Republican voters were older than the nonvoting Republicans. Both voting Republicans and Democrats also were better educated and had higher incomes than nonvoters. Union members were not disproportionately represented among voting or nonvoting Democrats, nor were blacks or Hispanics. A contrasting picture emerges on the Republican side. None of the black or Hispanic Republicans voted, but few blacks or Hispanic Republicans existed among the nonvoters as well. In summary, the demographic composition of the Super Tuesday voting electorate mirrors that found in other lower turnout elections. Voters were somewhat older, better educated, and wealthier than nonvoters.

Comparing Democratic voters in table 4.9 with Republican voters

Table 4.9: Demographic Composition of Southern Super Tuesday
Primary Electorates

	Democratic Nonvoters[a]	Voted in Democratic Primary[b]	Voted in Republican Primary[c]	Republican Nonvoters[d]
Age (ave. in yrs.)	44.3** (258)	48.6 (413)	47.3** (240)	41.6 (311)
Education (ave. in yrs.)	12.5** (257)	13.7* (411)	14.1* (239)	13.6** (309)
Income (ave. in $1,000)	$28.1** (250)	$32.9** (399)	$38.9** (299)	$34.9** (296)
Black	18% (254)	17%** (408)	0%** (239)	3%** (307)
Hispanic	5% (256)	3%** (409)	0%** (237)	3% (309)
Union member	13% (256)	14%** (411)	6% (238)	8% (309)

Figures in parentheses are number of cases.

 * = statistically significant difference at .05 level
** = statistically significant difference at .01 level

[a]significance tests noted in this column are between Democratic nonvoters and voters in Democratic primaries
[b]significance tests noted in this column are between voters in Democratic and Republican primaries
[c]significance tests noted in this column are between Republican nonvoters and voters in Republican primaries
[d]significance tests noted in this column are between Democratic nonvoters and Republican nonvoters

Source: NES Super Tuesday Survey.

reveals distinctions between participants in the two parties' primaries. Democratic voters were less educated, made less money, and were more likely to belong to a union than Republican voters. Whereas 17 percent of Democratic voters were black, less than one-half of 1 percent of Republican voters were black. Similarly, Hispanics participated more often in the Democratic primaries. One should not, however, be misled to assume that the prevalence of blacks and Hispanics in the Democratic electorate indicates that white southerners opted for the Republican primaries. Twenty-one percent of whites cast ballots in Republican primaries, 31 percent voted in Democratic primaries, and 48 percent did not vote. Rather than being more unrepresentative, the heterogeneous Democratic voters represented all elements of the Democratic coalition: blacks and whites, Hispanics and Anglos. The southern Democratic primary electorate on Super Tuesday contained all elements of the national party. The homogeneous Republican voters matched neither nonvoting Republicans nor Democratic voters. We will now turn to one other demographic trait, that of religion.

Religion

Pat Robertson pinned his presidential hopes on a Super Tuesday victory led by an invisible army of conservative religious voters. The religious right, however, is not a cohesive body. Important distinctions flourish, leaving Robertson the preferred candidate of only a portion of the religious right. Robertson, along with Jim and Tammy Bakker and Jimmy Swaggart, is associated with the Pentecostal faction. Pentecostals, like fundamentalists, believe the Bible is without errors and is literally true. Unlike fundamentalists, Pentecostals and charismatics believe God uses the Holy Spirit to guide people's lives. The gifts of the Holy Spirit include speaking in tongues, faith healing, and prophecy. Many fundamentalists violently disagree with these Pentecostal tenets. To them, God's wishes can only be learned from studying the Bible. Jerry Falwell is perhaps the best-known fundamentalist leader. Pentecostals differ from charismatics in that the former are isolated within specific denominations, most notably Assembly of God, while charismatics are found scattered among religious moderates in many different religious denominations; for instance, there may be charismatic Lutherans. Evangelicals comprise the third component of the religious right. They believe the Bible is the inspired word of God but that some parts of the Bible may be meant as parables rather than as literally true.

These doctrinaire distinctions between religious conservatives muddy the search for Robertson's supporters. All three types of religious conservatives believe in being "born again" in Christ. Both fundamentalists and Pentecostals view the Bible as literally true. With this understanding, table 4.10 examines the effects of two religious traits: (1) whether people consider themselves born-again Christians and (2) how they interpret the Bible. Approximately half of the southerners interviewed considered themselves born-again Christians, but they were equally as likely not to vote as to vote. Those who voted split themselves equally among the Democratic and Republican primaries, leaving born-again beliefs to have no impact on participation patterns. Southerners' interpretations of the Bible were measured on the following scale: (1) the Bible is the actual word of God and is to be taken literally, word for word; (2) the Bible is the word of God but not everything in it should be taken literally, word for word; and (3) the Bible is a book written by men and is not the word of God. Republican voters' positions on this scale averaged at 2.3, closest to a nonliteral interpretation. Additionally, opinions on the Bible did not affect participation in Republican primaries. Biblical interpretations did affect Democratic participation, but those with the most liberal beliefs, not the religious conservatives, voted more often.

To uncover the impact of Robertson's "invisible army" of conservative religious voters we may have to isolate specific religious denominations.

Table 4.10: Religious Representativeness of Super Tuesday Primary Electorates

	Democratic Nonvoters[a]		Voted in Democratic Primary[b]		Voted in Republican Primary[c]		Republican Nonvoters[d]	
Born-again Christian	56%	(229)	54%	(366)	52%	(223)	47%	(279)
Bible views[e]	2.4*	(255)	2.2	(403)	2.3	(235)	2.3*	(301)
Denominations								
Evangelical	17%*		10%		8%		12%	
Pentecostal	5%		3%		4%		4%	
Southern Baptist	25%		25%		21%		20%	
Fundamental	6%		7%		7%		5%	
Other Protestant	25%		31%**		45%		38%**	
Catholic	17%		18%		14%		18%	
Jewish	2%	(245)	4%**	(390)	0%	(229)	1%	(296)

Figures in parentheses are number of cases.

* = statistically significant difference at .05 level
** = statistically significant difference at .01 level

[a]significance tests noted in this column are between Democratic nonvoters and voters in Democratic primaries
[b]significance tests noted in this column are between voters in Democratic and Republican primaries
[c]significance tests noted in this column are between Republican nonvoters and voters in Republican primaries
[d]significance tests noted in this column are between Democratic nonvoters and Republican nonvoters
[e]Biblical views: 1 = the Bible is a book written by men and is not the word of God; 2 = the Bible is the word of God but not everything in it should be taken literally, word for word; and 3 = the Bible is the actual word of God and is to be taken literally, word for word

Source: NES Super Tuesday Survey.

Ascribing individuals' beliefs from the denomination of the church they attend is at best precarious. Yet, given overlapping viewpoints on other survey questions, this may be the only available method to tap into the distinctions among the religious right. Religious denominations were categorized as evangelical, Pentecostal, or fundamentalist. Southern Baptists comprised a separate category, since both fundamentalists and evangelicals belong. Charismatics share some of the beliefs and behaviors of Pentecostals but are found scattered among a variety of Protestant denominations. Therefore, they cannot be isolated with denominational categories.

Table 4.10 presents the impact of religious denominations on the composition of the Super Tuesday electorate. Pentecostals were a small proportion of the population, and they did not participate at a higher or lower rate than other groups. Similarly, adherents from no other conservative denomination swelled the ranks of Republican voters. Only on the Democratic side did a pattern emerge, but once again in the negative direction. Evangelicals participated less often than other Democrats. The religious groups with the most distinctive participation patterns were mainstream Protestants and Jews, with the former being more predominant among Republicans and the latter among Democrats.

Robertson's invisible army remained invisible on Super Tuesday. None of the religiously conservative groups participated at unduly high rates. Yet the fact that they participated at rates similar to others may attest to some mobilization by Robertson's candidacy. Religious conservatives traditionally shunned politics. In addition, Pentecostals often come from lower social and economic strata. Since economic position significantly predicts participation in America, Pentecostals, based on their socioeconomic status, are unlikely participants for the low turnout, low stimulus presidential primaries. Robertson may not have mobilized religious conservatives to the extent that they were overrepresented among primary voters, but his candidacy may have mobilized them enough so that they were no longer underrepresented.

Partisan and Ideological Composition

Democratic planners of Super Tuesday hoped to retain the traditional Democratic voter in their primaries, while Republican leaders hoped to steal away wavering Democrats who had voted for Ronald Reagan in 1980 and 1984. Figures in table 4.11 should please Democratic leaders. Only 2 percent of Democrats voted in Republican primaries. Republican leaders' hopes for capturing Democratic voters went unfulfilled. Even more disheartening for Republican leaders was the news that 13 percent of Republicans voted in Democratic primaries.

Why would Republicans be voting in Democratic primaries? Some Republican identifiers may have had no choice because they were registered as Democrats and lived in closed primary states. As registered Democrats they could only vote in the Democratic primary. In most cases, party identifications match party registrations, with the former being how individuals generally views themselves in politics and the latter being the party they selected when registering to vote. In the South, however, discrepancies between the two may be more common than in other areas of the country. Two factors would contribute to this.

The first is the unique political history of the South. For over a century, from Reconstruction through the 1960s, one-party politics characterized the South. Most people considered themselves Democrats, and Democratic

Table 4.11: Percentage of Party Voters in Democratic and Republican Primaries

| | Party Identification | | |
	Democrats	Independents	Republicans
Democratic Primary	54	31	13
Republican Primary	2	14	36
Did Not Vote	44	56	51
Total %	100	101	100
Number of cases	(585)	(59)	(609)

$$X^2 = 338.98 \quad \text{sign.} = .00$$

Source: NES Super Tuesday Survey.

candidates won almost every election from the state legislature to the presidency. A few pockets of Republicanism flourished, but in most parts of the South the Republican party was almost nonexistent. As Democratic party dominance made general election outcomes predictable, the most important electoral decisions were made in Democratic primaries. In order to participate in these primaries, most people registered as Democrats. Though times have changed in the South, with a revitalized Republican party and more competitive general elections, the historical importance of Democratic primaries may keep some Republican identifiers registered as Democrats.

A second explanation for discrepancies between party identification and party registration may lie in rapid changes in the former but not the latter. Some southerners may be changing party identifications to match recent habits of voting for Republican candidates. Yet they have not reregistered as Republicans. Unless a person moves or stops voting, reregistration is not required for voting in general elections, and most people are unlikely to bother with reregistration just to change their party designation. This is not to say that Republican party registration has not risen in the South. In the six southern states where voters register by party, Republicans added 71,000 more voters than the Democratic party did between 1980 and 1988 (Cook, March 5, 1988). Yet changes in registration apparently still lag behind changes in identification. Data from the NES survey indicate that 20 percent of Republican identifiers in southern closed primary states were registered as Democrats compared to only 2 percent of Democratic identifiers being registered as Republicans. With Democratic registrations, some southern Republicans could only vote in Democratic primaries.

Republican leaders would be disappointed to learn that they also did not pick up Democratic voters in open primary states. Twelve percent of Republicans voted in Democratic primaries in open primary states, whereas 13 percent of Republicans voted in Democratic primaries in closed primary states. Legal registration kept Republicans voting in Democratic primaries in closed primary states, but what made them vote in Democratic primaries in open primary states? After all, these were the states in which Republican leaders hoped to make their biggest gains. Stanley and Hadley (1989) uncovered the reason by examining the effects of other election contests on Republican primary participation. In open primary states, when no congressional or other state elections were on the ballot, only 5 percent of Republicans voted in Democratic primaries. When there were other races on the ballot, 22 percent of Republicans voted in Democratic primaries (NES figures). Thus Republican leaders lost the battle to capture the support of Democratic voters. Democrats voted in Democratic primaries, along with one out of four voting Republicans.

Besides fighting over Reagan Democrats, Democratic and Republican leaders both pursued moderate-to-conservative southern voters. Once again, Democratic leaders should be pleased with the results. As table 4.12 illustrates, Democrats held on to 26 percent of the conservative voters and 38 percent of the moderates. Republicans captured the support of as many conservatives as the Democrats did, at 26 percent, but attracted only half as many moderate voters. Liberal voters, as would be expected, voted mainly in Democratic primaries.

Party identification and ideological preference often overlap. Republicans tend to be conservatives, whereas Democrats may be liberal, moderate, or conservative. That moderates were more likely to vote in Democratic primaries may simply be owing to the fact that more moderates are Democrats than Republicans. Party identification needs to be held constant to truly judge the effects of ideology on primary turnout. Figures from the bottom half of table 4.12 reveal ideology had little affect on turnout or on which primary a person voted in after holding party identification constant. The Democratic party did not lose its conservative voters to the Republican primaries. At best, conservative Democrats were less likely to vote than other Democrats, whereas conservative Republicans were more likely to vote than other Republicans.

Issue Representativeness

The architects of Super Tuesday hoped a regional primary would force candidates to address southern issues. The impact of these appeals would depend in part on whether Super Tuesday's voters reflected the issue positions of other southerners. Table 4.13 reveals that voters in the Democratic primaries represented nonvoting Democrats on six of seven issues. Only on affirmative action programs for minorities did significant differences arise, and then voters held more conservative positions than nonvoters. Voters in the Republican primary did not represent Republican nonvoters as well. On

Table 4.12: Percentage of Liberal, Moderate, and Conservative Voters in
Democratic and Republican Primaries

	Ideology		
	Liberals	Moderates	Conservatives
Democratic Primary	45	38	26
Republican Primary	9	15	26
Did Not Vote	47	48	49
Total %	101	101	101
Number of cases	(303)	(207)	(710)

$X^2 = 60.00$ sign. $= .00$

	Democrats			Republicans		
	L	M	C	L	M	C
Democratic Primary	59	59	47	15	13	13
Republican Primary	2	2	3	26	31	40
Did Not Vote	39	39	50	60	56	47
Total %	100	100	100	101	100	100
Number of cases	(201)	(97)	(253)	(82)	(91)	(424)

$X^2 = 7.74$ $X^2 = 8.03$
sign. $= .10$ sign. $= .09$

C = Conservatives
L = Liberals
M = Moderates

Source: NES Super Tuesday Survey.

four of the seven issues, Republican voters were more conservative than Republican nonvoters. The demographically heterogeneous Democratic voters better represented nonvoting Democrats on the issues than the more homogeneous Republican voters represented nonvoting Republicans.

Republican voters also did not reflect the issue positions of Democratic voters. On all seven issues, Republican voters were more conservative. Issue differences, however, did not occur just between voting Democrats and Republicans. On six issues, nonvoting Republicans were more conservative than nonvoting Democrats. Issue differences between the parties exceed any differences within a party.

Candidate Representativeness

Ultimately we are interested in representativeness in order to judge whether primary voters choose candidates acceptable to those who do not vote. The

Table 4.13: Average Issue Positions of Voters and Nonvoters Measured on Five-Point Scales with Five Being the Most Conservative Position

	Democratic Nonvoters[a]		Voted in Democratic Primary[b]		Voted in Republican Primary[c]		Republican Nonvoters[d]	
Governmment Spending	2.6	(165)	2.8**	(344)	3.4**	(204)	3.1**	(236)
Minority Aid	3.3	(188)	3.1**	(356)	3.5	(191)	3.6**	(256)
Central America Intervention	2.3	(190)	2.3**	(364)	3.2**	(199)	2.8**	(255)
Military	2.4	(251)	2.4**	(406)	3.4**	(238)	3.0**	(305)
Affirmative Action	3.7*	(241)	4.0**	(382)	4.5	(228)	4.3**	(297)
Abortion	2.8	(252)	2.7*	(408)	2.9*	(237)	2.7	(305)
International Trade	2.1	(161)	2.4*	(284)	2.7	(177)	2.8**	(200)

Figures in parentheses are number of cases.

 * = statistically significant difference at .05 level
** = statistically significant difference at .01 level

[a]significance tests noted in this column are between Democratic nonvoters and voters in Democratic primaries
[b]significance tests noted in this column are between voters in Democratic and Republican primaries
[c]significance tests noted in this column are between Republican nonvoters and voters in Republican primaries
[d]significance tests noted in this column are between Democratic nonvoters and Republican nonvoters

Source: NES Super Tuesday Survey.

most direct indicator of representativeness thus would be whether primary voters and nonvoters evaluated candidates in a similar manner. But before individuals can evaluate a candidate, they must be familiar with that candidate.

Tables 4.14 and 4.15 list evaluations of Republican and Democratic candidates as well as candidates who had already withdrawn from the race (du Pont, Haig, Babbitt), leading politicians who choose not to run (Nunn, Cuomo), and President Reagan. The second figure listed for each candidate is the percentage of people who did not recognize or could not rate the candidate. These vary from no Republican primary voters being unable to rate Reagan to 76 percent of Democratic nonvoters being unfamiliar with du Pont and Nunn.

A major difference between primary voters and nonvoters emerges on candidate awareness. Republican voters were more familiar than Republican nonvoters with six out of seven Republican candidates; Democratic voters were more familiar than Democratic nonvoters with all nine Democratic

Table 4.14: Evaluations of Republican Candidates and Politicians on Thermometer Scales and Percentage of Respondents Unable to Rate Each Political Figure

	Democratic Nonvoters[a]		Voted in Democratic Primary[b]		Voted in Republican Primary[c]		Republican Nonvoters[d]	
Bush	56*	10%*	51**	5%**	74*	0%**	70**	6%
Dole	52	22%**	52**	13%**	66**	3%**	62**	15%*
Robertson	43**	27%**	34**	13%**	48**	6%**	40**	19%*
Kemp	42	59%**	39**	39%**	56**	25%**	50**	52%
du Pont	42	76%**	41**	53%**	50*	42%**	46	64%**
Haig	43**	36%**	37**	26%	47	22%	45	29%
Reagan	57*	4%	51**	2%*	81**	0%*	76**	2%
Average number	(256)		(414)		(240)		(310)	

The first number is average thermometer rating. The second number is percentage unable to rate candidate.

 * = statistically significant difference at .05 level
** = statistically significant difference at .01 level

[a]significance tests noted in this column are between Democratic nonvoters and voters in Democratic primaries
[b]significance tests noted in this column are between voters in Democratic and Republican primaries
[c]significance tests noted in this column are between Republican nonvoters and voters in Republican primaries
[d]significance tests noted in this column are between Democratic nonvoters and Republican nonvoters

Source: NES Super Tuesday Survey.

politicians. Primary voters even knew the opposition candidates better. Republican voters better recognized eight of the nine Democratic candidates, while Democratic voters knew more about six of the seven Republicans than did their nonvoting partisans. Being more aware, however, is not a form of unrepresentativeness that we would deem detrimental to the presidential nomination system. In fact, we should wish that primary voters knew more about the candidates than they do. Nearly one-quarter of Republican Super Tuesday voters did not know Kemp; over one-third of Democratic voters could not rate Simon. Thus, while voters are more aware than nonvoters, even primary voters are not familiar with all of the candidates.

    How voters and nonvoters evaluated the candidates they did know is indicated by the top figure for each candidate in tables 4.14 and 4.15. Respondents to the NES survey were asked to think of a thermometer scale from 0 (very cold) to 100 (very hot) when rating each candidate. A com-

Table 4.15: Evaluations of Democratic Candidates and Politicians on Thermometer Scales and Percentage of Respondents Unable to Rate Each Political Figure

	Democratic Nonvoters[a]		Voted in Democratic Primary[b]		Voted in Republican Primary[c]		Republican Nonvoters[d]	
Dukakis	60	32%**	63**	17%	52	16%**	52**	30%
Gephardt	56	38%**	56**	20%	48	21%**	49**	35%
Gore	59	42%**	62**	19%	55	19%**	53**	34%
Jackson	53	10%**	55**	4%	42	2%**	45**	9%
Simon	53	52%**	49**	34%	41*	28%**	44**	44%
Hart	42**	18%**	32**	10%	24**	13%	32**	16%
Babbitt	41	69%**	40	52%**	42	43%**	39	67%
Nunn	57	76%**	54	59%**	52	48%**	47*	68%*
Cuomo	58	68%**	60**	43%	46	38%**	47**	58%*
Average Number	(256)		(415)		(240)		(310)	

The first number is average thermometer rating. The second number is percentage unable to rate candidate.

  * = statistically significant difference at .05 level
** = statistically significant difference at .01 level

[a]significance tests noted in this column are between Democratic nonvoters and voters in Democratic primaries
[b]significance tests noted in this column are between voters in Democratic and Republican primaries
[c]significance tests noted in this column are between Republican nonvoters and voters in Republican primaries
[d]significance tests noted in this column are between Democratic nonvoters and Republican nonvoters

Source: NES Super Tuesday Survey.

parison of average thermometer ratings assigned by voters and nonvoters will indicate whether these groups held similar candidate preferences.

Democratic voters represented Democratic nonvoters quite well. Except for Hart, whom Democratic voters rated lower, Democratic voters and nonvoters evaluated candidates similarly. Republican voters, however, differed significantly from Republican nonvoters. Republican voters felt more warmly toward the four remaining Republican candidates (Bush, Dole, Robertson, and Kemp), one of the candidates who had withdrawn from the race (du Pont), and President Reagan. Given these figures, one might expect that Democratic primary voters would select a candidate that pleased nonvoting Democrats but that Republican votes would choose a candidate toward whom Republican nonvoters would not feel as warmly.

The candidate selected by each party also would not be as favorably looked upon by rank-and-file voters from the opposition party. For all Democratic candidates and one of the noncandidates (Cuomo), Democratic voters rated the candidate more highly than did Republican voters. Similarly, Republican voters rated all Republican candidates higher than did Democratic voters. Once more, differences between voting Democrats and Republicans reflect differences between nonvoting Democrats and Republicans. On eight of the nine Democratic candidates and four of the seven Republican candidates, Democratic and Republican nonvoters held different evaluations. Democrats and Republicans, whether they voted or not, simply did not have the same feeling toward candidates.

SUMMARY

Super Tuesday encouraged more southerners to participate in selecting the Democratic and Republican presidential nominees. Switching from caucuses to primaries raised participation by over 25 percent. Even the more modest 5 percent gain among states previously holding presidential primaries produced an additional three million southern voters. Yet such increases should not be unexpected. Participation increases in the former caucus states came about because voting in primaries requires less commitment than the four to five hours required to select delegates at a local caucus. Turnout rose in the primary states as the early March date for Super Tuesday ensured a broader range of choice and a closer contest among the candidates.

Despite the general increase in participation rates across the South, participation rates continued to vary among the Super Tuesday primaries. Few Virginians voted in their first ever presidential primary. Turnout in Arkansas's Democratic primary neared the general election rate as exciting and important state and local races drew out more voters. In general, participation in Democratic primaries was highest when nonpresidential elections were held along with the presidential primary, and highest in Republican primaries in the winner-take-all states.

Voters in Super Tuesday's Democratic primaries matched the characteristics and preferences of nonvoting Democrats better than Republican voters corresponded to Republican nonvoters. Additionally, Democratic voters comprised a much more heterogeneous group than Republican voters. Voting in Democratic primaries were whites, blacks, and Hispanics; liberals, moderates, and conservatives; born-again Christians and those who felt the Bible was written by men, not God; and one out of four voting Republicans. Yet, ironically, the less representative, more homogeneous Republican electorate supported the winning presidential candidate.

5

Vote Choice

Voting in presidential primaries is unlike casting ballots in any other election in the U.S. Typically, more than two candidates' names appear on the ballot. Yet no easy voting cues, such as party labels, accompany this longer list of competitors. Perhaps as a result, preferences for candidates seeking presidential nominations do not appear to be very firmly anchored. Candidates' fortunes rise and fall throughout the course of the campaign. One only needs to remember recent elections to realize this point. In 1984, Gary Hart in just two weeks jumped from being the preferred candidate of 2 pecent of Democrats to being favored by 30 percent. Similarly, Jimmy Carter rose from being the first choice of less than 1 percent in January 1976, to 30 percent by March 16 (Geer 1989, 64, 79). Changing public preferences often seem to follow candidates' changing electoral fortunes, as contestants win or lose early primaries and caucuses. Winning candidates capture momentum. Losing candidates soon fade from the field. Even after the initial winnowing of candidates, volatility still characterizes many candidates' fortunes. After surging to the forefront in 1984, Hart suffered a setback when Mondale queried "Where's the beef?" In 1976, Jimmy Carter jeopardized his loyal support from black Americans when he attempted to placate other Americans' desires for ethnic neighborhoods. Campaign crises such as these arose as the nomination season progressed from one state's primary to another. Super Tuesday, however, cut short the time available for such events to unfold. Half the 1988 delegates would be selected in less time than it took for the Hart story to unfold in 1984 or for Carter to assume the front-runner position in 1976.

One of the most frequently debated questions about the development of candidate preferences in presidential primaries is that of the role of momentum. Without momentum, Carter would not have won the 1976 Democratic nomination, Bush would not have emerged as the major challenger to Reagan in 1980, and Hart's fortunes would not have risen and fallen in 1984. One school of scholars attests that momentum is translated into votes as individuals incorporate candidates' chances of victory into their decision-making processes. Voters may weigh either the viability of candidates—e.g. the likelihood of winning the nomination—or they may consider the electability of candidates—e.g. the likelihood of winning the fall presidential election (see, for example, Abramson, Aldrich, Paolino, and Rohde 1990; Abramowitz 1987; Bartels 1985, 1988, 1989; Brady and Johnston 1987). Voters supposedly consider these estimates of viability and electability along with general preferences for each candidate when deciding whom to support. Some voters may actually vote strategically. That is, they cast their ballots for their second preferred candidate rather than their most favored candidate because the second candidate has greater viability or electability. Abramson, Aldrich, Paolino, and Rohde (1990) estimated strategic voting occurs about 10 percent of the time. More often, voters' preferences match their estimates of which candidate is most viable or electable. Perhaps these estimates affect voters' preferences or else voters unconsciously engage in projection or rationalization. With projection, voters let their preference for a candidate color their estimates of viability or electability, such that voters believe the candidate they prefer also has the best chance of winning. Rationalization occurs when voters develop preferences for the candidate they believe has the best chance of winning. Past research presents evidence supporting both projection and rationalization (Bartels 1988; Abramson, Aldrich, Paolino, and Rohde 1990).[1]

Other scholars view momentum as affecting presidential primary voting through its influence on the level and type of information voters possess about candidates (Geer 1989; Bartels 1989; Popkin 1991). Under this argument, voters do not consciously consider viability when making their choices because many voters are unable to distinguish the chances of each candidate or because they perceive several candidates as having equal likelihoods of winning (Geer 1989, 73). Instead, momentum affects primary voting by increasing familiarity with one candidate. As mentioned previously, Patterson (1980, 116) found Jimmy Carter gained an additional 12 percent of the vote in the 1976 Pennsylvania primary simply because he was better known than other candidates as a result of the more extensive media coverage he received after his earlier primary victories. In general, scholars in this camp argue that the positive news coverage received by winning candidates influences voters with weak or no preferences to jump aboard the advantaged candidate's bandwagon. This phenomenon may only occur, however, for previously unknown candidates (Geer 1989, 80; Patterson 1980, 126). Better-known candidates already have public images that cannot be easily altered by new information. As the nomination season progresses, momentum-driven rises in popularity diminish even for originally lesser-known candidates. As these candidates become more serious contenders for the nomination, the press begins to take a more critical view of them. News coverage of these candidates is no longer all positive. This more critical coverage may slow or halt candidates' rises in popularity, bringing to a close the advantages of momentum.

Popkin (1991) illustrates this argument with his discussion of Hart's momentum during the 1984 campaign. Popkin discovered Hart's ascent came as people dissatisfied with Mondale moved toward Hart after his second-place finish in Iowa and Hart's victory in New Hampshire made him appear as the most viable alternative to Mondale. This shift to Hart involved some judgments of viability, but voters who switched to Hart did not believe he had a better chance to win the nomination than Mondale. Rather, Popkin ascribed changes in preferences to voters learning new information about Hart. As the campaign progressed, voters discovered more about which types of people supported Hart and Mondale and about what types of presidential traits characterized each candidate. A great deal of projection also occurred. Those who switched to Hart immediately after the New Hampshire primary claimed Hart possessed a greater ability to deal with the Soviet Union than did Mondale, though no foreign policy positions were advocated or stressed in commercials or news coverage at that point in the campaign. Hart's decline, according to Popkin, occurred as questions arose about his abilities to govern. For instance, voters began to question how effective Hart would be as president after they learned of inconsistencies in issue positions and Hart's inability to control his own campaign organization. Hart's decline came about without any changes in estimates of his electability.[2] Rather, the public changed their minds about Hart's experience and competence as campaign events unfolded.

Besides momentum, other factors may affect voter preferences in presidential primaries. The creators of Super Tuesday obviously felt ideology played a role, as they hoped a southern regional primary would advantage a moderate or conservative Democratic candidate. Meanwhile, southern Republican leaders relished the thought that a liberal candidate might be aided by a small Democratic primary electorate. Yet, as we saw in Chapter 4, ideological orientations did not distinguish Super Tuesday voters from nonvoters in the South. In Chapter 2 we discovered voters had difficulty placing candidates on an ideological scale, including misplacing lesser-known candidates such as du Pont. Still, some political scientists aver ideology dictates voter preferences in presidential primaries (Lengle 1981; Polsby 1983). Other scholars, however, argue against the influence of ideology, noting that since candidates rarely stress ideological labels in their campaigns, voters are unfamiliar with the positions of the various contenders (Abramowitz 1987; Geer 1989, 70).

Similar to the debate over the role of ideology is one focusing on the impact of issues. While some argue for the primacy of issues (Bartels 1985; Brady and Johnston 1987; Brams 1978; Hedlund 1977), most empirical studies find issues have little influence on voters' choices in presidential primaries (Geer 1989; Gopoian 1982; Marshall 1984; Norrander 1986b; Williams et al. 1976). Even the small effect that issues do apparently have must be discounted because of evidence of voters placing the same candidate on different sides of an issue. Candidate misplacement occurs as supporters tend to move their preferred candidate toward their own diverse issue positions (Bartels 1989).

Besides momentum and ideology, a third set of factors that may influence candidate preferences entails the personal and political characteristics of candidates. Voters ask, "Does this candidate possess the traits necessary to make a good president?" Many studies indicate candidate characteristics to be the most consistently related factor to voting preferences (Abramowitz 1987; Geer 1989; Gopoian 1982; Marshall 1984; Norrander 1986b; Williams et al. 1976). One reason for the predominance of candidate traits in voting decisions may be the predominance of candidate traits in advertisements and news coverage. In 1988, Dole proclaimed he was "one of us" and that he possessed a record, not a résumé. Dukakis championed his abilities to manage the government. With candidates stressing such themes, voters learned about candidates' personal and professional qualifications, not their issue positions. Alternatively, voters from the same party may view all of their party's candidates as reflecting their policy preferences, leaving voters to differentiate between candidates on the basis of personal characteristics. The influence of personal characteristics on vote choice, however, is not unique to presidential primaries. In presidential elections, personal characteristics and party identification dominate voters' decisions (Niemi and Weisberg 1984, 89).

Finally, differing characteristics of voters within each party may underlie varying candidate preferences. Popkin (1991) and Bartels (1988) both ascribe preferences for Hart and Mondale in 1984 to generational and economic splits within the Democratic party. College-educated, white-collar Democrats preferred Hart, while blue-collar Democrats preferred Mondale. These divisions even extended to divergent lifestyles, such that Hart supporters were more likely than Mondale voters to drive Japanese cars and work with computers. Voters' social and economic distinctions lead to varying political concerns. White-collar Democrats fear inflation, while blue-collar Democrats fear for their jobs. White-collar Democrats deem restrictive trade sanctions as raising the price of consumer goods in the U.S.; blue-collar Democrats regard trade restrictions as protecting their jobs.

Among the distinguishing traits of presidential primary voters is where they live. As primaries are conducted in a state-by-state manner, candidates may fare better in their own regions or home states. Super Tuesday's architects viewed southern voters as having different preferences than Iowans or New Hampshirites. These southern politicians resented the fact that voters in those two states often narrowed the field of choices for southern voters participating in later primaries. Southern Democrats hoped that Super Tuesday would help protect the chances of a southern or moderate candidate. The significance of candidates' home regions to voting patterns in presidential primaries is confirmed by Grofman and Glazer (1988).

In summary, presidential primaries constitute an unusual setting for American voters making decisions about whom to support. Numerous candidates, and the lack of party labels, present primary voters with a difficult and unfamiliar task. How voters accomplish this task is hotly debated, but four factors receive the most attention. Momentum is the first of these factors, though the actual process by which momentum affects vote choice splits political scientists into two camps. Some ascribe momentum's effects to changing evaluations of candidate viability or electability; others argue that media attention to early primary victors affects how voters learn about the candidates. The second possible factor influencing voting decisions in presidential primaries is ideology, though we have seen in previous chapters that ideological positions do not characterize primary voters nor are primary voters particularly adept at classifying candidates on ideological scales. Candidate traits form the third possible influence on voting decisions, with their importance being augmented by the content of campaign commercials. The characteristics of primary voters constitute the final set of potential factors. Generational and lifestyle division among the Democrats, and religious distinctions among Republicans may explain varying candidate preferences.

MOMENTUM AND CANDIDATE PREFERENCES ON SUPER TUESDAY

Momentum leads a larger number of primary voters to support one advantaged candidate, but whether this movement is owing to changing opinions on viability or simply to learning of the existence of a candidate is yet to be decided. Super Tuesday and the 1988 campaign provide an ideal setting for attempting to resolve this debate. On the Democratic side, a large number of unknown candidates sat poised for a momentum-spawned run for the presidency. In contrast, on the Republican side, five candidates vied to dethrone Bush from his position at the top of the polls.

To judge the influence of momentum on Super Tuesday voters, we first need a general indication of changing preferences among southerners. Fortunately, the *Atlanta Constitution* polled southern voters five times prior

to Super Tuesday, beginning one year in advance in March 1987. Between
the first poll and Super Tuesday many aspects of the 1988 campaign
changed. Hart dropped out and then reentered the campaign, Biden pla-
giarized Labour leader Neil Kinnock, Dole's manager kicked subordinates
off the campaign plane, and Babbitt, du Pont, and Haig exited the race.

Despite numerous changes during the campaign, figures in table 5.1
reveal extraordinarily stable preferences among Republicans. A little over
half of southern Republicans preferred Bush in March 1987, and the same
number voted for him on Super Tuesday. (See tables A.5 and A.6 in the
appendix for each candidate's state-by-state vote totals.) Dole's misfortunes
on the campaign trail apparently had little impact on his supporters. One-
fifth of southern Republicans preferred Dole throughout the campaign.
Dole's mismanaged campaign, however, may be a reason for the stability of
Republican preferences. Dole never gave voters a reason to switch from Bush
to himself. Preferences for Robertson may have risen slightly. Meanwhile,
Kemp's failure to lure conservative Republicans to his cause is depicted in
the continual decline in those preferring Kemp. Despite some movement in
support for Kemp and Robertson, the overall picture for candidate preferences among southern Republicans is one of stability.

More significant changes occurred among southern Democrats. Preferences for Jackson remained the most stable, though a gradual increase in
support for Jackson did occur between the first poll, where he was favored by
21 percent, to his Super Tuesday vote of 30 percent. Once again, these
changes in preferences followed the tempo of the campaign, as the media
reported Jackson doing unexpectedly well in early primary and caucus states
despite the fact that few blacks resided in those states. Similarly, support for
Dukakis and Gephardt jumped in February after their victories in Iowa and
New Hampshire, but preferences for Gore also rose during this time despite
his having "skipped" those two events. Evaluations of Gore's viability would
be unlikely to change with no record of victories or losses, but awareness of
Gore could rise because of his more extensive southern campaign. Few
southerners preferred Simon in March 1987, and even fewer preferred him in
March 1988. Finally, Hart's volatile campaign is reflected in southern
opinions. In March 1987, Hart clearly held the front-runner position, being
preferred by over one-third of Democrats polled. When he reentered the race
after the Donna Rice incident, Hart fell to second place behind Jackson, but
by February 1988, preferences for Hart dropped to 6 percent. As Hart began
to be portrayed more as a celebrity than a serious presidential candidate,
southern preferences for Hart declined. In addition, southerners were learning more about the alternatives to Hart: Dukakis, Gephardt, and Gore.

The stability of preferences among Republican candidates leaves little
room for momentum to have an effect, although one might attribute this lack
of change to the Bush campaign's ability to stave off successful challenges

Table 5.1: Percentage of Candidate Support in Southern States

	March 1987	September 1987	January 1988	February 1988	March 1988	Actual Vote
Democrats						
Babbitt	—	3	1	—	—	1
Biden	—	3	—	—	—	0
Bumpers	6	—	—	—	—	0
Dukakis	—	9	6	19	20	25
Gephardt	4	5	4	14	12	10
Gore	—	13	13	18	20	31
Hart	35	—	20	6	5	3
Jackson	21	27	22	25	29	30
Nunn	11	—	—	—	—	0
Simon	—	5	4	3	2	2
undec./none	22	35	30	15	12	
Republicans						
Bush	53	46	52	53	56	59
Dole	17	19	17	21	21	21
du Pont	1	2	1	—	—	0
Haig	—	6	2	—	—	0
Kemp	10	7	4	4	4	5
Robertson	9	10	7	15	14	14
undec./none	11	11	16	7	5	

States included: Alabama, Arkansas, Florida, Georgia, Kentucky, Louisiana, Mississippi, North Carolina, South Carolina, Tennessee, Texas, Virginia.

— = name not included in poll

Source: *Atlanta Constitution* poll data published March 15, 1987; October 4, 1987; January 31, 1988; March 6, 1988; and March 8, 1988.

from his opponents. The movement in the Democratic race suggests earlier campaign events did affect Super Tuesday voting, but we cannot tell how this effect was manifested. Did the increase in preferences for Dukakis and Gephardt come at the expense of other candidates, or did voters move from the undecided category to support these candidates?

To better understand the movement and stability in the Democratic races we will examine preferences of individual voters prior to and after Super Tuesday. The NES Super Tuesday survey included questions on candidate preference, knowledge, evaluations, and estimates of viability in both the pre-election and post-election surveys. By comparing respondents' answers across time we can judge the effects of the campaign and previous events— i.e., Iowa and New Hampshire—on Super Tuesday voters.

First we will examine the patterns of candidate preferences between the pre-election and post-election polls. Respondents' candidate preferences in the pre-election survey will be compared to their actual votes as reported in the post-election follow-up. If the pre-election preference matches the reported vote, the respondent is placed in the "same" category. If the respondent preferred another candidate in the pre-election poll than he actually voted for on Super Tuesday, he is classified as a "switcher." The respondent who had no preference at the time of the pre-election poll is assigned to the "develop" category. Finally, the respondent who preferred a candidate not running for the presidency in the party in whose primary he voted was classified under the "noncandidate" category. For our analysis, respondents are additionally divided by the time of their pre-election interviews into four groups: (1) those interviewed prior to Iowa, (2) those interviewed after Iowa and before New Hampshire, (3) those interviewed after New Hampshire until the end of February, and (4) those interviewed in the first week of March. Voters in the first group experienced the entire early campaign between the time they answered the pre-election poll and the time they answered the post-election questions.

As figures in table 5.2 reveal, preferences among individual Republican voters remained as constant as the aggregate figures of table 5.1. Seventy percent of Republicans had the same preference in the pre-election poll as they did on election day. Thus, the campaign had no effect on the majority of Republican voters. About 20 percent of Republicans changed their minds during the course of the campaign, switching from one of the major candidates to another. Another one in ten voters developed a preference as the campaign proceeded. Almost none expressed a preference for a candidate who was not seeking the Republican spot on the presidential ballot.

The Democratic picture again demonstrates much more movement. Only 29 percent of those interviewed before Iowa held their same preference by the time Super Tuesday arrived. The number adopting and then retaining the same preference increased with time, such that nearly 60 percent of those interviewed the week prior to Super Tuesday had definitely decided which candidate to support. In each time period, the remaining Democratic voters tend to fall equally among the other three categories. Of those interviewed in the pre-Iowa period, about 25 percent changed their minds and voted for another candidate, another quarter moved from the no preference category, while another quarter preferred a candidate not seeking the Democratic nomination.[3] Nearly half of southern voters (46 percent) who preferred such a noncandidate favored Cuomo, while 12 percent favored Nunn and 17 percent preferred Kennedy. Another 9 percent favored a Republican candidate for the Democratic nomination![4]

Which candidates benefited from changing preference is examined in table 5.3. In this table only those whose preferences were gauged prior to the Iowa caucuses are included, in order that we may judge the full impact of the campaign on preferences for each candidate. Once again, the Republican

Table 5.2: Development of Candidate Preferences by Super Tuesday Voters

	Pre-election interview conducted			
	Before Iowa	Between Iowa & N.H.	After N.H. unitl Feb. 29	March 1 to March 8
Voted in Democratic Primary				
% Same	29	33	42	56
% Switch	25	29	21	17
% Develop	23	23	17	11
% Noncandidate	23	15	20	16
	(128)	(73)	(92)	(71)
		$X^2 = 18.74$	sign. $= .0275$	
Voted in Republican Primary				
% Same	72	71	64	71
% Switch	17	20	26	17
% Develop	10	5	10	10
% Noncandidate	1	5	0	2
	(96)	(41)	(50)	(42)
		$X^2 = 6.56$	sign. $= .6827$	

Figures in parentheses are number of cases.

Same = preferred same candidate at time of pre-election interview as voted for on Super Tuesday

Switch = preferred another candidate at time of pre-election interview than voted for on Super Tuesday

Develop = had no preference at time of pre-election interview but eventually voted on Super Tuesday

Noncandidate = preferred candidate not running (Cuomo, Nunn, Kennedy, or candidate from other party) at time of pre-election interview and voted for someone else on Super Tuesday

Source: NES Super Tuesday surveys.

picture is one of constancy for all candidates. Two-thirds of the voters for each candidate preferred that candidate before the campaign began. The Democratic side reveals considerable variation across candidates. Support for Dukakis changed the most. Only 11 percent of his voters preferred him before the campaign began. One-fourth of his supporters favored another candidate, while another one-fourth favored a candidate not contesting the Democratic nomination. Finally, one-third of Dukakis's voters had no preference before the campaign began. The movement of voters toward Dukakis fits the model describing momentum as resulting from growing awareness of candidates, since most of Dukakis's increased support came from those with no early preference for one of the 1988 contenders. In contrast to Dukakis's new base of supporters, over half of Jackson's supporters remained loyal to

Table 5.3: Changing Preference for Super Tuesday Voters Interviewed before the
Iowa Caucus

	Eventually voted for			
	Dukakis	Gephardt	Gore	Jackson
% Same	11	31	29	55
% Switch	28	31	21	21
% Develop	35	8	18	21
% Noncandidate	26	31	32	3
	(46)	(13)	(34)	(29)
		$X^2 = 24.13$	Sign. $= .0041$	

	Bush	Dole	Kemp	Robertson
% Same	77	67	57	69
% Switch	14	13	43	23
% Develop	8	21	0	8
% Noncandidate	2	0	0	0
	(52)	(24)	(7)	(13)
		$X^2 = 8.81$	Sign. $= .4551$	

Figures in parentheses are number of cases.

Same = preferred same candidate at time of pre-election interview as voted for on Super Tuesday
Switch = preferred another candidate at time of pre-election interview than voted for on Super Tuesday
Develop = had no preference at time of pre-election interview but eventually voted on Super Tuesday
Noncandidate = preferred candidate not running (Cuomo, Nunn, Kennedy, or candidate from other party) at time of pre-election interview and voted for someone else on Super Tuesday

Source: NES Super Tuesday surveys.

him throughout the campaign.[5] The remaining Jackson voters were evenly split between those who switched from another candidate and those who had no preference when the campaign began. Since Jackson was well known at the start of the campaign, the movement toward him followed increasing evaluations of his chances of electoral victory.[6] Between Jackson and Dukakis fell Gephardt and Gore. Both enjoyed the support of approximately one-third of their voters throughout the campaign. Changes in individual preferences for Democratic candidates hint momentum results both from increasing awareness of candidates and from changing preferences incorporating aspects of viability.

A more precise judgement on the effects of momentum can be gained by examining the influence of Iowa and New Hampshire on the preferences of Super Tuesday voters. Table 5.4 illustrates the effects of voters knowing

Table 5.4: Effects of Awareness of Iowa and New Hampshire Results on Candidate Preference Before Super Tuesday and on Actual Vote on Super Tuesday

Democratic Voters			
Know Gephardt won Iowa			
No	Yes	X^2	sign.
Prefer Gephardt: 13%	24%	3.83	.05
Vote Gephardt: 12%	13%	.00	1.00
(146)	(88)		

Know Dukakis won New Hampshire			
No	Yes	X^2	sign.
Prefer Dukakis: 11%	24%	4.05	.04
Vote Dukakis: 22%	39%	4.78	.03
(85)	(71)		

Republican Voters			
Know Dole won Iowa			
No	Yes	X^2	sign.
Prefer Dole: 23%	31%	.48	.49
Vote Dole: 16%	23%	.54	.46
(43)	(91)		

Know Bush won New Hampshire			
No	Yes	X^2	sign.
Prefer Bush: 57%	61%	.01	.91
Vote Bush: 38%	48%	.50	.48
(34)	(56)		

Figures in parentheses are number of cases. Preference is from pre-election interview; vote, from post-election report.

Source: NES Super Tuesday surveys.

which candidates won these two events on preferences for the winning candidates. Knowing that Gephardt won the Iowa caucuses increased pre-Super Tuesday preferences for Gephardt (24 percent of those who knew versus 13 percent of those who were unaware), but such knowledge did not affect the voting on Super Tuesday. Gephardt's Iowa "bounce" diminished quickly, such that on Super Tuesday he did not gain from knowledge of his early victory, receiving votes from 13 percent of those who knew he won Iowa and 12 percent from those who did not. Meanwhile, Dukakis's victory in New Hampshire remained more on the minds of Super Tuesday voters. His support increased by 17 percentage points among those who knew of his victory.[7] Knowledge of previous victories, however, had little influence on the Republican race. Knowing Dole won the Iowa caucuses did not increase support of Dole before or on Super Tuesday. Similarly, knowing Bush won New Hampshire did not affect Super Tuesday voters. Thus, knowledge of early victories increased the likelihood of voting for only one candidate on Super Tuesday. However, these early victories did affect voting on Super Tuesday by keeping candidacies alive. If Gephardt had lost to Simon in Iowa, he probably would not have remained a presidential candidate until Super Tuesday. Similarly, a loss by Dole to Bush in Iowa would have brought the Republican race to a close as soon as it began.

Although we have uncovered hints that both increasing awareness and changing evaluations incorporating estimates of viability may account for changing preferences among Democratic candidates, we have not examined each influence separately. Figures in table 5.5 do just that. Once again, the four categories of changing candidate preferences are incorporated, and the sample is restricted to only those interviewed prior to the Iowa caucuses. Because this greatly reduces the number of cases, Democratic and Republican voters are combined. Specifically, in table 5.5 we will examine average changes in levels of knowledge, favorableness, and viability for the candidate each respondent supported on Super Tuesday. The ratings respondents gave in the pre-election survey to the candidate they voted for on Super Tuesday were subtracted from ratings given to these same candidates in the post-election survey. The NES knowledge variable designates five levels of awareness. Evaluations and estimates of viability were gauged on 100-point scales. Feeling thermometers were used to measure overall evaluations, while viability was measured on a scale where 100 indicated absolute certainty that a candidate would win the nomination.

As is obvious from table 5.5, those voters who remained loyal to one candidate throughout the campaign did not change their opinions about that candidate. They knew him as well in January as they did in March. They maintained their favorable evaluation of the candidates despite the very slight tendency to realize that this candidate might be less likely to win the nomination.[8] Increasing knowledge played the most significant role for those originally preferring a candidate not seeking the nomination, increasing evaluations occurred the most for those developing a preference, and changing viability mattered most to those switching from one declared candidate to another.[9] Once again, all three momentum factors seem to account for changing candidate preferences.

Those voters who switched from one declared candidate to another constitute perhaps the most intriguing category. It seems logical that those with no original preference could be easily swayed by campaign events, but

Table 5.5: Effect of Changing Knowledge, Evaluations, and Expectations of
Victory on Candidate Choice on Super Tuesday

	Change in Knowledge	Change in Evaluation	Change in Viability
Same	.1	3.1	− 1.4
Switch	.9	10.4	13.2
Develop	1.0	12.1	9.5
Noncandidate	1.2	9.0	11.3
	(224)	(177)	(170)
sign.	.0000	.0292	.0112

Figures in parentheses are number of cases. All other values are average differences
between ratings given to candidate voted for on Super Tuesday in the post-election
interview and the pre-election interview. Evaluations and viability were gauged on a 100-
point scale; knowledge, on a 5-point scale. The table includes only those respondents first
interviewed prior to the Iowa caucuses.

Source: NES Super Tuesdays surveys.

those with a pre-election favorite would supposedly be more immune. What
caused them to change their minds? The most obvious possibility is that
their pre-election favorite is no longer an active candidate, one forced out of
the race by poor showings in Iowa or New Hampshire. Figures in table 5.6,
summarizing the source of movement for those who switched candidate
preferences, indicate that only 10 percent of these switchers originally
favored a candidate who was no longer seeking the presidency. The demise
of Haig's, du Pont's, and Babbitt's candidacies did not upset many southern
voters, since few supported these candidates in the early stages of the
campaign. The largest proportion of switchers moved away from failing
candidacies, such as Hart and Simon on the Democratic side and Kemp and
Robertson on the Republican side. Not to be forgotten, however, are those 24
percent of original Hart supporters, 25 percent of original Simon supporters,
56 percent of original Kemp supporters, and 89 percent of original Robertson supporters who still cast ballots for these candidates on Super Tuesday.
Nevertheless, movement away from failed and failing candidacies constituted over half of the reasons for changing preferences among declared
candidates as the campaign progressed.

The remaining 46 percent of switchers changed preferences among the
"viable" candidates. About a quarter of these moved to a candidate they now
rated more highly than their original choice, another quarter moved to a
candidate they now ascribed as more viable than their first choice, with
another quarter moving to a candidate they began to both like better and view
as having a better chance of winning the nomination. The remaining quarter
followed no expected pattern. Thus, figures in table 5.6 suggest that 50

Table 5.6: Categorization of Those Who Switched Candidate Preferences from
Time of Pre-Iowa Interview to Super Tuesday

Left candidate who withdrew from race	10%
Left candidate with failing campaign	44%
Moved to candidate rated more highly than previous choice	13%
Moved to candidate given a higher chance of winning the nomination	8%
Moved to candidate rated higher and given a better chance of winning the nomination	13%
Some other pattern	13%
Number of cases	(48)

Source: NES Super Tuesday survey.

percent of the movement between candidates is caused by the demise of
some candidacies in the early campaign, and movement among the other 50
percent is owing equally to changing evaluations and changing estimates of
viability.

The pre-Super Tuesday campaign mattered, though knowledge of specific events—i.e., results in Iowa or New Hampshire—did not appear to be
an important factor. Rather, the more general timber of the race—news
reports, presence or absence of campaign advertisements, failing or soaring
candidacies—are responsible for changing preferences. Most changes in
preferences, however, are not between competing candidates. Rather, they
arise from voters who had no preference or preferred a noncandidate when
the campaign commenced. Additionally, many voters retained their preferences throughout the campaign. This was especially true on the Republican
side, where voters were quite familiar with the major contestants at the
beginning of the nomination race. The early rounds of the 1988 campaign
had very little effect on voters' support for Bush, Dole, or Robertson. With a
large field of unknowns on the Democratic side, more changes in preferences occurred. But once again, these changes were mostly characterized by
the development of preferences, not by changes in preferences.

Having examined changes in candidate preferences over time, we now
need to investigate factors underlying voter preferences on Super Tuesday.
Besides momentum advantages, why did some Democrats prefer Dukakis,
others Jackson, Gephardt, or Gore? As mentioned earlier in this chapter, the
four most frequently considered factors include ideology, issues, candidate
qualities, and demographic traits of voters.

IDEOLOGY AND THE VOTE

The fear that previous Democratic nominees were too liberal for southern
voters underpinned the movement toward Super Tuesday. Mondale in 1984

and McGovern in 1972 won the Democratic nomination through primary victories but failed to win any southern state in the fall election. Overlooked in the southern leaders' reasoning is the fact that these two candidates won only three states and the District of Columbia between them. Only Jimmy Carter in 1976 carried the South in the fall election, and only Jimmy Carter since the 1960s won enough of the rest of the states to claim the White House for the Democrats. Yet, in the minds of southern leaders, the South was an essential component to any successful Democratic candidate. After all, the South possessed 165 electoral college votes, 60 percent of the total needed for victory, and had been the historical base of the Democratic party. To recapture this base, southern leaders reasoned, the Democratic party needed to nominate more moderate candidates that southern voters could support in the fall election. The question remains whether southern voters were as concerned about the ideological position of the candidates as their leaders were.

The effects of ideology on voting is most often examined under a system publicized by Anthony Downs (1957). According to his spatial model of voting, individuals cast ideological votes if they support the candidate they place closest to themselves on an ideological scale (see Wattier 1983 for an application to presidential primaries). The Downsian model of ideological voting, however, excludes a significant portion of voters by eliminating those who fail to classify themselves or the candidates on an ideological scale. Using a variety of public opinion polls, Geer (1989) found that up to 22 percent of primary voters do not place themselves on an ideological scale, up to 48 percent are unable to place the candidates, while up to 34 percent place two or more candidates at the same spot. As a result, the number of potential ideological voters ranged from a low of 33 percent among Pennsylvania Democratic voters surveyed in 1976 to a high of 71 percent among California Republican voters in that same year. In contrast, on average 68 percent of voters in presidential elections fit the criteria of placing themselves and the candidates on ideological scales and assigning different positions to the two candidates. Besides ignoring those incapable of assigning ideological identities, the Downsian model focuses solely on the relative placement of candidates and individual voters, not on the accurate classification of candidates as liberals, moderates, or conservatives.

Other political scientists who investigate ideological voting incorporate a voter's own ideological position as one of the factors that predict vote choice (e.g., Levitin and Miller 1979). Some of these scholars began to question the meaning of ideology because it retained an effect on candidate choice even after controlling for a variety of issue positions. If ideology entails a summary of, or causes, an individual's position on issues, ideology should not retain a separate influence on vote choice. This anomaly led several scholars to reconsider ideology as a symbolic label unrelated to most issues. Individuals who identified with the conservative label did so because they associated it with such groups as the middle class, Protestants, police, and military; those who identified with the liberal label associate it with blacks, Hispanics, and the women's and civil rights movements (Conover and Feldman 1981).

No one measure will allow us to separate the components of ideology or gauge the precise effects of each. But since Super Tuesday's architects were most concerned with finding a moderate or conservative Democratic candidate, a plausible approach for studying ideological voting on Super Tuesday would be to investigate voters' actual placement of candidates and themselves, rather than their relative placement. To uncover these ideological classifications, we will use the "CBS News"/*New York Times* exit poll of Super Tuesday voters. Over 8,000 Democratic voters and 7,000 Republican voters were surveyed, allowing us the luxury of a candidate-by-candidate breakdown. The question measuring ideological positions of respondents was quite standard: "On most political matters, do you consider yourself: liberal, moderate, conservative?" The question ascertaining ideological position of candidates, however, is somewhat unusual and asks, "Would you describe your choice today for president as a: liberal, moderate, conservative?" Nevertheless, by combining these two questions we can search for matches between respondents' positions and the positions they assigned to their candidates. We will not be able to accurately judge the Downsian model of voting for the closest candidate, since we do not have placements for the other candidates. But knowing whether matches exist between respondents' and candidates' ideologies provides a partial answer. Additionally, by knowing the actual placement, rather than the relative placement, we may gain some insight into the meaning of ideology for primary voters. If a significant portion of voters are willing to vote for a candidate whom they assign a different ideological label from their own, ideology would appear to be a relatively unimportant consideration. Of course, this mismatch between voter and candidate may reflect a reluctant choice, with the chosen candidate being perceived as the closest to the voter's own ideological position.

Table 5.7 provides the evidence about Democratic voters. Respondents are separated by which candidate they supported and the ideological labels they assigned to themselves and their candidates. Figures in the first column reveal that approximately 10 percent of voters supporting each Democratic candidate felt uncomfortable with or were unable to assign ideological labels. With 10 percent admitting unfamiliarity with these labels, we might reasonably assume another 10 percent essentially guessed at their answers, randomly ascribing labels to themselves and their candidates. The 25 percent of the respondents in the "mismatch labels" column of table 5.7 also demonstrate a lack of ideological voting in that they voted for candidates with different ideological persuasions than their own. Individuals in the middle three columns might represent ideological voting in that they voted

Table 5.7: Ideological Votes for Each Candidate on Super Tuesday

	% Missing Labels	% Both Liberal	% Both Moderate	% Both Conservative	% Mismatch Labels	Number
Democrats						
Dukakis	9	15	39	10	28	(2,253)
Gephardt	7	8	42	17	26	(1,140)
Gore	8	5	40	19	27	(2,230)
Hart	12	17	27	15	29	(226)
Jackson	12	24	26	13	25	(2,642)
Simon	5	21	35	7	31	(182)
Republicans						
Bush	5	3	24	45	22	(3,934)
Dole	5	3	31	36	25	(1,919)
Kemp	4	2	18	60	16	(420)
Robertson	4	2	10	72	12	(1,047)

Missing Labels = respondent failed to classify either self or candidate with ideological label
Both Liberal = respondent classified self and candidate voted for as liberal
Both Moderate = respondent classified self and candidate voted for as moderate
Both conservative = respondent classified self and candidate voted for as conservative
Mismatch labels = respondent classified self under one label and candidate voted for under another
Source: "CBS News"/*New York Times* Super Tuesday Primary Election Exit Polls, 1988.

for candidates with the same ideological positions as their own. Yet some of these voters ascribed their candidates as liberal, while others labeled the same candidates as conservative. Obviously, confusion existed about the ideological positions of candidates for some 5 to 15 percent of Democratic voters. Finally, not to be overlooked is that a plurality of these ideological Democratic voters described both themselves and their candidates as moderate. This even held true for Jackson voters! Of course, the number of moderate voter/moderate candidate matches varies from candidate to candidate in a somewhat predictable fashion, with Gephardt and Gore voters having the most of these matches. Still, the preponderance of these moderate-moderate matches among all candidates' voters casts doubts on the role of ideology in presidential primary voting.

Republican patterns duplicate Democratic patterns except that the most prevalent match is conservative voters supporting conservative candidates. Once again, this match increases predictably from a low of 36 percent for Dole voters to a high of 72 percent for Robertson voters. Nevertheless, we are left questioning the impact of ideology on presidential primary voting when most voters either do not answer the ideology question, assign themselves and their candidates different labels, or assign themselves and their candidates common labels (i.e, moderates for Democrats and conservatives for Republicans) regardless of which candidate they support. The prevalence of the latter pattern lends credence to a symbolic definition of ideology. Democrats in the South identified with the moderate label and assigned it to their chosen candidate, while Republicans identified with and assigned the conservative label.

ISSUES AND THE VOTE

If ideology is used as a symbolic label by primary voters, then issues could play a separate role in influencing voting decisions. Perhaps southern voters disliked Mondale and McGovern because of their issues positions: raising taxes and dovishness on Vietnam. Problems also could arise for Democratic prospects in the fall election if supporters of one candidate held distinctly different issue concerns than other primary voters. Would such voters be able to transfer their loyalties to another candidate if he won the Democratic nomination? However, none of these would be a problem if issues were not consistently related to voters' candidate preferences. As mentioned earlier in this chapter, most research on presidential primary voting found issues to have limited impact on primary choices. One reason for this lack of influence is the preoccupation of the press with the horse-race aspects of the contest: who is expected to win the next primary, whose campaign staff are bickering among themselves, and so on. Additionally, candidates are often thought to play down issues in their campaigns, especially in commercials, so as not to alienate any potential constituency.

We will search for a role for issues in voting decisions on Super Tuesday by making use of the "CBS News"/*New York Times* exit polls. Once again the large number of cases will allow us to examine each candidate's supporters with some confidence that what we are viewing accurately reflects other supporters. The "CBS News"/*New York Times* issues question, however, is somewhat unusual. Instead of asking respondents where they stand on specific issues, the poll asks, "Which issues mattered most in deciding how you voted?" The question was followed by nine categories, and respondents were instructed to pick two of these.[10] Such a question format does not lend itself to a causal analysis of voting decisions, but it will allow us to see if each candidate's supporters possessed a unique set of concerns. Table 5.8 presents the percentage of each candidate's supporters who were concerned about each issue.

On the Democratic side, Jackson voters held the most distinctive issue concerns. They chose unemployment and problems of the poor as their dominant issues, while being much less concerned with defense and foreign

Table 5.8: Percentage of Each Candidate's Supporters Citing Specific Issues as Reasons for Their Votes

Democratic Voters						
	Dukakis	Gephardt	Gore	Hart	Jackson	Simon
Unemployment	29	28	23	26	51	21
Oil Tax	6	8	7	8	2	4
Foreign Trade	13	29	18	12	7	11
Federal Deficit	40	30	36	23	16	43
Nicaragua	11	6	6	9	6	11
Social Security	30	32	30	30	24	24
Poor	20	15	14	21	55	24
Defense	13	11	18	19	5	15
None of Above	7	9	10	12	4	13
	(1,996)	(1,009)	(2,048)	(205)	(2,468)	(164)

Republican Voters			
	Bush	Dole	Kemp	Robertson
Missile Treaty	13	11	10	8
Oil Tax	6	7	8	3
Foreign Trade	13	18	11	9
Federal Deficit	40	47	42	30
Nicaragua	16	13	18	13
Social Security	21	21	12	11
Moral Issues	17	15	28	69
Federal Tax	27	20	31	14
None of Above	13	13	9	5
	(3,422)	(1,669)	(378)	(920)

Respondents could choose up to two reasons. See note 10 for complete issue options. Figures in parentheses are number of cases.

Source: "CBS News"/*New York Times* Super Tuesday Primary Election Exit Polls, 1988.

policy issues than other Democratic voters. The problems of the "have nots" in Jackson's Rainbow Coalition dominated the issue reasons given by his supporters. Dukakis, Gephardt, and Gore voters appeared quite similar in their issue concerns. Approximately one-third of each candidate's voters selected the federal deficit or Social Security as reasons for supporting their candidate. Hart voters joined Dukakis, Gephardt, and Gore voters on the social security issue, while Simon voters entered the fold on the question of the federal deficit. The similarity of issue concerns among these five candidates' supporters indicates a lack of issue distinctiveness, with one exception. Gephardt voters, picking up on his campaign theme, selected unfair foreign trade more often than other voters. The Gephardt and Jackson examples demonstrate that issues can be related to voting preferences if such issues fit into a dominant campaign theme.

On the Republican side, similarity in issue concerns also predominates. Bush, Dole, and Kemp supporters often cited the same issues for their support. The slightest distinctiveness occurred for Dole voters, with these Republican voters being slightly more concerned with the federal deficit and slightly less concerned with not raising federal taxes. Perhaps Bush's bid to paint Dole as a politician unwilling to commit to a "no-new-tax" pledge played a role in Dole voters being less likely to select this issue option. The most distinctive set of Republican voters supported Robertson. An over-whelming concern for traditional moral values characterized his supporters. Once again, issues are related to candidate preferences if those issues conform to the dominant campaign image of a candidate. Not all attempts to create such an image, however, are successful.

CANDIDATE QUALITIES AND THE VOTE

Past research often found candidate qualities most distinguished one candidate's supporters from the others'. The lack of issues and the dominance of images in news coverage and campaign commercials constitute the chief explanations for these findings. Additionally, similar issue preferences among voters from the same party are thought to lead voters to concentrate on candidate qualities in deciding which candidates to support.

The "CBS News"/*New York Times* exit polls asked about candidate qualities in the same format as the question they used in asking about issues. Respondents were asked, "Which qualities of your candidates mattered most in deciding how you voted?" Nine categories followed, with instructions to select two.[11] As with the analysis of the issue question, the percentage of each candidate's supporters selecting each item are presented in table 5.9.

As with issue concerns, Jackson voters cited the most distinctive set of candidate qualities as their reasons for supporting him. They noted Jackson's honesty, leadership, and concern for people. They were much less likely than others to cite experience as a reason for their vote choice. This list of characteristics reflects Jackson's campaign themes of caring for the have-nots and providing bold new leadership. Candidate qualities also tended to distinguish Simon voters. Honesty and intelligence predominated among the concerns of Simon's supporters, reflecting his bespectacled, bow-tied image of a thinking person's politician. Dukakis's supporters also cited reasons that reflected his campaign image: management skills and electability. Hart voters present an interesting case of why voters continue to support a candidate on the slide; they simply disliked the other options. Hart voters may have cast protest votes. Gephardt voters were indistinguishable by the

Table 5.9: Percentage of Each Candidate's Supporters Citing Specific Candidate Qualities as Reasons for Their Votes

			Democratic Voters			
	Dukakis	Gephardt	Gore	Hart	Jackson	Simon
Honest	40	48	46	26	52	72
Intelligent	30	26	30	23	22	42
Leadership	29	25	27	29	38	8
Experience	22	12	10	19	4	19
Cares	14	26	20	25	40	23
Win in November	11	8	6	5	4	0
Management	17	6	6	8	5	5
Own Region	2	6	12	3	2	1
Dislike Others	12	15	13	24	6	8
	(2,031)	(1,028)	(2,074)	(217)	(2,477)	(167)

		Republican Voters		
	Bush	Dole	Kemp	Robertson
Honest	34	41	49	75
Intelligent	22	28	30	29
Real Conservative	9	9	37	27
Experience	51	30	9	5
Leadership	13	39	15	22
Win in November	10	10	3	2
Reagan Heir	29	8	14	10
Own Region	1	2	2	1
Dislike Others	10	13	15	8
	(3,544)	(1,723)	(384)	(927)

Respondents could choose up to two reasons. See note 11 for complete list of options. Figures in parentheses are number of cases.

Source: "CBS News"/*New York Times* Super Tuesday Primary Election Exit Polls, 1988.

candidate qualities cited. Gephardt's image in the South remained with his dominant issue—unfair foreign trade. Gore's distinction came from those citing region as a concern, but only 12 percent choose this option. Either Gore failed to cement his image as the southern candidate or southern voters simply were not very concerned with the origins of candidates.

Candidate qualities distinguished Republican voters in much the same manner as one would expect, given the themes of their campaigns. Bush's position as Reagan's vice president resulted in his voters citing experience and being Reagan's heir more often than other candidates' voters. Meanwhile, Dole successfully transmitted to his supporters his claim that while Bush languished in the White House, Dole provided true leadership in the Senate. Bush and Dole shared the image of best being able to win in

November, but only 10 percent expressed such a concern. Kemp convinced his supporters that he was a real conservative, while Robertson's supporters cited his honesty.

Both candidate qualities and issues distinguished some candidates' supporters from others. Yet in many cases supporters of all or many of a party's presidential contenders appeared alike in their reasons for the votes. The issues and qualities that distinguished one candidate's supporters from another's were those hammered home by dominant campaign themes. Gephardt voters cited his foreign trade theme, while Dukakis voters cited his management skills connected with his reputation as the force behind the Massachusetts Miracle. Jackson's Rainbow Coalition emerged in the issue concerns of the have-nots and the caring image that accompanied this concern. Gore picked up a few votes by being a southerner. Hart benefited from a protest vote by those who disliked all the other candidates. Finally, Simon's meager support in the South came from those who liked his honesty, intelligence, and concern with the budget deficit.

The images and issues that dominated Democratic voting on Super Tuesday did not reflect those of Super Tuesday's architects. These Democratic leaders feared the party's image of being weak on defense resulted in Democratic candidate losses in the South. But few Democratic voters on Super Tuesday expressed concern for the foreign issues of Nicaragua or the national defense. Rather, domestic concerns predominated: the deficit and social security. Even the foreign trade issue is basically a domestic concern, as blue-collar workers feared for their jobs. Among image concerns, southern Democratic voters were spectacularly unconcerned with the regional origins of the candidates or their winning ability in November. Rather, subjective images of honesty, intelligence, and leadership characterized the concerns of most Democratic voters.

Most Republican voters were not dedicated to finding a true conservative to bolster their party's chances; their reasons for support followed the campaign themes of the candidates. Bush and Dole voters often appeared alike, except that Bush's supporters cited his connections with Reagan and Dole's supporters cited his leadership and concern for the federal deficit. Only Kemp's supporters expressed interest in finding a true conservative who would not raise taxes. Robertson's ministerial background led his supporters to view him as more honest and more concerned with moral issues.

DEMOGRAPHICS AND THE VOTE

The final aspect of the Super Tuesday vote that needs examining is the pattern of candidate preferences among different demographic groups. Bartels (1988) maintains that demographic traits represent basic divisions in each party. These divisions may be closely related to candidate preferences. If they are, these distinctions may foreshadow problems for the fall election. Basic internal divisions within the party will need to be reconnected to make victory in the fall possible. For this final analysis, we will continue to use the "CBS News"/*New York Times* exit polls. To maintain compatibility with previous tables, the percentages of each candidate's supporters coming from each group are presented in tables 5.10 and 5.11.

Southern Democratic leaders desired a candidate that southern voters could support. Among the 1988 candidate field, two candidates received disproportionate support from native southerners. Gore benefited from the southern vote, but so did Jackson. Southern blacks form a significant proportion of the southern Democratic electorate, and their support in 1988 went to Jackson. Unions form another traditional component of the Democratic electorate. Gephardt, with his advocacy of protectionist trade legislation, received 29 percent of his vote from union members, but Jackson benefited from an equal proportion of union support. Thirty-two percent of union members in the South are black; white union members were no more likely to support Jackson than were whites who did not belong to a union. Jackson's vote in the South came mainly from black voters, but black voters in the South constitute significant proportions of other important constituent groups, such as unions and native southerners. Dukakis, Gephardt, and Gore supporters resembled each other, except in that Gephardt received more support from union members than did the other two and Gore received more support from native southerners than did Gephardt or Dukakis. Simon's support came from highly educated, high-income voters, whereas Hart's constituency fell at the other end of the socioeconomic scale.

Robertson received support from the most unique group of Republican voters. His religiously oriented backers were predominantly fundamentalist and frequent church attenders. He was unable to expand his coalition to include conservative Catholics. His fundamentalist supporters also tended to be native southerners with lower incomes than other Republican voters. Meanwhile, Kemp attracted younger and better-educated Republicans to his fold. Bush's backers were older, while Dole's support derived proportionately from all segments of the Republican electorate.

SUMMARY

Having examined voting patterns by southern Democrats and Republicans, one must conclude that the pre-Super Tuesday campaign mattered. Not because southern voters knew who won Iowa and New Hampshire and followed suit, but rather because the pre-Super Tuesday campaign affected

Table 5.10: Percentage of Each Democratic Candidate's Supporters from Specific Demographic Groups

	Dukakis	Gephardt	Gore	Hart	Jackson	Simon	All
Female	55	51	47	48	55	51	52
Black	3	3	2	9	79	1	26
Hispanic	4	2	1	4	2	2	2
White	93	95	97	86	18	95	71
18-29	13	11	13	19	17	15	14
Over 60	33	31	32	22	19	21	28
College Degree	38	26	32	24	32	51	33
Over $35,000	44	39	40	33	28	52	38
Under $12,500	11	12	13	21	25	8	16
Union family	19	29	18	21	27	22	23
Fundamental	6	10	12	9	6	7	8
Catholic	28	23	10	26	29	20	17
Jewish	10	12	12	15	1	7	4
Weekly Church	37	42	46	43	45	43	43
Southerner	39	39	69	46	59	34	53

Source: "CBS News"/*New York Times* Super Tuesday Primary Election Polls, 1988. Over 8,000 Democratic voters responded to these questions.

the fates of candidates and the general timber of the campaign. Events prior to March 8 provided Republican voters with few reasons to switch from their original preferences. Bush, Dole, and Robertson were well known before the race, and three-fourths of their supporters remained with them until Super Tuesday. Few southern Republicans were forced to switch preferences when Haig's, du Pont's, and Kemp's campaigns faded, because few southerners knew or supported these candidates in the beginning months of 1988.

The fates of the Democratic contenders shifted with the campaign but not because people switched their preferences among the main contenders as each candidate won or lost earlier events. Rather, much of the change came about because half of the Democratic voters had no preference at the beginning of the campaign, including about 25 percent who preferred Cuomo, Nunn, Kennedy, or some other candidate not seeking the Democratic nomination. Only one-quarter of Democrats switched preferences among the 1988 Democratic candidates, with about half of these leaving the failed, or failing, candidacies of Babbitt, Hart, and Simon. The other half of the "switchers" moved among Gephardt, Dukakis, Gore, and Jackson because of changing attitudes about the attractiveness and viability of these candidates. One-fourth of Democratic voters remained loyal to their candidates throughout the campaign.

Table 5.11: Percentage of Each Republican Candidate's Supporters from Specific Demographic Groups

	Bush	Dole	Kemp	Robertson	All
Female	45	50	40	52	47
Black	2	3	5	4	3
Hispanic	2	2	0	2	2
White	95	95	94	94	95
18-29	17	17	21	16	17
Over 60	30	23	21	18	26
College Degree	37	40	49	31	38
Over $35,000	50	51	53	42	49
Under $12,500	8	8	7	9	8
Union Family	11	12	13	14	12
Fundamentalist	11	15	24	66	21
Catholic	20	18	16	7	18
Jewish	2	4	2	1	2
Weekly Church	44	45	49	70	48
Southerner	47	41	43	50	45

Source: "CBS News"/*New York Times* Super Tuesday Primary Election Polls, 1988. Over 7,000 Republican voters responded to these questions.

   The campaign mattered also in presenting people with reasons for their choices. Depending upon what factors a candidate stressed in his campaign, some of these reasons were based on issues, whereas others focused on candidate qualities. Gephardt voters cited the unfair foreign trade issue emphasized in his Hyundai commercial. Dukakis's claim to the Massachusetts Miracle led his voters to cite competent management as a major reason for their choice. Jackson's Rainbow Coalition emerged in his supporters' choice of issue concerns (i.e, unemployment) and desired candidate qualities (i.e, caring). Robertson's supporters highlighted their concerns with moral issues; Kemp's, with taxes. Nevertheless, most of the major issues of the day, including the federal deficit, events in Nicaragua, and concerns for Social Security, did not distinguish among candidate supporters because candidates did not adopt distinguishing positions. The same was true for candidate qualities, as supporters of all candidates saw in their choices the desired traits of honesty, intelligence, and leadership.
   Despite these similarities, divisions within each party continued to be reflected in candidate preferences. Black Democrats supported Jackson; white union members backed Gephardt. Native southerners, being both black and white, split their votes among Gore, Jackson, and, less frequently, the remaining Democratic candidates. Demographic distinctions were less

prevalent among supporters of Republican candidates, with the exception of Robertson. His support remained totally within the confines of the white, Protestant religious right.

These findings about candidate support do not coincide with the concerns of Super Tuesday's creators. Southern Democratic leaders felt liberal Democratic candidates kept winning the presidential nomination because Iowa and New Hampshire possessed too much clout and the South too little. Expectations about the effects of momentum, ideology, and regionalism emerged from these southern concerns. Evidence in this chapter, however, demonstrates that these three factors affected voting in a manner inconsistent with the southern leaders' fears. Events in Iowa and New Hampshire did not cause many southerners to change their minds, because on the Democratic side one-half began 1988 undecided while on the Republican side three-quarters remained committed to their candidate throughout the campaign. The attrition of candidates after the two early contests also did not affect many southern voters, as few knew of or supported these candidates. Nevertheless, the development of preferences among many Democrats, and a few Republicans, was influenced by changing evaluations of candidates and their fates.

Southern voters did not use ideology in a manner consistent with an issue-based definition, an assumption upon which southern leaders based their fears of a too liberal Democratic nominee. Rather, southern voters employed ideological labels symbolically and indiscriminately. Most of the Democratic "ideological" voters, including a scant plurality of Jackson voters, viewed themselves and their candidates as moderates. Most Republicans viewed themselves and their candidates as conservatives.

Regional concerns did not resonate in the minds of many southern voters as they had among Super Tuesday's architects. Only 10 percent of Gore voters cited his southern identity as a reason for their support, although 70 percent of Gore's support did arise from native southerners. However, a southern identity and regional concern were the only traits that distinguished Gore supporters from Dukakis and Gephardt backers. Even losing 10 percent of his support would push Gore into third place in subsequent contests. Knowledge of Gore's victory in the South would not make up for this loss of regional support. Just as Iowa and New Hampshire victories did not resonate in the minds of southern voters, Super Tuesday victories would not dominate calculations of subsequent voters. Southern roots also characterized Jackson's supporters, but the issues and candidate qualities associated with his theme of a Rainbow Coalition, which provided southerners with reasons to support Jackson, would also provide northerners in subsequent primaries with similar incentives to cast their ballots for Jackson.

6

Winning the Nomination

Each nomination season brings a new crop of candidates and then proceeds to eliminate most within a few weeks of the New Hampshire primary. Meanwhile, momentum boosts the fortunes of some candidates, though many of these candidates, such as Bush in 1980 and Hart in 1984, fall short of the ultimate goal. Time is the common element allowing both winnowing and momentum to unwind. Both processes occur as the primary season rolls from one state to the next. An essential characteristic of all presidential nominations, therefore, is time. Super Tuesday truncated the time span of the 1988 nomination process. The selection of 50 percent of all delegates would begin by March 8. Did this truncated nomination season expedite or delay winnowing and momentum and thus change the date by which the nominee was ultimately chosen?

In addition to altering time, Super Tuesday was designed to change who won the nomination by giving the South more clout. The early, simultaneous selection of an immense bloc of delegates would force candidates and the media to pay attention to the South. More candidate attention would give southern voters a better choice. More media attention would increase the impact of southern choices on subsequent primaries, just as the extensive coverage of Iowa and New Hampshire multiplies the impact of their decisions. But were southern wishes ignored in the past, and did Super Tuesday increase the influence of the South on the Democratic or Republican presidential nomination?

In this chapter we will explore the effects of Super Tuesday on the final choices of the Democratic and Republican parties in 1988. First, we will concentrate on Super Tuesday as a regional primary that could potentially alter the timing of the nomination. Second, we will examine Super Tuesday as a *southern* regional primary. In other words, what effect did the South have on the selection of presidential nominees?

TIME AND WINNING THE PRESIDENTIAL NOMINATION

Candidates earn presidential nominations because they win votes and accumulate delegates, but they also win nominations because other candidates drop out of the race. Thus, three elements unfold over time to
determine the ultimate victor: attrition of candidates, voters jumping on
winning candidates' bandwagons, and candidates trying to accumulate the
50 percent of convention delegates needed to secure the nomination. Super
Tuesday altered the calendar of the 1988 nomination season, but how
would it alter the timing of these three processes? Some commentators felt
Super Tuesday would delay the Democratic nomination until the national
convention, as no candidate would be able to accumulate sufficient delegates after Jackson polled his portion of the Super Tuesday vote (Apple,
January 3, 1988; Barnes, March 19, 1988; Barnes, March 21, 1988; Udall,
January 10, 1988; Wicker, February 19, 1988). With 50 percent of the
delegates already chosen, not enough delegates would be available after
Super Tuesday for any candidate to pull together a majority. This scenario,
however, neglected the process of candidate attrition, which makes available
the already selected delegates of failed candidates to be redistributed among
the remaining contestants. Thus, all three elements (candidate attrition,
voters bandwagons, and delegate accumulation) need to be examined over
time.

Attrition of Candidates

Al Haig exited the 1988 Republican race on February 13, three days before
New Hampshire's primary. Bruce Babbitt and Pete du Pont soon followed
on February 18. Super Tuesday eliminated two more candidates, with the
withdrawals of Gary Hart and Jack Kemp. Gephardt and Dole failed to
revive their candidacies after disappointing results on Super Tuesday, so
Gephardt left the 1988 nomination race on March 28 and Dole followed a
day later. Paul Simon ran out of scenarios on April 7, and Al Gore's failure
to win northern votes forced him from the race on April 21. Pat Robertson
formally disbanded his campaign on May 16, though he had ceased
campaigning much earlier. Three candidates remained to make their bids
before the national conventions: George Bush, Michael Dukakis, and Jesse
Jackson.

Each candidate's withdrawal from the race rejuggled the stakes for the
remaining players. As we saw in Chapter 5, 10% of the respondents to the
NES Super Tuesday survey had to abandon their pre-Iowa favorites as these
candidates left the race. Another 44 percent left the sinking ships of
candidates such as Hart, Simon, and Kemp. In Chapter 2, we saw how the
composition of Iowa's convention delegation shifted as candidates who won

support in the earliest rounds no longer remained active candidates as the later rounds arrived. Thus, candidate attrition accounts for many of the changes in voter preferences and delegate acquisition.

The question remains whether Super Tuesday altered the rate of candidates' withdrawals. Table 6.1 traces the attrition of candidates from 1976 to 1988—except for the constant two-man races on the Republican side in 1976 and the Democratic side in 1980—by listing the number of original candidates competing at various time periods. By Super Tuesday, the 1988 Democratic race already lost one candidate; the Republican, two. A week later, Democrats and Republicans each witnessed one more of their parties' candidates withdraw his name from consideration. Such an early reduction in candidates, however, is not unusual. The 1988 Democratic and 1980 Republican contests both commenced with seven candidates and proceeded to winnow them at identical paces. The sole exception occurred at the end of the primary season, as Bush's withdrawal left Reagan as the lone candidate in 1980, whereas Jackson continued to contest Dukakis's nomination up to the Democratic convention. The 1988 Republican and 1984 Democratic fields, although starting with slightly different numbers, also lost the bulk of their members in March. At best, Super Tuesday slightly quickened the pace of withdrawals in the 1988 Republican race, with half of the candidates leaving by mid-March. The reduction of the candidate field by half usually does not occur until the beginning of April. Still, this change represents only a two-week difference. Super Tuesday did not alter the fact that candidate attrition is a central process by which presidential nominations are decided.

This gradual attrition pattern was not fully institutionalized in the 1976 campaign. Instead, some candidates selectively entered and avoided primaries, much as candidates did in the pre-reform era. "Scoop" Jackson shunned New Hampshire to concentrate on Massachusetts; Frank Church and Jerry Brown did not declare their candidacies until mid-March and did not compete in any primary until April. Under the pre-reform system, candidates used primary victories in selected states to persuade uncommitted delegates and party elites to support their candidacies. Jimmy Carter convincingly demonstrated, however, that under the post-reform system candidates capture the nomination by entering every primary in order to gradually accumulate the number of committed delegates necessary to win the presidential nomination. Since 1976, avoiding primaries has been a sign of weakness rather than an indication of an astute strategy. Simon's dodging of Super Tuesday was forced on him as poor showings in earlier contests led to a lack of funds. Gore's stated avoidance of Iowa and New Hampshire followed disappointing pre-caucus poll results. Under the post-reform system, candidates compete early and often until

Table 6.1: Number of Candidates Remaining in Races for Republican and
Democratic Nominations at Various Time Periods

	Democratic			Republican	
	1976	1984	1988	1980	1988
Pre-Iowa	10	8	7	7	6
March 1	8	7	6	7	4
March 8	8a	5	6	6	4
March 15	8b	4	5	5	3
March 23	8	3	5	4	3
April 1	8	3	4	4	2
April 16	7	3	3	3	2
May 1	7	3	2	2	2
May 16	6	3	3	2	2
June 1	5	3	2	1	1
At convention	2	3	2	1	1
Total number of candidates	12	8	7	7	6

aBayh left race; Brown entered.
bShapp left race; Church entered.

poor results force them from the race or good results propel them to
victory.

Jumping on Candidates' Bandwagons

With seven Democrats and six Republicans at the start of the 1988 races,
none could expect to win a large percentage of the vote. One hundred
percent divided by seven leaves few voters supporting any one candidate.
But as attrition occurs, the percentage of voters casting ballots for the
remaining candidates naturally increases. Which candidates benefit from
this rejuggling of preferences significantly influences who wins the nomination. At some point before the end of the primary season, voters appear to be
jumping on the bandwagon of one candidate, who then moves on to become
the nominee.[1]

Figures 6.1 and 6.2 trace the support of voters for the four most
successful candidates on each side in 1988. These graphs chart the average
vote for each candidate on each primary day, combining voting percentages
from all states on multiple primary dates such as Super Tuesday. As highlighted by figure 6.1, March 8 set Bush on an unstoppable bandwagon.
Thereafter, he never won less than 50 percent of the vote, mostly because
only Robertson remained as a declared candidate, and a weak one at that. By
April, Bush's vote totals hovered around the 75 percent mark. The Demo-

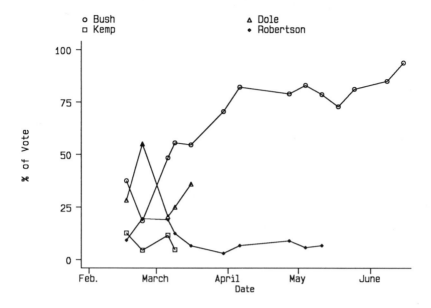

Figure 6.1: Average Primary Vote for Republican Candidates in 1988

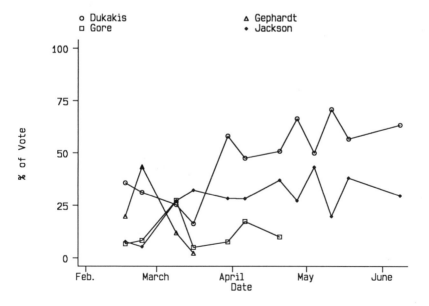

Figure 6.2: Average Primary Vote for Democratic Candidates in 1988

cratic race, depicted in figure 6.2, indicates a later and weaker bandwagon for Dukakis. His vote totals did not approach the 50 percent mark until April, when only Jackson and Gore remained as challengers. Once Gore left the race, Dukakis's vote percentage remained high, fluctuating in reverse image to Jackson's. However, Dukakis's vote never topped the 75 percent mark, as Bush's did, as a result of the continual presence of Jackson in the race.

How did Dukakis's and Bush's bandwagons compare to those in earlier years? Before answering this question, we must establish the appropriate cases for comparison. One might compare all Democratic races to one another and all Republican races to one another, but a better classification exists. What determines the patterns of a nomination race is not which party it falls in, but the nature of the candidate field. Some races have only two candidates, as in 1976 when Reagan challenged Ford and in 1980 when Kennedy confronted Carter.[2] The opposite extreme is a multicandidate race with no one candidate in the lead. Such "open races" occurred for the Democratic party in 1988 and 1976. In between are multicandidate races with front-runners, with Bush leading the Republican pack in 1988, Mondale ahead at the start of the 1984 Democratic race, and Reagan the presumed front-runner in the 1980 Republican contest (see Bartels 1988; and Keech and Matthews 1976 for similar classifications of presidential nomination races).

Voting patterns in open races, as depicted in figure 6.3, began with the ultimately successful candidate capturing around 25 percent of the vote. The next plateau is to near the 50 percent mark. Dukakis reached this point by the beginning of April. Carter's percentage of the vote reached 50 percent earlier but also declined afterwards as additional candidates entered the Democratic race. Carter's vote leveled off to about 35 to 45 percent of the vote, while Dukakis's remained 5 to 10 percent higher. With only two years for comparisons, and with some elements of the 1976 race hearkening back to the older style of campaigning, making generalizations about open-race bandwagons is difficult. Carter's less successful final half of the race was owing to the entrance of new challengers, a pattern that has not been repeated. His quick rise in March coincided with southern primaries in Florida and North Carolina. Given the difference between the two races, Super Tuesday does not appear to have affected the nature of voter bandwagons in open races.

Voting patterns in races with front-runners, depicted in figure 6.4, suggest a greater effect for Super Tuesday. Once Bush achieved 50 percent of the vote on Super Tuesday, his vote percentage never fell below that point and climbed to near 75 percent by April 1. In contrast, Reagan surpassed the 50 percent mark in early March but then fell back to 30 percent of the vote by late March only to climb and fall twice more. Meanwhile, Mondale struggled, fluctuating between 25 and 40 percent of the vote throughout the

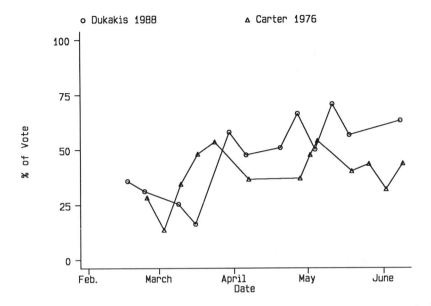

Figure 6.3: Average Primary Vote for Leading Candidate in Open Races

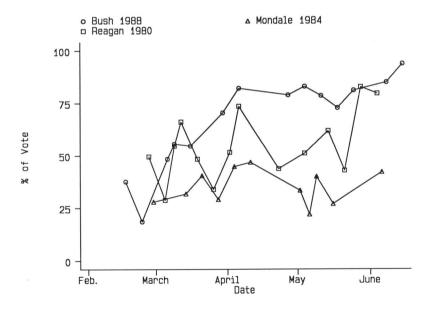

Figure 6.4: Average Primary Vote for Leading Candidate in Races with
Front-Runners

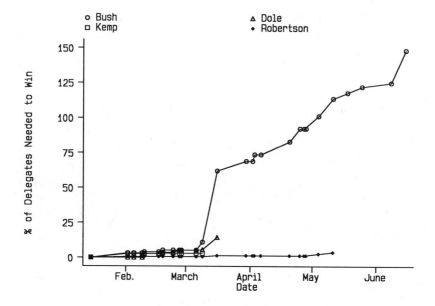

Figure 6.5: Delegates Won by Republican Candidates in 1988

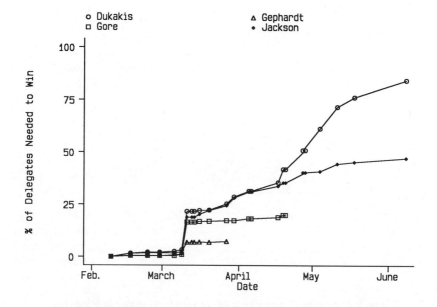

Figure 6.6: Delegates Won by Democratic Candidates in 1988

campaign. The Reagan and Bush bandwagons make the best comparison, as both candidates had strong public support and overflowing campaign coffers. Bush, however, in one blow eliminated his rivals. Reagan eventually eliminated his, but not until the closing series of primaries. A victory by a front-runner in a single regional primary may be sufficient for capturing the nomination. A series of regional primaries, of course, would produce a different scenario.

Accumulation of Delegates

Winning primary votes is only a means to an end, with the ultimate goal being the accumulation of delegates. Super Tuesday selected one-third of the 1988 convention delegates. As figure 6.5 demonstrates, Super Tuesday vastly increased the number of Bush delegates, while adding only meagerly to Dole's collection. Super Tuesday decisively altered the 1988 Republican race for convention delegates.

Figure 6.6 illustrates a completely different pattern for the Democratic field. Super Tuesday equally augmented the delegate folds of Dukakis, Gore, and Jackson. Only after Super Tuesday did the Democratic delegate race begin to sort itself out. Gore failed to add delegates after Super Tuesday and, therefore, was surpassed by Dukakis and Jackson. Those two candidates remained neck and neck in the delegate count until late April when Gore dropped out of the race. At that point, Dukakis began to break away from Jackson. Super Tuesday did not decide the Democratic delegate race, but it did establish the three major players for the last half of the primary season.

Figures 6.7 and 6.8 compare the rates of delegate accumulation in 1988 to the appropriate contests in earlier years. In both figures, the Super Tuesday boost in total delegates is quite clear. Excluding these jumps in delegate totals on March 8, however, the patterns across the years are remarkably similar. In the open races, both Carter and Dukakis accumulated delegates at a gradual pace until the first of May. At that point, the two candidates began to capture the remaining delegates at a slightly faster pace. Races with front-runners, depicted in figure 6.8, take off in early March when the first significant number of delegates become available. Front-runners quickly gather a number of delegates in March, after which they continue gradually to increase their delegate support. Super Tuesday altered the delegate accumulation game by increasing the number of early March delegates, but the amassing of all other delegates repeated the patterns of earlier years.

Winning the Nomination

The ultimate goal of all candidates is to win 50 percent of the delegates in order to guarantee attaining the presidential nomination on the first ballot at

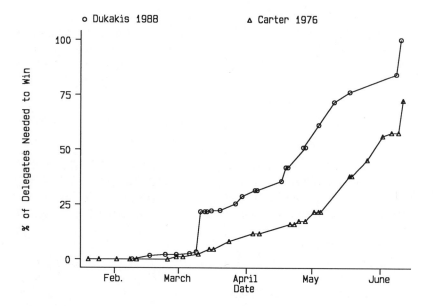

Figure 6.7: Delegates Won by Leading Candidate in Open Races

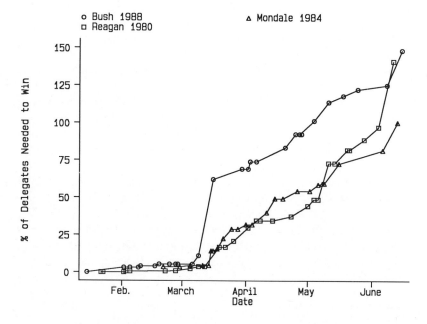

Figure 6.8: Delegates Won by Leading Candidate in Races with Front-Runners

the national convention. Bush accumulated 50 percent of the Republican delegates by late April, while Dukakis had to wait for the results of the last series of primaries on June 7. Yet these candidates were considered de facto nominees prior to this point. At what point were their nominations guaranteed, and did this point occur earlier or later in the campaign season than for previous nominees?

Gamson (1962), working with data from national conventions, asserted a candidate was guaranteed victory once he captured 41 percent of the delegates. Collat, Kelley, and Rogowski (1981) contend that the 41 percent figure is sometimes misleading. Instead, Collat and his colleagues suggest that the nomination is guaranteed when the number of delegates added to a candidate's coalition at a single point in time is approximately equivalent to one-third of delegates not already committed to this candidate. Specifically, they assert that a candidate's nomination is guaranteed when his gain-deficit ratio exceeds .36. The gain-deficit ratio is measured by

$$\frac{D_t - D_{t-1}}{W - D_t}$$

where D_t is the number of delegates currently committed to the candidate; D_{t-1} is the number committed to the candidate after the previous series of primaries or caucuses, and W is the number of delegates needed for the nomination. The gain-deficit ratio takes on a large value when "a candidate makes a small gain when close to victory, or a large gain when not" (428). Bush's gain-deficit ratio equaled 1.33 after Super Tuesday when his delegate total jumped from 126 to 705, with 1,139 delegates needed for the Republican nomination. Thus, Bush provides an example of winning the nomination by posting a large gain in delegates when the nomination was previously wide open. Dukakis provides an example of obtaining a critical, but smaller, group of delegates when the nomination race is closer to the end. Dukakis's delegate count rose from 1,276 to 1,494 on May 3, with 2,082 delegates needed for the Democratic nomination. With the addition of 218 delegates, Dukakis scores a gain-deficit ratio of .37, just over the minimum needed.

Table 6.2 lists the dates from 1976 to 1988 that candidates met all three criteria for victory: (1) controlling 50 percent of delegates, (2) controlling 41 percent of delegates, or (3) attaining a gain-deficit ratio exceeding .36. As noted previously, Bush attained the support of 50 percent of the 1988 Republican delegates on April 26, after the Pennsylvania primary, but he reached the 41 percent mark two weeks earlier on April 5, at the time of the Wisconsin primary. Super Tuesday, on March 8, however, may have previously secured Bush's nomination, according to the gain-deficit ratio. Thus, on the Republican side, Super Tuesday indeed was decisive. Comparing Bush's fate to earlier front-runners also suggests that Super Tuesday

Table 6.2: Three Criteria for Winning the Nomination Measured Both on Actual
Calendar Date and Percentage of Delegates Chosen

		Majority of Delegates	41% of Delegates	Gain-Deficit Ratio > .36
Front-runners				
Bush	1988	April 26 (61%)	April 15 (52%)	March 8 (42%)
Mondale	1984	post primary[a]	May 15 (83%)	April 10 (53%)
Reagan	1980	June 3 (90%)	May 13 (57%)	May 6 (53%)
Open races				
Dukakis	1988	June 7 (93%)	May 17 (88%)	May 3 (86%)
Carter	1976	post primary[b]	post primary[b]	June 8 (85%)

Values in parentheses are percentage of delegates chosen.

[a]Mondale ended the primary season with 47% of the delegates; 97% of Democratic delegates had been selected.
[b]Carter ended the 1976 primary season with 36% of the delegates; 85% of Democratic delegates had been selected.

accelerated the process. Table 6.2 lists both the dates on which candidates met the various criteria and the percentage of convention delegates selected by those dates. The latter is important because the front-loading of the primary season means more and more delegates are chosen at an earlier point in time. The number of delegates chosen acts as a partial control for this front-loading. Regardless, using either the actual date or the percentage of delegates chosen, Bush reached each of the three criteria before either Reagan or Mondale. Perhaps the most interesting criteria is the gain-deficit ratio, which indicated both Mondale and Reagan won the nomination when 53 percent of the delegates were chosen. Bush met the gain-deficit criterion when only 42 percent of the 1988 delegates were selected. No matter what indicator is employed, Super Tuesday expedited the victory of the front-running Republican candidate in 1988.

On the Democratic side, the 50 percent and 41 percent delegate accumulation figures suggest that Dukakis achieved the nomination during the primary season but that Carter in 1976 did not. Nevertheless, Carter's major competitors chose to withdraw from consideration after the final series of primaries. Perhaps the gain-deficit ratio that Carter achieved on the last primary day, June 8, cemented the notion that he had the nomination tied up. Of course, voters, delegates, and other candidates do not precisely calculate a gain-deficit ratio. But if a candidate increases his delegate count significantly in relationship to the number of delegates still available and needed, which is what the gain-deficit ratio measures, many voters and delegates will conclude that this candidate is the one that will eventually win the nomination. If such is true, Dukakis and Carter, although reaching this point on different dates, attained the significant increase in delegates at approximately the same place in the campaigns, when 85 percent of the delegates were chosen. In that case, Super Tuesday had no apparent affect on the timing of the open race among the Democratic contenders for the presidential nomination, except that with more delegates chosen earlier 85 percent were selected by an earlier calendar date.

Super Tuesday did not change the basic process by which candidates captured the Democratic and Republican presidential nominations. The winnowing of candidates, switching of voters' preferences, and accumulation of delegates continued to combine to select de facto nominees before the close of the primary season. Super Tuesday nevertheless did alter the timing of some of these processes. Candidates appeared to have been winnowed at a normal pace on the Democratic side in 1988, while Republican candidates left the race at a slightly faster than usual rate. Perhaps this is the difference between an open race and a front-runner race in conjunction with a single regional primary, especially when that regional primary is held in an area favorable to the front-runner. The swift demise of Bush's competitors produced a quick and huge bandwagon effect in voting in subsequent primaries. With only Robertson presenting token opposition, Bush captured 75 percent of the vote. Bush's bandwagon surpassed those of previous front-runners, such as Reagan and Mondale. Dukakis's bandwagon did not appear until April, when the Democratic field also narrowed. Apparently, the winnowing of candidates is a necessary condition for bandwagons to appear. As Super Tuesday affected the candidate attrition rate on the Republican side, the southern regional primary affected the timing of Bush's bandwagon. With the more normal attrition rate on the Democratic side, Dukakis's bandwagon appeared within the normal time frame.

Ultimately, the nomination struggle centers on the accumulation of delegates. Super Tuesday gave both Bush and Dukakis a large number of delegates. Dukakis, however, faced Gore and Jackson, who captured as many delegates from Super Tuesday as he did. This three-way tie did not guarantee any candidate the victory. However, as Gore failed to follow up his Super Tuesday victories in the Big State Showdowns, Dukakis's slight lead increased. By the beginning of May, Dukakis's increasing delegate count signified victory under the gain-deficit criterion. Carter reached this point at a later calendar date, but when the same 85 percent of delegate had been selected. Dukakis positively secured the nomination on June 7 when he acquire the support of 50 percent of the delegates. Only in this manner was his victory slightly easier than Carter's uphill battle in 1976. In contrast, Super Tuesday definitely clinched Bush the nomination at an earlier point in time than for previous front-runners. In fact, by one indicator, Bush wrapped up the Republican nomination on Super Tuesday.

Thus, Super Tuesday altered the timing of one out of two nomination contests in 1988.

THE SOUTH'S INFLUENCE ON PRESIDENTIAL NOMINATIONS

The ultimate goal of Super Tuesday was to give the South more clout in the presidential nomination process. The size of a regional primary would force candidates, the media, and the nation to pay attention to the South. The boost its 1,173 Democratic and 639 Republican delegates could give to one candidate could send him on his way to capturing the nomination. Media coverage accompanying that victory would influence voters in subsequent primaries. Combined, the South's increased influence would temper the Democratic nomination process such that a more moderate candidate would head the ticket in the fall election. Such a candidate would once again allow a Democratic presidential candidate to carry the South and win the White House.

Media Coverage of Super Tuesday

One very basic question is "Did the South receive additional media coverage with the onset of Super Tuesday?" Table 6.3 provides an answer.[3] The amount of coverage devoted to southern states did not increase in the *New York Times* from 1980 to 1988. However, the *Los Angeles Times* did offer 5 percent more stories, almost all combined stories under the Super Tuesday heading. A more elaborate study by Gurian (1990) comparing media coverage in 1988 to 1984 found southern states received less attention in 1988, 9 percent of all coverage versus 26 percent in 1984. More confirmation of the patterns of media coverage in 1988 comes from Lichter, Amundson, and Noyes's (1988) content analysis of television network newscasts. They counted 228 mentions of Super Tuesday, 285 references to Iowa, and 210 statements about New Hampshire. Iowa received extraordinary attention from the media, just as it had from the candidates. As other scholars have noted, the media follow the lead of the candidates as to which primaries and caucuses to cover (Robinson and Sheehan 1983, 179). As the 1988 candidates paid more attention to Iowa, so did the media. Losing the media wars in 1988 were all primary states other than Super Tuesday or New Hampshire. Their coverage dropped by nearly half in the *New York Times* and by 14 percentage points in the *Los Angeles Times*.

While Super Tuesday states did not receive a large increase in media attention, that does not necessarily mean that the South's impact on the nomination process did not increase. In fact, the opposite may have hap-

Table 6.3: Percentage of News Articles Covering Specific Primaries or Caucuses

	New York Times		Los Angeles Times	
	1980	1988	1980	1988
Iowa	9	19	14	23
New Hampshire	11	17	15	11
South Carolina	2	4	2	2
Super Tuesday		11		16
Alabama	2	0	1	—
Arkansas	1	—	1	—
Florida	4	2	2	0
Georgia	2	1	1	0
Kentucky	1	0	0	—
Louisiana	0	—	1	—
Maryland	1	0	1	—
Mississippi	1	—	—	—
Missouri	1	1	1	0
North Carolina	1	1	1	0
Oklahoma	1	0	1	—
Tennessee	1	—	1	—
Texas	2	3	3	3
Virginia	1	1	0	0
Total Super Tuesday	20	21	15	20
Other Primaries	50	29	46	32
Other Caucuses	8	11	8	11
Number of Stories	965	524	245	348

Source: James Moore compiled this media count for the author.

pened. The media coverage southern states received in 1988 was compacted within a narrow time frame. The American public is often quite inattentive to political news, such that a concentrated, inundating story is needed before most Americans remember an event. Super Tuesday provided such an intensive, concentrated story. Its coverage rivaled Iowa and New Hampshire and surpassed the attention given to any other state.[4]

The South's Influence at Democratic Conventions

Many commentators concluded that Super Tuesday failed because Dukakis, not Gore, won the Democratic nomination (Galston 1988; Hadley and Stanley 1989). But how much influence did the South have on the 1988 nomination, and how much did it have in the past? If candidates supported by southern primary voters in the past always lost the Democratic nomination and the southern favorite lost in 1988, Super Tuesday had no effect. If southern favorites won in the past but lost in 1988, Super Tuesday had a negative effect. Thus, we will not be able to judge Super Tuesday's true influence on candidate selection without making historical comparisons.

The complaint that southern interests have been short-shrifted in recent Democratic nominations is not new. William Crotty (1978, 256) attributes the decline in the South's leverage over Democratic nominations to the 1970s reforms. However, Reiter (1985) eloquently refutes this argument. Tables 6.4 and 6.5 present Reiter's findings along with updates for 1988. Table 6.4 reveals that southern representation at Democratic national conventions dropped from 1948 to 1976. This decline came about because the Democratic party allocates seats at its conventions based on a formula incorporating both the size of a state's population and how strongly that state supported Democratic candidates in the last election. Since southern voters began deserting the national Democratic ticket as early as 1948 and continued to do so throughout the 1960s and 1970s, their representation at Democratic conventions fell. This trend, however, reversed itself in 1980, when southern representation at Democratic conventions rose as southerners supported Carter in both 1976 and 1980. Even after Mondale's losses in the South, southern states still continued to gain in seats at the Democratic convention.

As for candidates selected at Democratic national conventions, southerners had more to complain about in the 1950s than they did in the 1970s or 1980s. As table 6.5 indicates, southern preferences were ignored at Democratic conventions from 1948 to 1960. Since that time, the candidate supported by the majority of southern delegates won five out of six times. Included among these victories was the nomination of the first candidate from the Deep South since the Civil War. The idea that the South has been neglected by Democratic conventions has been most certainly overstated.

Southern Choices and Presidential Nominations

While preferences of southern convention delegates were not ignored, perhaps the wishes of southern voters were not as well represented. In recent years, very few candidates remained as contenders until the convention. Southern favorites may have been eliminated at earlier stages. One simple method of determining whether the favorite candidates of southern voters have lost recent nominations to candidates preferred by voters in other regions of the country would be to compare the average vote for specific candidates in southern primaries with voting averages in primaries held in the rest of the nation. Table 6.6 presents the average vote major Democratic candidates received in both primaries and caucuses held in various regions of the country. Dukakis did not top the South's list of preferred candidates in

Table 6.4: Representation of the South in Democratic Conventions, 1948-1988

Year	Percentage of votes	Absolute change	Percentage change
1948	24.1		
1952	23.6	− 0.5	− 2.1
1956	24.3	+ 0.7	+ 3.0
1960	23.1	− 1.2	− 4.9
1964	22.5	− .06	− 2.6
1968	20.1	− 2.4	− 10.7
1972	19.7	− 0.4	− 2.0
1976	19.2	− 0.5	− 2.5
1980	21.0	+ 1.8	+ 9.4
1984	23.7	+ 2.7	+ 12.9
1988	24.3	+ 0.6	+ 2.5

Figures given are percentage of votes at Democratic national conventions held by eleven former Confederate states.

Source: Values for 1948 to 1984 from Reiter 1985, 18.

Table 6.5: Support for Democratic Nominee at National Conventions by Southern and Nonsouthern Delegations

Year	Nominee	Percentage of southern vote for nominee	Percentage of nonsouthern vote for nominee
1948	Truman	4.4	97.5
1952	Stevenson[a]	3.1	33.6
1956	Stevenson	47.6	71.9
1960	Kennedy	2.7	68.9
1968	Humphrey	83.5	63.0
1972	McGovern	23.6	65.6
1976	Carter	89.3	70.9
1980	Carter	86.7	57.6
1984	Mondale	53.6	56.4
1988	Dukakis	60.6	71.8

[a]second ballot; all other nominees' votes on first ballot

Source: 1948 to 1984 from Reiter 1985, 18.

1988. About 22 percent of southern primary voters and caucus attenders supported Dukakis, placing him third, behind Jackson and Gore. Dukakis was, however, the top choice of voters in Iowa, New Hampshire, and all other sections of the country. While southern preferences did not prevail in 1988, in 1976, 1980, and 1984, southern voters' wishes were not ignored. The

Table 6.6: Average Voting Percentage for Democratic Candidates in Primaries and Caucuses Divided by Region

	South & Super Tuesday	Iowa & New Hampshire	East	Midwest	West	sign.
1988						
Dukakis	22 (3)	28 (1)	53 (1)	42 (1)	49 (1)	.0001
Gephardt	12 (4)	24 (2)	6 (3)	14 (3)	5 (4)	.3880
Gore	30 (2)	4 (6)	4 (4)	8 (5)	10 (3)	.0002
J. Jackson	32 (1)	9 (4)	31 (2)	26 (2)	29 (2)	.2196
1984						
Glenn	14 (4)	9 (4)	4 (5)	—	1 (4)	.0479
Hart	24 (2)	26 (2)	40 (2)	38 (2)	53 (1)	.0000
J. Jackson	24 (3)	4 (6)	13 (3)	10 (3)	7 (3)	.0003
Mondale	36 (1)	36 (1)	41 (1)	44 (1)	31 (2)	.0855
1980						
Carter	66 (1)	53 (1)	40 (2)	50 (1)	47 (1)	.0004
Kennedy	21 (2)	34 (2)	50 (1)	32 (2)	32 (2)	.0001
1976						
Brown	25 (2)	—	65 (1)	—	41 (1)	.6838
Carter	41 (1)	29 (1)	37 (2)	41 (1)	15 (3)	.0041
H. Jackson	8 (5)	1 (7)	23 (3)	8 (6)	15 (4)	.7438
Udall	7 (6)	14 (2)	14 (5)	18 (3)	14 (5)	.6114
Wallace	19 (4)	—	9 (6)	11 (5)	3 (6)	.0161

Percentages listed average state percentages of votes in primaries or caucuses for regions in which candidates competed. Since not every candidate competed in all primaries and caucuses within a region, the percentage of support for all candidates within one region do not sum to 100 percent. Numbers in parentheses are each candidate's ranking, comparing his average vote in a region to all other candidates. Significance tests are for percentages, not rankings.

— = candidates did not compete in any primary or caucus in the region

plurality of southern voters supported the eventual nominee in all cases. In contrast, eastern and western voters' wishes were overlooked when Hart, Kennedy, and Brown failed to win the Democratic nomination.

Table 6.7 provides the same type of analysis for Republican candidates. In 1988, southern voters lined up with eastern, midwestern, and western voters in support of George Bush. Dole's larger vote advantage in Iowa than Bush's edge in New Hampshire produced a vote advantage for Dole in the Big Two Openers' average. This early advantage had little effect on the 1988 Republican nomination. In 1980, Reagan's victory fulfilled southern voters' wishes, as it did the wishes of voters in all other regions of the country.

Table 6.7: Average Voting Percentage for Republican Candidates in Primaries and Caucuses Divided by Region

	South & Super Tuesday	Iowa & New Hampshire	East	Midwest	West	sign.
1988						
Bush	59 (1)	28 (2)	73 (1)	61 (1)	51 (1)	.1602
Dole	25 (2)	33 (1)	24 (2)	47 (2)	23 (3)	.1380
Kemp	5 (4)	12 (4)	6 (3)	12 (3)	7 (4)	.0120
Robertson	13 (3)	17 (3)	6 (4)	11 (4)	33 (2)	.0107
1980						
Anderson	6 (5)	7 (4)	18 (3)	24 (3)	1 (5)	.1430
Baker	33 (2)	14 (3)	5 (4)	7 (4)	1 (5)	.1150
Bush	25 (4)	27 (2)	34 (2)	25 (2)	30 (2)	.9136
Reagan	69 (1)	40 (1)	54 (1)	59 (1)	71 (1)	.0748
1976						
Ford	43 (2)	47 (1)	72 (1)	53 (1)	44 (2)	.0023
Reagan	56 (1)	45 (2)	31 (2)	44 (2)	51 (1)	.0307

Percentages listed average state percentages of votes in primaries or caucuses for regions in which candidates competed. Since not every candidate competed in all primaries and caucuses within a region, the percentage of support for all candidates within one region do not sum to 100 percent. Numbers in parentheses are each candidate's ranking, comparing his average vote in a region to all other candidates. Significance tests are for percentages, not rankings.

Southern and western supporters of Reagan in 1976, however, were disappointed. Neither the Republican party nor the Democratic party disproportionately ignored the wishes of southern voters when naming their recent presidential candidates. Only in the 1988 Democratic contest and the 1976 Republican race did the southern favorite not win the nomination. Eastern and western favorites were ignored more often.

The final argument asserting the South's ineffectualness in influencing presidential nominations contends that southerners' preferred candidates were eliminated before southerners had a chance to vote. Under this argument, outcomes in Iowa and New Hampshire eliminated southerners' favorite candidates. Glenn's virtual elimination by those two contests in 1984 initiated the Super Tuesday movement. But was Glenn the early favorite of southern voters? Table 6.8 examines voter preferences in four regions of the country prior to the New Hampshire primary in 1980 and 1984. Early preferences of Southerners in 1988 are also included. These data come from respondents to the 1980, 1984, and 1988 NES year-long panel, continuous monitoring, and Super Tuesday polls.

Table 6.8: Percentage Support for Democratic Candidates by Democratic
Identifiers Interviewed Prior to the New Hampshire Primary

		1988			
		Southern preferences			
Babbitt	2		Dukakis		6
Gephardt	8		Gore		7
Hart	13		J. Jackson		11
Simon	2		Other		18
Don't know	34				(472)

	1984			
	East	Midwest	South	West
Mondale	32	46	34	34
Glenn	8	9	16	9
J. Jackson	6	7	8	8
Hart	3	6	5	4
Other	17	15	15	26
Don't know	33	18	23	19
	(63)	(55)	(80)	(53)
	$X^2 = 29.82$		sign. $= .6266$	

	1980			
	East	Midwest	South	West
Carter	50	66	67	61
Kennedy	38	27	29	30
Other	4	7	3	9
Don't know	8	1	2	—
	(165)	(206)	(334)	(137)
	$X^2 = 62.92$		sign. $= .0000$	

Nationwide, preferences for other candidates in 1984 were as follows: Cranston, 1%;
McGovern, less than 1%; Hollings, 1%; Kennedy, 12%; Reagan, 3%; Baker, 1%,
unspecified, 1%. In 1980 preferences for other candidates included 2% for Brown and 3%
for Mondale. Values in parentheses are number of survey respondents.

Source: NES surveys.

The early demise of Glenn's 1984 candidacy thwarted the wishes of only
16 percent of southern Democrats, a figure statistically similar to the number of early Glenn supporters in other regions of the country. Instead, Mondale was the early plurality favorite among southerners and voters across the
country. Additionally, more southern Democrats in 1984 expressed no
candidate preference at the start of the campaign than espoused support for
Glenn. Southern preferences simply were not ignored in 1984. In contrast, in
1980 early southern preferences for Carter prevailed, along with those of

Table 6.9: Percentage Support for Republican Candidates by Republican
Identifiers Interviewed Prior to the New Hampshire Primary

1988			
Southern preferences			
Bush	44	Dole	23
du Pont	0	Haig	1
Kemp	5	Robertson	7
Other	4	Don't know	16
			(483)

1980			
	East	Midwest	South	West
Anderson	5	2	2	4
Baker	4	4	10	4
Bush	13	20	19	15
Reagan	31	38	34	49
Other	44	34	34	27
Don't know	2	1	2	—
	(121)	(152)	(200)	(114)
$X^2 = 31.08$		sign. = .1514	

Nationwide Republican preferences for other candidates in 1980 included 30% for Ford,
5% for Connally, and less than 1% for Crane. Values in parentheses are number of survey
respondents.

Source: NES surveys.

midwesterners and westerners, against easterners' preferences for Kennedy.
Thus, in 1980, the early preferences of southerners also were not neglected.
The now familiar 1988 story centers on the lack of preferences by many
southerners in the early stages of the campaign. The demise of Babbitt's and
Simon's campaigns disillusioned few southern supporters. Southern claims
of discrimination because of the elimination of candidates at early stages
in the campaign does not hold up against the data presented in table 6.8.

Table 6.9 presents a similar analysis for Republican voters. In 1980
Reagan held the top post among Republicans in all areas of the country. His
nomination satisfied more southern Republicans than any other possible
choice. Similarly, in 1988 more southern Republicans preferred Bush in the
early stages of the campaign than any other candidate. In both years,
southern wishes prevailed.

SUMMARY

Analyzing the outcome of Democratic and Republican presidential nominations involves two central questions: who won and how? Super Tuesday

influenced the how by affecting the timing of the nomination. On the Republican side, a strong front-runner used the southern regional primary to bring the contest to a swift close. In the more open Democratic nomination fight, Super Tuesday made Dukakis's victory more difficult. Dukakis eventually won the war by avoiding the winnowing process that characterizes the presidential primary season. Dukakis's fate improved as the candidate field narrowed. With fewer competitors, his average primary vote rose to nearly 50 percent, helping him to accumulate larger and larger numbers of delegates. By the last series of primaries, Dukakis controlled the 50 percent of delegates needed to guarantee him the nomination, but his ultimate victory was foretold earlier, around the first week in May. Super Tuesday expedited the 1988 Republican nomination but had little effect on the progress of the Democratic race.

Super Tuesday also had little effect on who won the nomination. Super Tuesday's architects started with the false premise of southern neglect in the choice of previous Democratic presidential nominees. Southern wishes were not ignored at the convention or during the primary season. Neither were southern favorites winnowed before the South had a chance to vote. Only in 1988 did the southern favorite not win the nomination. But Dukakis became the first choice of voters in every other region of the country. To ignore these voters in order to fulfill the wishes of a divided South is unquestionably unfair and would not guarantee a Democratic victory in the fall presidential election.

7

Super Tuesday:
Success or Failure?

Newsweek magazine, tongue in cheek, kept track of the 1988 presidential race with Conventional Wisdom (CW) reports. In the fall of 1988, *Newsweek* issued the following report on Super Tuesday:

> The pundits' assessment of the huge Southern primary illustrates how fickle the CW can be. Initially the experts expected that Super Tuesday would accomplish the goal of its Southern creators and boost the fortunes of a centrist Democrat such as Albert Gore. Then, as Iowa and Jesse Jackson loomed larger, the CW flipped 180 degrees. Suddenly Super Tuesday was seen as a disaster for its centrist planners. "It's not working out at all the way they hope," wrote The Washington Post's David Broder. The very morning of Super Tuesday, NBC's Ken Bode went on the air to reassert that Gore would be the day's loser. Within hours, Gore had won seven states and catapulted himself into the top tier of contenders. Then he proceeded to fade as if the Southern primaries had never been held. Now the CW on Super Tuesday seems hopelessly confused. (Alter and Kaus, October 31, 1988, 23)

Let's see if we can unconfuse the conventional wisdom. In this final chapter we will review reactions to and judgments about Super Tuesday, before comparing those conclusions to those found in this book. A discussion on the future of Super Tuesday will close out the chapter.

REACTIONS TO SUPER TUESDAY

John Traeger, the leader of the Southern Legislative Conference during the creation of Super Tuesday, judged the nation's first regional primary a success: "The important thing is that the voter turnouts were generally big, the South saw more presidential candidates than it has seen in the last five presidential elections, and all of them were forced to take positions on regional issues." Traeger's Republican counterpart, Haley Barbour, the director of the Southern Republican Primary Project, came to the opposite conclusion: "I think the Democrats realize it was very beneficial to the Republican Party, quite divisive to the Democrats, and it demonstrated to Southerners that the people who dominate the [Democratic] party in the Deep South are the same ones who dominate it in New York and Massachusetts" (both quotes from Mashek and Baxter, March 10, 1988, 12). Lee Atwater, Bush's campaign manager, averred that for the Democratic party, Super Tuesday was "the biggest political boo-boo of the decade" (Oreskes, March 10, 1988). Given the stake of these three gentleman in the outcome of Super Tuesday, divergent reactions are not unexpected. Let us now turn to the assessment of various politicians, journalists, and political scientists, some who viewed Super Tuesday as a success, whereas others described the nation's first regional primary as a failure.

The Success of Super Tuesday

Several themes dominate the comments in support of Super Tuesday. Early positive commentaries centered on the success of Super Tuesday in launching Gore's candidacy. Georgia House Speaker Tom Murphy asserted Super Tuesday helped conservative Democrats by providing a candidate—i.e., Gore—"who gets a chance to sell our views outside the South" (Mashek and Baxter, March 10, 1988). Hastings Wyman, Jr., a southern political consultant, chimed in with the conclusion that Super Tuesday "proved that it was possible for a candidate to start in the South. And . . . that a Democrat who wants to present a more moderate message can benefit from it" (McQuaid, March 10, 1988). On the heels of Super Tuesday, the *New Republic* endorsed Gore as the man for the Democratic party, their rationale being that the Democratic party needed the South to win the presidency and only Gore could accomplish this task (After Super Tuesday, March 28, 1988).

A second positive evaluation of Super Tuesday noted a diminution of the importance of the Iowa caucuses. "Iowa? What Iowa?" asserted Charles Paul Freund in "The Zeitgeist Checklist," the *New Republic's* version of *Newsweek's* Conventional Wisdom reports (March 28, 1988, 8). Gephardt's and Dole's losses led many commentators to view the impact of the Iowa vote on Super Tuesday as nil (Galston 1988; Hadley and Stanley 1989). Along this vein, Al From, the executive director of the Democratic Leadership Council, asserted, "What Al Gore has proven is that the road to Atlanta [the cite of the 1988 Democratic convention] does not necessarily go through Des Moines" (McQuaid, March 10, 1988, 13). Others, such as Hodding Carter (March 13, 1988), think the devaluation of Iowa and New Hampshire will become even clearer in the 1992 campaign.

Increased interest in the southern primaries among candidates and voters rounds out the praises for Super Tuesday. Louisiana state Democratic Chairman Jim Brady asserted, "We wanted them [the candidates] to pay attention to us and they did. Not only did they come in many times, they began to speak to the issues that are of concern to Louisianians. Although we had a low turnout, it was still almost double what we had four years ago" (McQuaid, March 10, 1988, 13). Turnout increases also were cited on the Republican side. In Georgia, the number of Republican voters nearly doubled from 200,000 in the 1980 primary to 399,616 in 1988 (Mashek and Baxter, March 10, 1988). Hodding Carter (March 13, 1988) noted that while Republican turnout rose, the Democratic party still retained the loyalty of two-thirds of Super Tuesday's voters.

The Failure of Super Tuesday

Those who criticized Super Tuesday came to the opposite conclusion of its supporters. Critics averred that Super Tuesday helped liberal candidates, not conservative ones. Instead of concentrating on Gore's success in the South, the critics pointed to the victories of Jackson and Dukakis (McQuaid, March 10, 1988; Apple, March 8, 1988). Germond and Witcover (1989, 278-90) described Super Tuesday as a failure because it eliminated Gephardt from the race and Gephardt was a moderate Democrat who could win voter support within and outside of the South. Meanwhile, the divided outcome on Super Tuesday, with Gore, Jackson, and Dukakis finishing even in primary victories and delegate counts, diminished the impact of the South on subsequent primaries (Hadley and Stanley, 1989; Apple, March 8, 1988).

In a similar vein, the format of Super Tuesday was criticized for leaving Gore with no friendly territory to build on his March 8 success (Galston 1988). Having done reasonably well in the South, Gore was then forced to compete against Dukakis and Jackson in the more liberal eastern and midwestern primaries. The South had no further input in the Democratic race after Super Tuesday, with three months of the primary season left to unwind (Hadley and Stanley 1989). As David Broder concluded, "The South *is* too big, too complex and much too important to be kissed off in one day, and then forgotten for the rest of the primary campaign" (March 2, 1988, 21).

Critics of Super Tuesday also proclaimed that Iowa and New Hampshire were not overshadowed by the nation's first regional primary. Dukakis and Gephardt became major contenders on Super Tuesday because of the their victories in these earlier contests (Apple, March 8, 1988; Hadley and Stanley 1989). Other critics pinned the failure of Super Tuesday not so much on its design but on the fact that the right candidates did not run (Akerman, March 13, 1988; Galston 1988; Hadley and Stanley 1989). Neither Sam Nunn nor

Charles Robb entered the Democratic race. Both were cited as more conservative and more truly southern than Gore (Kuttner, March 21, 1988). In addition, Gephardt's victory over Simon in Iowa presented southern voters with two moderate choices—Gephardt and Gore—rather than one moderate candidate, Gore, versus two liberals, Simon and Dukakis (Apple, March 8, 1988).

The common conclusion that Super Tuesday was simply too big underlay a number of criticisms. Both Paul Kirk, Democratic National Committee chairman, and Frank Fahrenkopf, Republican National Committee chairman, opposed Super Tuesday because of its size. Kirk concluded that Super Tuesday was "too large of an arena. It's too much like a general election already" (Democratic Leader Has Doubts About Super Tuesday Concept, March 5, 1988, 7). Fahrenkopf thought that too much of Super Tuesday's structure was set by the Democrats and that smaller states, such as his own home state of Nevada, became overlooked in regional primaries (Mashek and Baxter, March 10, 1988). Maryland's governor William Donald Schaefer also felt that his state got lost in the shuffle on Super Tuesday (Hadley and Stanley 1989).

The size of Super Tuesday also forced candidates to target specific constituencies rather than addressing southern issues as a whole (Galston 1988; Germond and Witcover, March 5, 1988). Furthermore, few southerners got to meet the candidates as they engaged in tarmac campaigning and media blitzes (Apple, March 8, 1988; Hadley and Stanley 1989; Reeves, March 9, 1988). In fact, the South, especially smaller states, saw less of the candidates than in previous years (Germond and Witcover, March 5, 1988). Super Tuesday's size also made money more important. Candidates needed millions of dollars by the start of 1988 to contest Iowa, New Hampshire, and sixteen primaries on Super Tuesday effectively (The Shock of Super Tuesday, March 10, 1988).

WHAT REALLY HAPPENED ON SUPER TUESDAY

Evidence from Chapters 2 through 6 will help us develop a more accurate conclusion about what really happened on Super Tuesday. Two of the concerns, candidate and media attention to the South and turnout on Super Tuesday, can be addressed quite simply and directly. Candidates did not forgo Iowa and New Hampshire to campaign in the Super Tuesday states. Rather, Iowa received even more attention than in previous years. As a result, most of the Super Tuesday campaign was condensed into the three-week period after New Hampshire. During those twenty-one days, candidates jetted across the South, making several quick airport stops each day. Accompanying their tarmac campaigning were negative commercials aimed at dissuading voters from supporting their competitors. The news media followed the candidates' lead to Iowa and New Hampshire, short-changing individual states on Super Tuesday. Nevertheless, Super Tuesday became one of the major stories of 1988 and, as such, had the potential to influence national public opinion.

Super Tuesday increased turnout in the South by 5 percent, with a greater increase in Republican than Democratic primaries. This increase in turnout was not owing to the regional primary structure but rather to the early date. Despite the larger rise in turnout on the Republican side, more people continued to vote in Democratic than Republican primaries. The resulting Democratic primary electorate was more representative and more heterogeneous than the Republican electorate. If Democratic leaders want to retain even more "presidential Republicans" (i.e. those who claim a Republican identification but often vote for Democrats for state offices), more southern states should combine their primaries for state offices with their presidential primaries. But as Arkansas discovered in 1988, state and local politicians dislike an early March date for their nomination campaigns.

A more difficult question to answer is the effect Super Tuesday had on the importance of Iowa and New Hampshire. In 1988 we did not see a candidate such as Hart in 1984, who nearly overtook the front-runner with a better-than-expected showing in Iowa followed by a victory in New Hampshire. Rather, the victors in Iowa—Dole and Gephardt—did not repeat in New Hampshire. Nor did Super Tuesday voters appear to consider consciously these early victories when deciding which candidates to support. Still, Iowa and New Hampshire affected Super Tuesday by winnowing the candidate fields. If Gephardt had not bested Simon in Iowa, Gephardt, not Simon, would have sat out Super Tuesday. If Dole failed to win in his own region, Bush's victory would have come even sooner.

An equally difficult question is whether Gore was helped by Super Tuesday or whether liberal candidates fared better. As it turns out, this question is not an either/or proposition. Both halves are true to some extent. Gore was helped by Super Tuesday; he came from nowhere to become one of three front-runners. But Dukakis and Jackson also were helped, with Dukakis perhaps gaining the most, as his victory was the least expected. With an understanding of the diversity of the southern electorate, Dukakis wisely planned to chip away at the corners of Super Tuesday to score his victories.

Finally, the huge size of Super Tuesday did produce negative effects, but also some positive ones. Individual states did not receive as much candidate or media attention as they had in previous years. Nevertheless, the cumulative media coverage of all southern states combined did produce a venerable story. Super Tuesday dominated reporting of the 1988 nomination races, placing fourth, after Iowa, New Hampshire, and Illinois. The story Super Tuesday had to tell, however, was not a simple one on the Democratic side.

Three victories is a muddled story, but less muddled than a four- or five-way split, which some originally expected. Super Tuesday was not too big for one Republican candidate to win. Whether it was too big for one Democratic candidate to win is another matter. The Republican race had a front-runner; the Democratic race did not. The Republican electorate in the South is homogeneous; the Democratic electorate is not. A Democratic front-runner may be able to win decisively in a future southern primary, but then again he may not. More than likely, candidates will be forced to target certain states and specific constituency groups because of the high costs of multiple-state campaigning, leading to further split decisions from the Super Tuesday states.

Neither naive architects nor unrealistic goals produced the muddled results of Super Tuesday. All recent reforms produced expected and unexpected results. Such divergent consequences arise because each group of reformers can change only one aspect of the presidential nomination system. Southern legislatures could change the date of southern primaries. They could not change the dates of the Iowa caucus or the New Hampshire primary. Super Tuesday's architects also could not dictate which candidates would run. Once candidates decided to run, they alone chose their strategies. Most followed the standard practice and turned first and foremost to Iowa and New Hampshire. Similarly, the southern planners of Super Tuesday could not dictate to the media how to cover the 1988 campaign. Even technological advances interfered with the Super Tuesday plan. Videocassettes and satellite television allowed candidates to reach more voters, but not in a face-to-face manner in which southerners could tell candidates what they desired. The structure and outcome of the quests for the presidential nominations are set by complex relationships among a wide variety of legal, technological, and individual factors. Changing only one aspect of the campaign structure can and will set off an unexpected chain reaction.

THE FUTURE OF SUPER TUESDAY

The shape of Super Tuesday in 1992 and beyond is in the hands of the same southern legislators that created our nation's first regional primary. Though these politicians still want their states to be able to influence presidential nominations, state legislators are concerned first and foremost with their own electoral fates and state budgets. Legislators in Arkansas found the March 8 date too early for their own renomination campaigns. Thus, despite Arkansas having the highest turnout on Super Tuesday, Arkansas's 1992 state and presidential primaries will be held on the fourth Tuesday in May. Kentucky, finding separate state and presidential primaries too expensive, also has left Super Tuesday. Alabama's legislature has acted to remove the state from the 1992 southern regional primary. Several states passed only temporary legislation to join Super Tuesday in 1988 and did not pass additional legislation to continue their participation. The Virginia legislature failed to reenact legislation for 1992.[1] As a result, seven southern states (Florida, Georgia, Louisiana, Mississippi, Oklahoma, Tennessee, and Texas) have primaries set for March 10, 1992. Missouri will hold local caucuses on that date. Thus eight of the original fourteen southern states remain in Super Tuesday 1992.

OTHER REFORMS FOR 1992

Super Tuesday spawned speculation of other states moving to regional primaries in 1992. Robert Bennett, chairman of the Ohio Republican party, called for a midwestern regional primary to include Illinois, Indiana, Michigan, Wisconsin, and Ohio (Rheem, July 28, 1988). Discussions of a midwestern regional primary, however, date back to the early 1970s.[2] None of these efforts have ever been successful. More concrete action toward another regional primary for 1992 has come in the Northwest. In March of 1989 the Washington state legislature enacted its first presidential primary law with anticipation of joining Oregon, Idaho, and Montana in a northwestern primary (Primary Stirs Hope for Regional Impact, April 1, 1989). However, these states failed to set their primaries on a mutual date. The trend toward more primaries continues unabated. Switching from caucuses to primaries in 1992 are Colorado, Kansas, Michigan, and Minnesota, along with Washington.

States continue to tinker with the presidential primary system with aspirations of gaining more clout. The saga of the attempt to change the date of the California primary in 1989-1991 provides a good illustration of how states continue to work under the old assumption that the earlier a state holds a primary the more clout it will have, ignoring any lessons from Super Tuesday. The California plan called for its primary to be moved to the first week in March from the first week in June, where Californians feel they have no impact on the campaign as the nomination struggle often appears to be over by that point in time. The proposed 1992 date would sandwich the California primary between New Hampshire and the remains of Super Tuesday. The national Democratic party even expanded the window for 1992 to allow California to adopt the early date.

The primary bill, however, floundered in the California legislature as one partisan battle after another scuttled the plan. The first stumbling block was the added cost of moving the primary forward. California traditionally holds its congressional and state primaries on the same date as the presidential primary. Separating the two primaries would cost the state $42 million, the fee for holding two elections rather than one. Republican Governor George Deukmejian vetoed an earlier attempt to move the California primary for just this reason, though in 1989 he dropped his opposition.

To avoid the added costs of two elections, a bill was proposed to move both primaries to early March, but then opposition to an early state and congressional primary began to foment. Democratic leaders in the legislature began to worry about the difficulties of raising campaign funds prior to a March primary. Republicans began to worry that the redistricting of state legislative and U.S. congressional seats would not be completed by March of 1992. Republicans hoped to gain from this redistricting. They demanded that primaries for Congress and the state legislature be held back until the traditional June date. Finally, Republicans even began to back away from an early presidential primary. Recent Californian elections contain numerous initiatives. Constitutionally, initiatives can be placed on any election ballot. Republican legislators began to fear that in 1992, with no race expected on the Republican side because of President Bush's high popularity, the presidential primary electorate would be composed solely of Democrats and liberals. These groups would distort the voting on initiatives, the Republicans feared. A measure to ban initiatives from the early presidential primary date failed to gain enough votes. The California presidential primary bill saga came to a close, at least for a while (Webb, August 17, 1989; Berke, February 15, 1990; California Is Split on Early Primary, February 23, 1990; In California Question Arises on Plan to Move Up Primary, August 31, 1990).

In March 1991, California Democrats passed a plan at their state convention to select one-third of their 1992 delegates at caucuses scheduled for the first Sunday in March. The remaining delegates would be selected at the traditional June primary. Leaders of both the national party and the Democratic Leadership Council opposed California's early caucus plan because they felt only liberal activists would attend the caucuses, advantaging liberal candidates (Bishop, March 10, 1991), just the type of candidate Super Tuesday was designed to prevent from gaining the nomination. The Executive Board of the California state Democratic party voted down the caucus plan, ending that option. Meanwhile, in the summer of 1991, the early primary bill was once again being considered in a committee of the California legislature. This bill also floundered, and California's 1992 primary is set for June 2. At no time during this long saga did the state of California consider the lessons of Super Tuesday. First, an early date does not guarantee that the favored candidate of a state's or region's voters will become the ultimate nominee. Second, candidates cannot afford to conduct intensive in-person campaigns in large arenas, such as California or the South, as they can in the more manageable Iowa caucus and New Hampshire primary. Finally, the early primaries, including Super Tuesday 1988, only serve to narrow the candidate field. The crucial decisions as to who ultimately becomes the nominee are made in late March and early April as one candidate slowly but surely wins sufficient delegates to clinch the nomination.

While some states continued to jockey for "better" positions on the 1992 nomination calendar, other Democratic politicians, from both the North and South, concluded from Super Tuesday 1988 that the problem was not the nomination rules but the party's message. Few internal battles were fought over the 1992 rules in Democratic National Committee meetings: "To many longtime Democrats, settling the nominating rules swiftly was less a sign of unity than an expression of the consensus that it is not the party's rules, but its political message, that has prevented it from producing winning Presidential candidates" (Oreskes, March 25, 1990, 26). The Democratic Leadership Council (DLC), one of the original advocates of Super Tuesday, came to a similar conclusion. Still dissatisfied with Democratic presidential nominees, these more moderate Democratic leaders plan to stress their desired issue positions prior to the 1992 campaign. The DLC wants to convince the American voter that Democratic policies can bring about economic growth, make American goods competitive in the world market, and protect the victims, not the perpetrators, of crimes (Toner, March 25, 1990).

ADVICE TO SOUTHERN STATES FOR THE 1990s

What can southern politicians do if they still want to increase their influence on the Democratic nomination? First they need to decide what they want to influence. If they want more influence in order to force the Democratic party to nominate more conservative candidates, they need to focus on the latter goal. The first step in attaining the Democratic nomination for a more conservative candidate is to find a strong candidate with the desired positions. A strong candidate is not a candidate with the correct record or reputation in Washington, D.C. A strong presidential candidate in the 1990s, as has been true for a long time, is a candidate who can win support in a majority of the states. The presidential nomination is secured by focusing on delegate acquisition. Delegates can and need to be picked up in the Big Two Openers, Super Tuesday, and especially in the Showdown states in late March and early April.

This moderate-to-conservative candidate cannot take the South for granted. Being a southerner will gain a candidate at most 10 percent of the vote. Being a true conservative also will not pay off, because primary voters use ideological terms symbolically rather than as sophisticated summaries of issue positions. The preferred label among southern Democrats is the moderate label, which voters will ascribe to themselves and candidates as diverse as Gore and Jackson. A candidate's being a southerner and a conservative will not guarantee him votes. Votes must be earned. No candidate will enjoy widespread support in the South at the beginning of an open-race campaign. Many southerners do not even recognize such southern conservative favorites as Sam Nunn or Charles Robb. The successful conservative candidate must raise his name recognition among southern voters, but his campaign must also have a message beyond ideology or regional pride. Every successful candidate's campaign needs a dominant theme that voters can latch on to. This theme may involve an issue or an image, but it needs to be consistent and repeated often to penetrate the collective consciousness of the American public.

Besides focusing on who runs, southerners need to perceive the nomination race as a war of attrition. Momentum happens and is important, but the attrition of candidates determines the ultimate victor. Although one big knockout punch may be thrown in a nomination race, as Bush did on Super Tuesday, this is unusual. Winnowing characterizes most struggles for the nomination, and the key to a conservative candidate winning the nomination is to avoid being winnowed out. This means the conservative candidate needs to survive not only round one (Iowa and New Hampshire) and round two (Super Tuesday) but also rounds three, four, and five. Southern legislatures may want to stagger southern primaries across all of these rounds to keep the conservative candidate in a winning mode.

Ultimately the presidential nomination is won by accumulating delegates. The South should contemplate the best method to award more delegates to their preferred candidate. Proportional representation rules do not provide large blocs of delegates to any candidate. Jesse Jackson won an early commitment from the Democratic National Committee for all primaries in 1992 to be conducted under proportional representation rules (Cook, July 2, 1988).[3] Nevertheless, other methods of distributing delegates, such as loophole or bonus primaries, can award larger blocs of delegates. But southern leaders need to be certain that their conservative candidate is capable of winning a majority of southern votes before they pursue delegate distribution rules that advantage front-runners. Tinkering with the rules, however, will not be an adequate substitute for a committed, well-financed campaign by the South's elusive dream candidate.

An often forgotten fact about recent Democratic nominees is that they do not start out as unpopular with the American public. One month after Super Tuesday, Dukakis matched Bush's popularity in the Gallup Poll, 43 percent to 45 percent. Dukakis trailed Bush by only 2 percentage points in the South and by only 5 percentage points among white voters. By May, Dukakis led Bush 54 percent to 38 percent and was seen as closer to the public on nine out of eleven issues. Dukakis continued to lead Bush in the polls until August (Gallup Poll, April 1988; May, 1988; September 1988). Dukakis lost his advantage during the fall campaign. Recent Democratic nominees do not lose because of the nomination process, they lose when they fail to convince voters in the fall that they would make a better president than their Republican opponents. Perhaps Democratic party leaders, from both the South and the North, should stop worrying about the nomination phase and concentrate on the general election phase of the presidential selection process.

CONCLUSIONS

Super Tuesday was neither a total failure nor a total success. As with every reform of the presidential nomination process, Super Tuesday produced some desired results and some unexpected consequences. Turnout increased as hoped, and the Democratic party managed to keep many southern voters in its primaries, even conservative white southern voters. Yet the Democratic party's primary electorate also contained liberals, blacks, transplanted northerners, and so on. Such diverse groups will rarely prefer the same candidate. Super Tuesday did indeed launch Gore's campaign. He became one of three major contenders for the Democratic nomination. Gore's collapse after Super Tuesday lay in his failure to provide northerners with a reason to support a southern candidate. The heterogeneous southern Democratic electorate also gave boosts to the campaigns of Dukakis and Jackson. Super Tuesday did not convince the candidates and the media to forgo Iowa and New Hampshire. But neither did the candidates and the media ignore Super Tuesday. Few southern voters met the candidates as they jetted from one airport to the next, but then most voters do not have the chance to meet presidential candidates in the fall election, or senatorial or gubernatorial candidates, for that matter. The media did not give individual southern states as much coverage as when these states held isolated primaries, but the Super Tuesday story was extensively covered in a concentrated period of time. Such an inundating story has a greater chance of affecting public opinion. Finally, despite Super Tuesday's Democratic origins, the Republican party also benefited. Turnout increased in their primaries, though the resulting electorate was homogeneous and unrepresentative. Nevertheless, their actions guaranteed the nomination of the next president of the United States.

A significant portion of southern states will stick with the Super Tuesday format for the 1992 nomination. A few states from other regions of the country will adopt new presidential primary legislation, while others, including some of the 1988 Super Tuesday states, will revert to caucuses. This is nothing new. Each election calendar brings such changes. But only 1988 produced the massive change of clustering twenty events—fourteen southern primaries, two northern primaries, and four western caucuses—on one day. As such, March 8, 1988 truly was super, despite its mixed results.

APPENDIX

Table A.1: Democratic Delegates Won on Super Tuesday

	Dukakis	Gephardt	Gore	Jackson
Southern primaries				
Alabama	0	0	27	29
Arkansas	10	0	19	9
Florida	90	7	6	33
Georgia	10	0	31	36
Kentucky	12	0	37	6
Louisiana	6	3	23	31
Maryland	47	0	0	20
Mississippi	1	0	15	24
Missouri	1	62	0	14
North Carolina	17	0	34	31
Oklahoma	7	13	23	3
Tennessee	0	0	56	14
Texas	72	9	35	67
Virginia	15	0	22	38
Total	288	94	328	355
Northern primaries				
Massachusetts	78	0	0	20
Rhode Island	19	0	0	3
Total	97	0	0	23
Western caucuses				
Hawaii	12	0	0	8
Idaho	8	0	0	4
Nevada	5	0	7	3
Washington	38	0	0	27
Total	63	0	7	42
Grand Total	448	94	335	420

Source: *Congressional Quarterly Weekly Reports,* March 12, 1988, 638.

Table A.2: Republican Delegates Won on Super Tuesday

	Bush	Dole	Kemp	Robertson
Southern primaries				
Alabama	35	3	0	0
Arkansas	14	7	1	5
Florida	82	0	0	0
Georgia	48	0	0	0
Kentucky	27	11	0	0
Louisiana	34	0	0	0
Maryland	41	0	0	0
Mississippi	27	2	0	2
Missouri	19	19	0	0
North Carolina	29	25	0	0
Oklahoma	33	3	0	0
Tennessee	29	11	0	0
Texas	111	0	0	0
Virginia[a]	45	0	0	5
Total	574	81	1	12
Northern primaries				
Massachusetts	30	13	3	2
Rhode Island	15	6	0	0
Total	45	19	3	2
Western caucus				
Washington	2	0	1	38
Grand Total	621	100	5	52

[a]Virginia's Republican delegates were selected in a separate caucus-convention process not connected with the primary vote on Super Tuesday

Source: *Congressional Quarterly Weekly Reports,* March 12, 1988, 639.

Table A.3: Spending in Dollars by Democratic Candidates in Iowa,
New Hampshire, South Carolina, and Super Tuesday

	Dukakis	Gephardt	Gore	Hart	Jackson	Simon
Iowa	756,411	751,157	262,037	207,159	195,032	791,257
New Hampshire	438,650	366,824	438,074	336,974	72,892	447,550
South Carolina	40,830	35,021	113,974	1,000	40,510	967
Southern primaries on Super Tuesday						
Alabama	69,663	120,688	227,627	2,346	25,500	6,900
Arkansas	102,527	57,975	127,161	5,000	14,500	19,480
Florida	738,219	318,247	187,147	582	31,000	24,543
Georgia	135,971	152,601	241,562	4,655	44,851	33,621
Kentucky	60,219	1,352	122,039	0	39,532	4,615
Louisiana	27,424	82,765	75,044	0	28,000	4,475
Maryland	244,880	3,002	40,211	0	19,300	12,059
Mississippi	5,334	7,487	91,324	0	22,300	4,000
Missouri	3,581	292,678	357	1,000	4,000	12,212
North Carolina	345,024	23,740	357,123	0	72,151	59,546
Oklahoma	80,681	94,343	158,684	2,500	0	6,424
Tennessee	13,498	931	28,476	200	12,000	4,341
Texas	1,069,536	447,050	948,468	40,268	73,500	55,437
Virginia	88,568	1,607	216,422	0	20,500	22,799
Northern primaries on Super Tuesday						
Massachusetts	271,885	181,340	416	6,635	4,000	59,549
Rhode Island	14,989	687	0	0	2,500	372
Western caucuses on Super Tuesday						
Hawaii	8,636	1,681	1,500	1,500	7,379	0
Idaho	1,824	224	16,456	0	0	0
Nevada	11,536	64	30,373	0	320	0
Washington	110,469	50	6,444	461	2,000	5,475

Note: FEC-imposed state spending limits for Hawaii, Idaho, and Nevada were set at
$461,000. For all other states' limits, see table A.4.

Source: *FEC Reports on Financial Activity: 1987-1988.*

Table A.4: Spending in Dollars by Republican Candidates in Iowa,
New Hampshire, South Carolina, and Super Tuesday

	Bush	Dole	Kemp	Robertson	State Limit
Iowa	774,696	793,228	765,145	781,658	775,217
New Hampshire	481,329	462,458	425,965	446,483	461,000
South Carolina	580,553	339,859	455,248	384,395	916,099
Southern primaries on Super Tuesday					
Alabama	87,788	216,712	17,137	196,456	1,093,861
Arkansas	85,961	78,817	22,511	67,448	642,081
Florida	1,118,471	304,388	13,745	707,211	3,436,847
Georgia	253,135	292,991	21,823	233,852	1,654,436
Kentucky	115,223	88,893	1,059	90,715	1,007,192
Louisiana	158,086	195,373	5,210	241,621	1,159,876
Maryland	115,704	274,734	1,574	37,839	1,257,608
Mississippi	188,005	82,785	4,194	132,720	676,010
Missouri	318,962	423,290	5,259	95,645	1,399,227
North Carolina	203,524	705,782	7,042	165,913	1,756,026
Oklahoma	180,802	306,366	5,613	141,284	877,375
Tennessee	116,055	268,033	383	169,172	1,329,155
Texas	420,493	158,489	18,540	978,121	4,353,684
Virginia	55,267	75,416	4,635	310,856	1,638,947
Northern primaries on Super Tuesday					
Massachusetts	905,878	1,003,643	725,531	213,760	1,666,607
Rhode Island	65,871	77,587	0	10,942	461,000
Western caucus on Super Tuesday					
Washington	94,109	343,005	4,706	101,683	1,242,487

Source: *FEC Reports on Financial Activity: 1987-1988.*

Table A.5: Percentage Vote for Candidates in Democratic Primaries and
Caucuses Held on Super Tuesday

	Dukakis	Gephart	Gore	Hart	Jackson	Simon
Southern primaries						
Alabama	8	7	37	2	44	1
Arkansas	19	12	37	4	17	2
Florida	41	14	13	3	20	2
Georgia	16	7	32	3	40	1
Kentucky	19	9	46	4	16	3
Louisiana	15	11	28	4	36	1
Maryland	46	8	9	2	29	3
Mississippi	8	5	33	4	44	1
Missouri	12	58	3	1	20	4
North Carolina	20	6	35	2	33	1
Oklahoma	17	21	41	4	13	2
Tennessee	3	2	72	1	21	1
Texas	33	14	20	5	25	2
Virginia	22	4	22	2	45	2
Northern primaries						
Massachusetts	59	10	4	2	19	4
Rhode Island	70	4	4	2	15	3
Western caucuses						
Hawaii	55	2	1	1	35	1
Idaho	38	1	8	0	22	7
Nevada	26	2	30	1	23	1
Washington	44	1	2	0	35	4

Source: Primary votes from Scammon and McGillivray 1989, and caucuses votes from
Congressional Quarterly Weekly Reports, March 12, 1988, 638.

Table A.6: Percentage Vote for Candidates in Republican Primaries and
Caucuses Held on Super Tuesday

	Bush	Dole	Kemp	Robertson
Southern primaries				
Alabama	65	16	5	14
Arkansas	47	26	5	19
Florida	62	21	5	11
Georgia	54	24	6	16
Kentucky	59	23	3	11
Louisiana	58	18	5	18
Maryland	53	32	6	6
Mississippi	66	17	4	14
Missouri	42	41	4	11
North Carolina	45	39	4	10
Oklahoma	37	35	6	21
Tennessee	60	22	4	13
Texas	64	14	5	15
Virginia	53	26	5	14
Northern primaries				
Massachusetts	59	26	7	5
Rhode Island	65	23	5	6
Western caucus				
Washington	24	26	8	39

Source: Primary votes from Scammon and McGillivray 1989, and caucuses votes from
Congressional Quarterly Weekly Reports, March 12, 1988, 639.

NOTES

CHAPTER 1

1. Various other names were auditioned for the southern regional primary—including Hyper Tuesday, Mega Tuesday, Mega-Super Tuesday, Super-Duper Tuesday, Super-Grits, Titanic Tuesday, and Awesome Tuesday—before settling on the previously used Super Tuesday (Stanley and Hadley 1987; Will, January 12, 1986).

2. Some speculated Jesse Jackson and Pat Robertson hoped for brokered conventions in which they could bargain for concessions. Others suggested some candidates might hope to emerge as dark horses in a brokered convention. Yet party leaders, such as Democratic chair Paul Kirk, dreaded the prospects of a brokered convention.

3. Nelson Rockefeller campaigned between October and December 1959, but, finding Nixon had already shored up the support of the Republican party elite, he withdrew from the race (White 1961).

4. Tracking the increase in presidential primaries is exceedingly difficult. Alternative sets of numbers are available in Stanley and Niemi's *Vital Statistics on American Politics* (1990, 134) and Congressional Quarterly's *Guide to the Presidency* (Nelson 1989, 166). Normally reliable sources, such as *Congressional Quarterly,* neglected in the past to include states, such as Alabama and New York, that held delegate-selection primaries without any presidential preference ballots. Also, some counts include Puerto Rico's primary, while others do not. Puerto Rico is excluded from the count in table 1.1.

5. For an opposing view see Polsby (1980), who viewed the McGovern-Fraser Commission as being dominated by the party's left.

6. Less change occurred in the Republican party because the national party was viewed more as an association of state parties and party rules are harder to change. Also the success of Republican presidential candidates led to little demand for changing the system (Fraser 1980).

7. The $1,000 maximum contribution limit has not been changed since the law was written in 1974. The amount of money candidates can spend, however, has been adjusted for inflation. The original limits for 1976 were $10.1 million; in 1980, $14.7 million; in 1984, $20.2 million; and 1988 candidates could spend $23 million for the campaign and an additional $4.6 million for fund-raising.

8. Four nineteenth-century presidents did not seek renomination; five others were defeated in their bids. Six won renomination, but two had to fight off strong challengers. From 1900 to 1964, only one sitting president (Taft in 1912) was challenged (Pomper 1963, 97).

9. Democratic nominations also required more ballots prior to 1936 because party rules required a two-thirds vote for nomination. Current Democratic and Republican rules only require a majority vote.

10. In two other cases the polls did not indicate a clear favorite. In 1940 Dewey's popularity was slipping fast, such that Wilkie actually led in the final poll. In 1964, Goldwater tied for first place in the polls (Keech and Matthews 1976).

11. If no candidate wins an absolute majority of the vote, most plans for a national primary call for a subsequent runoff primary between the top two candidates.

12. Morris Udall (D-Ariz.) made the first of these proposals in 1967, when his bill H.R. 1412 would require presidential primaries to be held after June 1. Other variants include John Ashbrook's (R-Ohio) plan in 1977 (H.R. 4329), allowing states to choose from four primary dates with the Federal Election Commission providing the list of candidates and delegates allocated by proportional representation. Sander Levin (D-Mich.) proposed a plan for six interregional primaries, requiring regional balance among the states holding their primaries on the same date (Levin, April 6, 1986).

13. The idea of regional primaries may be increasing in popularity. Those feeling regional primaries were a good idea in previous Gallup polls numbered 44 percent in 1982, 45 percent in 1984, and 40 percent in 1985 (Gallup Poll, March 1988, 11).

14. The Southern Legislative Conference, headquartered in Atlanta, represents state legislatures in fifteen southern states plus Puerto Rico. Organized in 1947, the Southern Legislative Conference is part of the Council of State Governments (SLC Fact Sheet, n.d.).

15. The Democratic Leadership Council (DLC) was formed in 1985 to advocate more moderate positions for the Democratic party. Virginia Governor Charles Robb and Senator Sam Nunn of Georgia led in the formation of the DLC. Richard Gephardt was its first chairman; Bruce Babbitt and Al Gore were also members (Germond and Witcover 1989).

CHAPTER 2

1. Democrats first imposed restrictions on delegate selection dates with the McGovern-Fraser rule that all delegates must be selected within the election year. In 1980 Democrats imposed the first "window" with a three-month time span from the second week in March to the second week in June but leaving Iowa's caucus scheduled for January 21 and New Hampshire's primary for February 26. In 1984 the national party convinced Iowa to move its caucus to the last week in February and New Hampshire to hold its primary the first week in March, reducing the actual time frame by five weeks (Lengle 1987).

2. Unofficial estimates of candidate strengths in Minnesota's Democratic caucus were immediately available based on the candidate affiliations of persons chosen as delegates to the county conventions. Similarly, although South Dakota's Democratic primary results were technically nonbinding, everyone suspected that delegates chosen at the March 12 caucuses would reflect the primary outcome.

3. Arizona Republicans likewise began their delegate selection process in 1986 with the election of precinct committee members on September 16. Only these precinct

committee members would be allowed to participate in the county and legislative district caucuses.

4. The percentage of delegates available in each period is based on the starting date of local caucuses and the actual date of primaries. All delegates from these states may not have been allocated by the date assigned, especially in caucus states where delegates often are selected at later county or state conventions. However, the ultimate selection of delegates rests on events at the first stage, and, therefore, those dates are used to demonstrate the front-loading of the election calendar.

5. In Michigan, Bush forces won a court decision allowing additional participants at county conventions, besides those selected to attend in 1986 precinct caucuses. Robertson and Kemp supporters upset by this ruling walked out of one-fifth of the county conventions, selecting their own delegates at separate meetings. With two different sets of delegates, long credential battles loomed on the horizon for the state and national conventions (Bush Wins a Round in Michigan, January 16, 1988, 135). At the state convention, Robertson's supporters walked out, held their own convention, and selected their own set of delegates for the national convention. A credential battle at the national convention was avoided as Bush and Robertson supporters in Michigan reached a compromise in July. Robertson received five more delegates in the official delegation, and the rest of his unofficial delegates could attend the convention as non-voting delegates (Benenson, August 6, 1988).

As Hawaii is a heavily Democratic state, local Republican leaders expected few participants in their caucuses originally scheduled for January 27. Robertson supporters, however, initiated a registration drive that swelled the number of eligible Republican voters from 10,000 to 17,000. Party officials, mostly backers of Dole and Bush, decided to delay the caucuses, citing the need to develop rules for challenging the credentials of new voters. After a barrage of negative publicity and a threatened lawsuit by Robertson, Republican leaders decided to reschedule the caucus for February 4 (Hawaii Republicans Reset Caucuses, January 30, 1988). Robertson won 82 percent of the delegates elected at these caucuses.

6. Bonus proportional representation rules were first allowed in 1984.

7. Loophole primaries were banned for the 1980 Democratic convention but reinstated for 1984.

8. PEOs were first introduced for the 1980 convention, in which they constituted 10 percent of each state's delegation.

9. 1984 was the first year Super Delegates were chosen.

10. Hammond (1980) argues that winner-take-all rules advantage candidates in their home regions but hurt them in other areas of the country. Conversely, proportional representation rules disadvantage a candidate in his own region while helping him in the rest of the country. In contrast to Lengle and Shafer (1976), Hammond argues that proportional representation rules advantage centrist candidates and winner-take-all rules help out more liberal or conservative candidates. Large northern states, according to Hammond, retain the most clout over Democratic nominations regardless of the rules used.

11. Additional Democrats contemplating bids or spoken of as possible candidates included Senator Bill Bradley of New Jersey, Chrysler Corporation chairman Lee A. Iacocca, Representative Patricia Schroeder of Colorado, former Governor Robert Kerrey of Nebraska, Senator Ernest F. Hollings of South Carolina, Ohio Governor Richard Celeste, Governor Rudy Perpich of Minnesota, Representative James A. Traficant of Ohio, and William Farley, a major Fruit of the Loom stockholder. Among the Republican possibilities were Governor Thomas Kean of New Jersey, syndicated columnist Pat

Buchanan, Governor James Thompson of Illinois, former Defense Secretary Donald Rumsfeld, former U.N. ambassador Jeane Kirkpatrick, and former Pennsylvania Governor Richard Thornburgh. Additionally, various fringe candidates announced they would seek the Republican or Democratic nomination, including former Ku Klux Klan member David Duke, former 1940s boy-wonder governor of Minnesota and perennial Republican presidential candidate Harold Stassen, and Lyndon LaRouche. In total, over one hundred individuals submitted their names to the Federal Election Commission as possible candidates.

12. Baker established a precandidacy PAC and conducted some preliminary campaigning. Yet even before his decision to join the Reagan White House, many commentators felt that Baker was wavering about entering the presidential race because of the poor health of his wife.

13. Michael Dukakis's campaign manager and longtime confidant, John Sasso leaked the videocassette to the press. When public acknowledgment of the leak led to a brouhaha, Dukakis replaced Sasso with Susan Estrich. Sasso returned to help Dukakis's faltering presidential campaign in late August.

14. The ideological placement of candidates by respondents to the 1980, 1984, and 1988 NES polls is as follows: (1) for 1980, respondents to the first wave of the major panel (P-1, interviewed from January 22 to February 25) and the minor panel (C-1, interviewed from April 2 to May 22); (2) for 1984, those in the continuous monitoring poll interviewed between January 11 and June 1; and (3) for 1988, all respondents, including those from Massachusetts and Rhode Island, interviewed from January 17 to March 7. The placement of Democratic candidates came from respondents who were strong, weak, or leaning Democrats, while Republican classifications came from strong, weak, and leaning Republicans. Ideological placements in 1980 and 1988 were obtained from a question asking respondents to imagine a seven-point scale. In 1984, ideological placements came from two questions in formats similar to the traditional party identification questions. Respondents were first asked if a candidate was a liberal, moderate, or conservative. The second question asked whether the candidate was a strong or not very strong liberal or conservative or whether a moderate candidate leaned toward the liberal or conservative side.

15. These matching funds are accumulated through the one-dollar check-off on federal income tax forms. About 20 percent of American taxpayers check off the one-dollar contribution, which does not increase their tax obligation (Tolchin, February 12, 1991).

16. Candidates may spend an additional sum, equal to 20 percent of the limits, for fund-raising purposes. Additionally, there are no limits on the amount of money used for legal and accounting costs. None of these items count against the overall spending limits.

17. The first precandidacy PAC was organized by Ronald Reagan in 1977 to make use of surplus funds from his 1976 presidential campaign. Reagan and his advisers soon realized they could use his PAC, Citizens for the Republic, to finance the pre-election activities of Reagan for the 1980 campaign. Bush, Connally, and Dole followed Reagan's lead and formed their own PACs prior to the 1980 campaign. In 1984, Mondale, Cranston, Hollings, Glenn, and Reagan employed precandidacy PACs (Corrado 1990).

18. A tax-exempt foundation is not allowed to engage in partisan activities. In December of 1987 the IRS began an audit of the Freedom Council and CBN for possible violations in support of Robertson's campaign. Several Freedom Council officials admitted on national television that it served as a front for the Robertson campaign (Wilcox 1991).

CHAPTER 3

1. As we saw in Chapter 2 (tables 2.4 and 2.5), both Democrats and Republicans across the South picked approximately 60 percent of the delegates at the district level. In every case but one, the election district coincided with U.S. Congressional districts. Texas Democrats, the exception, employed state senate districts instead (O'Byrne, March 6, 1988).

2. The first candidate to parlay an intensive campaign in Iowa into favorable press was George McGovern in 1972, who turned an unexpected second-place finish into a moral victory over Edmund Muskie. Prior to 1972, the Iowa caucuses were held in the middle of the nomination season and received little attention (Winebrenner 1987).

3. This information on Dukakis's Florida strategy is from a conversation with Anthony Corrado, March 1989.

4. PACs actually play only a very small role in presidential nomination finances, as PAC contributions are not eligible to be matched by government funds. In 1988 only $3 million in PAC contributions was received by all the candidates, comprising only 1 percent of total funds raised. The Gephardt campaign did receive the largest percentage, at 5 percent of his campaign total (Wilcox 1991).

5. This delegate-acquisition aspect to the four-corner strategy was pointed out by Anthony Corrado in an October 8, 1990, letter.

6. Bush won all forty-eight Georgia delegates as a result of his victory in the primary, but Robertson supporters won a large number of the delegate slots at the state convention. For the state convention, party regulars evoked an obscure rule trying to disqualify many of Robertson's delegates, but state courts ruled against this strategy. The state party chairman tried to adjourn the convention. Failing that, he and the party regulars walked out. Robertson supporters remained and selected delegates for the convention. Meanwhile, the state central committee selected its own set of delegates, leading to further battles in the court. Eventually, the Republican National Committee ruled both delegate slates invalid. On August 8, a compromise delegation was established, including members from both the Robertson and state central committee slates (Benenson, August 13, 1988).

7. Candidate expenditures in each state are those reported to the Federal Election Commission. These figures contain some biases. Figures for Iowa and New Hampshire underreport actual expenditures, as candidate avoid exceeding the state spending limits by diverting costs to neighboring states. Additionally, candidates vary as to which expenses they attribute to state operations and which they allocate to the national headquarters. For instance, some candidates established phone banks in each state, while others ran these operations from Washington, D.C. (See Wilcox 1991 for more elaboration.) Nevertheless, FEC state spending figures still give us the relative importance each candidate placed on various states in his campaign.

8. Simon, as well as several other candidates, are reported as exceeding state spending limits in Iowa or New Hampshire. If these figures hold up through the final audits, they will be subject to relatively small fines.

9. Of course, candidates may have spent more money in states already favorable to themselves in order to secure a victory.

10. A regression analysis of Republican spending patterns in all fifty states plus the District of Columbia provides essentially the same results, except that the date of the primary or caucus also becomes an important factor. The standardized regression coefficients for this equation are as follows: .50 for Iowa; .54 for New Hampshire; $-.21$ for Super Tuesday, which is significant at the .10 level; $-.03$ for number of delegates;

− .42 for date; .27 for primary versus caucus; .06 for number of event on date; and − .02 for home state. R equals .91, and R^2 equals .82.

11. Connally's spending is not even included in the high expenditure figure for South Carolina in 1980. Since Connally did not accept federal matching funds, he was not required to report state spending figures to the FEC.

CHAPTER 4

1. Adding partisan division of the state legislature to the normal vote measure will increase Democratic proportions in the South, where state and local voting is still heavily Democratic. This, however, may be a proper addition reflecting the continued importance of the Democratic party and primaries in the South. Turnout figures in tables 4.1 and 4.2 indicate that, even with this possibly enlarged Democratic numeration, turnout in Democratic primaries in the South still exceeded turnout in Republican primaries.

2. Individual bivariate analyses, instead of one multivariate analysis, are used to explore the effects of rules and candidate strategies on turnout in the Super Tuesday states because of the small number of cases. Using only one party, the maximum number of cases is fourteen, allowing little more than one or two independent variables in a multivariate analysis. Even both parties combined present only twenty-eight cases.

3. Of course, correlations do not tell us the direction of a causal relationship. Candidates may have spent more in states they expected to have higher turnout rates, thinking that in these states their campaign expenditures would have a greater effect.

4. Caucus participation rates were calculated in the same manner as presidential primary turnout. Raw figures on numbers of caucus participants were obtained from *Congressional Quarterly Weekly Reports* (July 9, 1988, p. 1,895; August 13, 1988, p. 2,255; June 2, 1984, p. 1,317; July 26, 1980, p. 2,126; January 26, 1980, p. 187; March 1, 1980, p. 599; February 28, 1976, p. 462).

5. Kentucky, Mississippi, and Texas Democrats also held caucuses in 1984, but no turnout figures are available to compare with 1988 primary turnout rates.

6. Because of a problem with regression toward the mean, variables measuring change over time cannot be used as dependent variables in regression equations (Markus 1979, 45-48). States with higher turnout rates in 1980 would be less likely to increase their turnout rates in 1988 than would states that had lower turnout rates in 1980. This is true for the data in this analysis, where the correlation coefficient between turnout in 1980 and percentage change in turnout between 1980 and 1988 is − .65. Therefore, the dependent variable for the multivariate analysis of change in turnout will be turnout rates in 1988, while turnout in 1980 becomes one of the independent variables. Additionally, different variances in turnout in 1980 and 1988 make the use of standardized regression coefficients precarious. However, some comparison between the impact of different independent variables is desirable and can be obtained by converting all variables to base 10 logs. The unstandardized regression coefficients than give the percent change in the dependent variable with a one percent change in the independent variable. (See Barrilleaux 1986 for similar methodology.)

Percentage change formula were used to measure changes in closeness of the race, candidate expenditures, and number of candidates before conversion to base 10 logs. For measuring the closeness of the national race, John Aldrich's (1980) competitive standing measure was adopted. This measure takes on a value of one when a candidate has won enough delegates to be assured of winning the nomination on the first roll call at the convention. The formula is as follows (with d_1 = delegates committed to leading candidates, d_j = delegates committed to all other major candidates, and D = number of delegates needed to win the nomination):

$$\frac{d_1 - d_j}{D - d_1 - d_j}$$

Not included as delegates committed to major candidates are delegates selected as uncommitted or attached to minor candidates, as they are often available to be won by a national candidate.

An average candidate expenditure rate per state for each year was calculated based on Federal Election Commission (FEC) spending limits for each state. As these limits are based on state population sizes, their use controls for the size of the state. Each candidate's expenditures in a state was divided by the maximum allowed. Values for all candidates from each party in each state were summed and divided by the number of candidates competing to obtain average expenditures per candidate; those are the same figures found in the last columns of tables 3.2 and 3.3. The change formula was then used to measure percentage increases or decreases in candidate expenditures in a state between 1980 and 1988, before conversion to base 10 logs.

The number of candidates contesting a primary included only serious national candidates. That is, the candidate qualified for federal matching funds and was generally discussed by the national media as a contender. Once again, the change formula was employed to derive percentage increases or decreases in the number of candidates.

Three category variables were used to measure (with log values given) change in nonpresidential races on the ballot coded (0) away from other races, (.3) no change, and (.48) to other races on the ballot in 1988; change in home states coded (0) home state in 1980 but not 1988, (.3) no change, and (.48) home state in 1988 but not 1980; and change in beauty contests coded (0) beauty contest in 1980 but not 1988, (.3) no change, and (.48) beauty contest in 1988 but not 1980.

Changes in delegate distribution rules were based on the following scale for each year: (1) winner-take-all, (2) loophole, (3) beauty contest, (4) bonus proportional representation, and (5) proportional representation. Subtracting 1988 values from 1980 figures, produces a high value for states moving toward the proportional-representation end of the scale and a low value if they moved toward the winner-take-all direction.

Party and Super Tuesday were dummy variables. Party was coded (0) Republican and (.3) Democrat. Super Tuesday was coded (.3) southern Super Tuesday primary and (0) all other primaries.

7. This is the value for R^2 when 1988 turnout rates are regressed on 1980 turnout rates.

8. Geer (1988) found presidential primary voters to be more moderate than general election voters supporting a party's candidate. Norrander (1989) found some evidence that 1980 Republican presidential primary voters may have been more ideologically sophisticated—i.e, more likely to be ideologues—than Republican general election voters not participating in the primaries.

9. Ideally, a comparison to general election voters would be better. However, the Super Tuesday respondents were not repolled after the fall election to determine whether they voted and for whom. People who are registered, however, normally vote in presidential elections. Therefore, they will provide a sufficient substitute for general election voters.

10. This analysis excludes only forty respondents claiming a purely independent identification. Independents who leaned toward the Democratic or Republican party were combined with the appropriate group of partisans. Pure independents were not excluded if they voted in one of the primaries. All voters in the Democratic primary, whether they were Democrats, Republicans, or independents, constituted the Democratic electorate and were compared to Democratic identifiers who did not vote.

CHAPTER 5

1. Kenney and Rice (1990) find five different theories explain the effects of momentum on voting: (1) being caught up in the excitement, (2) pleasure from backing a winner, (3) strategic voting, (4) cue taking, and (5) reluctant support for an inevitable winner.

2. Abramowitz (1987) argues the contrary point, that changing opinions about the viability of Mondale and Hart accounted for declining preferences for Hart.

3. Most of these figures for Democratic voters are for white southerners. Only fifty-five black respondents are included in this analysis. Unlike white southerners, who were slow to make up their minds, about two-thirds of blacks kept their same candidate preference throughout the campaign, regardless of when they were interviewed.

4. Sixty-nine respondents fell in the noncandidate category, including both Democrats and Republicans voting in the Democratic primaries. The preference for a Republican candidate for the Democratic nomination, however, did not derive solely from Republican voters participating in Democratic primaries. Among these Republicans, six out of fourteen favored Cuomo, three preferred Kennedy, four preferred an unspecified other, and only one preferred a Republican candidate—Dole.

5. Eight of the Jackson voters were white. Two-thirds of these voters switched over to Jackson from another candidate. In contrast, 70 percent of Jackson's black supporters remained with him throughout the campaign.

6. Among those who switched to Jackson from another candidate or no candidate, significant increases occurred in their estimates of Jackson's viability between the pre-election and post-election interviews. On average, viability estimates rose 21.4 points on a 200-point scale. Evaluation ratings—i.e. thermometer scores—rose only 2.7 points, whereas knowledge rose .5 on a 10-point scale.

7. This analysis was unaffected by race, since none of the black respondents voted for Gephardt or Dukakis and only one black respondent had preferred Gephardt in the pre-Super Tuesday campaign.

8. Since the post-election survey was conducted after Super Tuesday, it may be that these lower estimates of viability were affected by Super Tuesday results. When voting actually occurred, these respondents may have felt their preferred candidates maintained higher probabilities of winning the nomination.

9. Only twenty-two black respondents are part of this analysis, most of whom remained loyal to Jackson throughout the campaign. Nevertheless, similar differences in mean values occur for black and white Democrats, and these differences are statistically significant for both groups.

10. The options for Democratic voters included (1) unemployment, (2) oil import fee or tax, (3) unfair foreign trade competition, (4) reducing the federal deficit, (5) U.S. role in Nicaragua, (6) protecting social security benefits, (7) problems of poor people, (8) national defense, and (9) none of these issues. The options for Republicans included (1) intermediate range missile treaty, (2) oil import fee or tax, (3) unfair foreign trade competition, (4) reducing the federal deficit, (5) U.S. role in Nicaragua, (6) protecting social security benefits, (7) traditional moral values, (8) not raising federal taxes, and (9) none of these issues.

11. The options for Democratic voters included (1) honest/has integrity, (2) intelligent, (3) strong leader, (4) experienced, (5) cares about people like me, (6) can win in November, (7) has management ability, (8) from my part of the country, and (9) I don't

like the other candidates. The options for Republicans included (1) honest/has integrity, (2) intelligent, (3) a real conservative, (4) experienced, (5) strong leader, (6) can win in November, (7) will advance Reagan's ideas, (8) from my part of the country, and (9) I don't like the other candidates.

CHAPTER 6

1. The term "bandwagon" classically refers to the point at which one candidate pulls ahead in the voting at a multiballot national convention, but the term has also been applied to voting results in sequential presidential primaries. (See Collat, Kelley, and Rogowski 1981 for a more complete discussion of the origins of the term.) In this chapter, "bandwagon" will be used in a mode similar to Aldrich (1980, 130), though not as precisely. Under this definition, bandwagon voting differs from momentum voting in that the former inevitably leads to the nomination while the latter may fall short of that goal.

2. Of course, Jerry Brown also competed in a few primaries in 1980, but his dismal performance led both voters and journalists to soon ignore him.

3. Figures in table 6.3 were obtained by identifying the state associated with each story as indexed by the *New York Times* and *Los Angeles Times*. Admittedly this is a rather crude method. One caveat is that the 1980 *New York Times* index listed the Democratic and Republican races separately, leading to a double count of some stories. However, these crude findings are replicated by Gurian's (1990) more sophisticated analysis. As is common with most media studies of presidential primary coverage, figures in table 6.3 do not include stories on the New York, Connecticut, and New Jersey primaries from the *New York Times* nor stories on the California primary from the *Los Angeles Times*.

4. Gurian's more elaborate count found Super Tuesday placing fourth in overall coverage, after Iowa, New Hampshire, and Illinois.

CHAPTER 7

1. This information comes from conversations with Pat Stafford of the Southern Legislative Conference, October 12, 1990, and March 19, 1991.

2. This information is from a phone conversation with John Kessel, October 11, 1989.

3. One aspect of the Jackson-Dukakis deal, which reduced the number of Super Delegates by eliminating automatic seats for Democratic National Committee (DNC) members, was reversed by the DNC in September 1989. Another provision, eliminating the 15 percent minimum vote requirement for winning delegates under proportional representation, also may be overturned before the 1992 convention (Rosenthal, September 29, 1989).

REFERENCES

Abramowitz, Alan I. 1987. Candidate Choice Before the Convention. *Political Behavior* 9:49-61.

Abramson, Paul R., John H. Aldrich, Phil Paolino, and David W. Rohde. 1990. "Sophisticated" Voting in the 1988 Presidential Primaries. Presented at the annual meeting of the American Political Science Association, San Francisco, Calif.

After Super Tuesday. March 28, 1988. *New Republic,* 7-9.

Akerman, Robert. March 13, 1988. This Tuesday Should Make It Plain What Super Tuesday Really Achieved. *Atlanta Constitution.*

Aldrich, John H. 1980. *Before the Convention: Strategies and Choices in Presidential Nominating Campaigns.* Chicago: University of Chicago Press.

Alexander, Herbert E. 1983. *Financing the 1980 Election.* Lexington, Mass.: Lexington Books.

Allin, C.D. 1912. The Presidential Primary. *Queens Quarterly* 20:92-99.

Alter, Jonathan, and Eleanor Clift. February 29, 1988. Gore's Message Gap. *Newsweek,* 23.
———, and Mickey Kaus. October 31, 1988. Reign of Errors: This Year's Conventional Wisdom Was Even More Wrong Than Usual. *Newsweek,* 22-24.

Ansolabehere, Stephen and Gary King. 1990. Measuring the Consequences of Delegate Selection Rules in Presidential Nominations. *Journal of Politics* 52:609-21.

Apple, R.W., Jr. January 3, 1988. A Nominee by Spring? Hart Makes It Tougher. *New York Times.*
———. January 28, 1988. The Sound of Politics in Iowa Town. *New York Times.*
———. March 8, 1988. Super Tuesday Offers a Muddled Experiment. *New York Times.*

Arterton, F. Christopher. 1978. Campaign Organizations Confused the Media Political Environment. In *Race for the Presidency,* ed. James David Barber. Englewood Cliffs, N.J.: Prentice-Hall.

Balzar, John. February 26, 1988. Two Dole Aides Fired in Shake-Up. *Los Angeles Times.*

Barnes, Fred. March 21, 1988. Blessed Are the Kingmakers. *New Republic,* 11-13.

Barnes, James A. March 19, 1988. The Brokering Game. *National Journal,* 724-31.

Barone, Michael, and Grant Ujifusa. 1987. *The Almanac of American Politics, 1988.* Washington, D.C.: National Journal.

Barrilleaux, Charles J. 1986. A Dynamic Model of Partisan Competition in the American States. *American Journal of Political Science* 30:822-40.

Bartels, Larry M. 1985. Expectations and Preferences in Presidential Nominating Campaigns. *American Political Science Review* 79:804-15.

————. 1988. *Presidential Primaries and the Dynamics of Public Choice.* Princeton: Princeton University Press.

————. 1989. After Iowa: Momentum in Presidential Primaries. In *The Iowa Caucuses and the Presidential Nominating Process,* ed. Peverill Squire. Boulder, Colo.: Westview.

Baxter, Tom. February 21, 1988. It's Bush v Robertson in S.C. Republican Race. *Atlanta Constitution.*

————. March 13, 1988. Robertson Supporters Make Waves at State GOP's County Conventions. *Atlanta Constitution.*

Beckel, Robert G. 1987. The 1988 Presidential Selection Process: Flirting with Disaster? *Election Politics* 4:2-5.

Benenson, Bob. March 12, 1988. A Quiet Settles Over Once-Stormy Maryland. *Congressional Quarterly Weekly Reports,* 664-65.

————. August 6, 1988. Thorny Georgia Credentials Dispute Looms. *Congressional Quarterly Weekly Reports,* 2154.

————. August 13, 1988. Georgia Credentials Dispute Settled. *Congressional Quarterly Weekly Reports,* 2249.

Beninger, James R. 1976. Winning the Presidential Nomination: National Polls and State Primary Elections, 1936-1972. *Public Opinion Quarterly* 72:22-38.

————. 1977. The Legacy of Carter and Reagan: Political Reality Overtakes the Myth of the Presidential Primaries. *Intellect* 105:234-37.

Berke, Richard L. December 27, 1987. Heeding Plato, Greek-Americans Aid in Effort to Raise Money for Dukakis. *New York Times.*

————. March 10, 1988. Dukakis Funds Mount as His Rivals Face Bills. *New York Times.*

————. May 21, 1988. Jackson Narrows Fund-Raising Gap. *New York Times.*

————. February 15, 1990. Two Major Parties Back California on an Early Presidential Primary. *New York Times.*

Bibby, John F., Cornelius P. Cotter, James L. Gibson, and Robert J. Huckshorn. 1983. Parties in State Politics. In *Politics in the American States,* 4th edition, eds. Virginia Gray, Herbert Jacob, and Kenneth N. Vines. Boston: Little, Brown.

Bishop, Katherine. March 10, 1991. California Democrats Adopt Early Caucus System. *New York Times.*

Black, Christine M., and Thomas Oliphant. 1989. *All by Myself: The Unmaking of a Presidential Campaign.* Chester, Conn.: Globe Pequote.

Black, Earl, and Merle Black. 1987. *Politics and Society in the South.* Cambridge, Mass.: Harvard University Press.

Bloom, Melvyn H. 1973. *Public Relations and Presidential Campaigns: A Crisis in Democracy.* New York: Thomas Y. Crowell.

Bode, Kenneth A., and Carol F. Casey. 1980. Party Reform: Revisionism Revised. In *Political Parties in the Eighties,* ed. Robert A Goldwin. Washington, D.C.: American Enterprise Institute.

Brady, Henry E., and Richard Johnston. 1987. What's the Primary Message: Horse Race or Issue Journalism? In *Media and Momentum,* eds., Gary R. Orren and Nelson W. Polsby. Chatham, N.J.: Chatham House.

Brams, Steven J. 1978. *The Presidential Election Game.* New Haven: Yale University Press.

Broder, David. March 2, 1988. No More Super Tuesdays. *Washington Post.*

Bush Wins a Round in Michigan. January 16, 1988. *Congressional Quarterly Weekly Reports,* 35.

California Is Split on Early Primary. February 23, 1990. *New York Times,* 9a.

Carleton, William. 1957. The Revolution in Presidential Nominating Conventions. *Political Science Quarterly* 72:224-40.

Carlson, Eugene. December 17, 1985. Southern States Have a Plan for Choosing Next President. *Wall Street Journal.*

Carroll, James R. January 1, 1988. Hart's Beleaguered Backers. *San Jose Mercury News.*

Carter, Hodding, III. March 13, 1988. A Dixie Gamble with "Super" Winnings. *Atlanta Constitution.*

Christensen, Mike. February 26, 1988. Dole Campaign Chief Fires 2 Top Aides, Boots Them Off Plane. *Atlanta Constitution.*

Churches and Church Membership in the United States, 1980. 1982. Atlanta: Glenmary Research Center.

Clendinen, Dudley. September 13, 1986. A Coy Robertson is Pioneering Era of Satellite Politics. *New York Times.*

Coleman, Kevin J. 1988. *The Presidential Nominating Process: The Regional Primary Movement and Proposed Reforms.* Washington, D.C.: Congressional Research Service.

Collat, Donald S., Stanley Kelley, Jr., and Ronald Rogowski. 1981. The End Game in Presidential Nominations. *American Political Science Review* 75:426-35.

Conover, Pamela Johnston, and Stanley Feldman. 1981. The Origins and Meaning of Liberal/Conservative Self-Identifications. *American Journal of Political Science* 25:617-45.

Cook, Rhodes. 1987. *Race for the Presidency: Winning the 1988 Nomination.* Washington, D.C.: Congressional Quarterly.

———. March 5, 1988. March 8 Offers Clues to South's Political Soul. *Congressional Quarterly Weekly Reports,* 569-74.

———. July 2, 1988. Pressed by Jackson Demands, Dukakis Yields on Party Rules. *Congressional Quarterly Weekly Reports,* 1799-1801.

———, with Dave Kaplan. June 4, 1988. In 1988, Caucuses Have Been the Place for Political Passion. *Congressional Quarterly Weekly Reports,* 1523-27.

Corrado, Anthony. 1990. An Old Game in a New Arena: PACs as Presidential Campaign Organizations. Presented at the annual meeting of the Western Political Science Convention, Newport Beach, Calif.

Crotty, William. 1978. *Decisions for the Democrats.* Baltimore: Johns Hopkins University Press.

———. 1983. *Party Reform.* New York: Longman.

Dart, Bob. March 5, 1988. Nunn Staying Neutral Until After Tuesday. *Atlanta Constitution.*

David, Paul T., Ralph M. Goldman, and Richard C. Bain. 1960. *The Politics of National Party Conventions.* Washington, D.C.: Brookings.

Davis, James W. 1967. *Presidential Primaries: Road to the White House.* New York: Crowell.

———. 1983. *National Conventions in an Age of Party Reform.* Westport, Conn.: Greenwood.

———. 1980. *Presidential Primaries: Road to the White House.* Westport, Conn.: Greenwood.

Democratic Leader Has Doubts About Super Tuesday Concept. March 5, 1988. *Atlanta Constitution,* 7a.

Dionne, E.J., Jr. February 10, 1987. Toward an Ideological Scorecard. *New York Times*.
———. January 17, 1988. After 20 Years of Infighting, the Democrats Grow Closer. *New York Times*.
———. March 20, 1988. Momentum Eludes Democrats, One by One. *New York Times*.
Downs, Anthony. 1957. *An Economic Theory of Democracy*. New York: Harper and Row.
Doyle, William. 1975. Regional Primaries: The Spirit of '76. *State Government* 48:141-44.
Drogin, Bob. March 1, 1988. Dukakis Faces Up to Problems in South. *Los Angeles Times*.
———. March 8, 1988. Upbeat Dukakis May Win Enough States Today to Hurt Rivals Badly. *Los Angeles Times*.
Eichel, Larry. March 8, 1988. Bush Seeks Near-Sweep in Primaries. *San Jose Mercury News*.
Eizenstat, Stuart E. March 5, 1988. Southern Democrats' Bold Step, Super Tuesday, Is Unlikely to Work for Party. *Atlanta Constitution*.
Elazar, Daniel J. 1984. *American Federalism: A View from the States,* 3rd edition. New York: Harper and Row.
Etherton, Shelly. March 1, 1988. For Staffers, Home is an Airport, Phone an Appendage. *USA Today*.
Federal Election Commission. April 12, 1988. Second Monthly Presidential Reports Show Spending Over $146 Million. Washington, D.C.: FEC Press Office Release.
———. August, 1989. *FEC Reports on Financial Activity, 1987-1988, Final Report*. Washington, D.C.: Government Printing Office.
Feeney, Susan. March 1, 1988. Candidates Milking Airports. *New Orleans Times-Picayune*.
———. March 2, 1988. Dole: Short of Time, Votes in the South. *New Orleans Times-Picayune*.
Fraser, Donald M. 1980. Democratizing the Democratic Party. In *Political Parties in the Eighties,* ed. Robert A Goldwin. Washington, D.C.: American Enterprise Institute.
Freund, Charles Paul. March 28, 1988. The Zeitgeist Checklist. *New Republic,* 8.
Gailey, Phil. March 8, 1986. Southern Democrats Press Plan for a Regional Primary. *New York Times*.
———. April 8, 1986. South Unifying '88 Primary Dates: Political Effects Debated. *New York Times*.
Gallup, George H. 1978. *The Gallup Poll: Public Opinion, 1972-1977*. Wilmington, Del.: Scholarly Resources.
Gallup Poll. December 1987. Bush Continues to Outpace Rivals for 1988 Republican Nomination. *Gallup Report* 267:8-9.
———. December 1987. Strenuous Campaigning Fails to Produce Strong Democratic Nominee. *Gallup Report* 267:9-10.
———. March 1988. Nationwide Presidential Primary Backed by Two-Thirds Majority. *Gallup Report* 270:9-11.
———. April 1988. Dukakis Runs Neck and Neck with Bush But Falls Behind with Jackson as V.P. *Gallup Report* 271:2-6.
———. May 1988. Dukakis Closer to Public's Views on Many Issues. *Gallup Report* 272:8-19.
———. September 1988. Dukakis's Lead Drops to Pre-Convention Levels. *Gallup Report* 276:2-3.
Galston, William. 1988. Did Super Tuesday Work? *Election Politics* 5:2-5.

Gamson, William A. 1962. Coalition Formation at Presidential Nominating Conventions. *American Journal of Sociology* 68:157-71.

Geer, John G. 1988. Assessing the Representativeness of Electorates in Presidential Primaries. *American Journal of Political Science* 32:929-45.

———. 1989. *Nominating Presidents.* New York: Greenwood.

Germond, Jack W., and Jules Witcover. 1989. *Whose Broad Stripes and White Stars? The Trivial Pursuit of the Presidency, 1988.* New York: Warner Books.

———, and Jules Witcover. March 5, 1988. Super Tuesday May Prove to Be a Political Flop. *National Journal,* 622.

Gillette, Robert. February 26, 1988. Jackson, Heeding Old Foe, Targets the "Little People." *Los Angeles Times.*

Glen, Maxwell. November 14, 1987. No Time for Brokers. *National Journal,* 2868-76.

Gopoian, J. David. 1982. Issue Preferences and Candidate Choice in Presidential Primaries. *American Journal of Political Science* 26:523-46.

Gorman, Joseph B. 1976. *Federal Presidential Primary Proposals, 1911-1976.* Washington, D.C.: Congressional Research Service.

Grofman, Bernard, and Amihai Glazer. 1988. A Simple Model of Candidate Support in the 1988 Democratic Presidential Primaries. Unpublished manuscript.

Gurian, Paul-Henri. 1986. Resource Allocation Strategies in Presidential Nomination Campaigns. *American Journal of Political Science* 30:802-21.

———. 1989. The Relationship Between Media Coverage and Resource Allocations in Presidential Campaigns. Presented at the American Political Science Association, Atlanta, Ga.

———. 1990. Less than Expected: Media Coverage of Super Tuesday, 1988. Presented at the annual meeting of the American Political Science Association, San Francisco, Calif.

Hadley, Arthur. 1976. *The Invisible Primary.* Englewood Cliffs, N.J.: Prentice-Hall.

Hadley, Charles D., and Harold W. Stanley. 1989. Super Tuesday 1988: Regional Results and National Implications. *Publius* 19:19-37.

Hagen, Michael G. 1989. Voter Turnout in Primary Elections. In *The Iowa Caucuses and the Presidential Nominating Process,* ed. Peverill Squire. Boulder, Colo.: Westview.

Hagstrom, Jerry, and Robert Guskind. July 30, 1988. Calling the Races. *National Journal,* 1972-76.

Hamilton, Howard D. 1971. The Municipal Voter: Voting and Nonvoting in City Elections. *American Political Science Review* 65:1135-40.

Hammond, Thomas H. 1980. Another Look at the Role of "The Rules" in the 1972 Democratic Presidential Primaries. *Western Political Quarterly* 33:50-72.

Harris, Ron. March 1, 1988. Gore Seen as Needing Big Victory in South but Trails Jackson There. *Los Angeles Times.*

Harvey, Steve, and Hal Straus. February 25, 1988. Simon to Bypass Primaries in South. *Atlanta Constitution.*

Hawaii Republicans Reset Caucuses. January 30, 1988. *Congressional Quarterly Weekly Reports,* 206.

Hedlund, Ronald D. 1977. Cross-Over Voting in a 1976 Presidential Primary. *Public Opinion Quarterly* 41:498-514.

Hertzke, Allen D. 1989. Pat Robertson's Crusade and the GOP: A Strategic Analysis. Presented at the annual meeting of the Midwest Political Science Association, Chicago, Ill.

Hyping Hyper Tuesday. March 28, 1986. *New York Times,* 34a.

In California, Question Arises on Plan to Move Up Primary. August 31, 1990. *New York Times,* 11a.

Ingwerson, Marshall. March 28, 1986. 1988's Mega-Super Tuesday. *Christian Science Monitor.*

Jacoby, Tamar, John McCormick, Vern E. Smith, and Margaret Garrard Warner. January 4, 1988. Is it Time to Take Pat Seriously? *Newsweek,* 21-22.

Jewell, Malcolm E. 1984. *Parties and Primaries: Nominating State Governors.* New York: Praeger.

Kamarck, Elaine C. 1987. Delegate Allocation Rules in Presidential Nomination Systems: A Comparison Between the Democrats and Republicans. *Journal of Law and Politics* 4:275-310.

Katz, Allan. March 8, 1988. La. Expects Less than Super Turnout. *New Orleans Times-Picayune.*

Katz, Gregory. February 17, 1988. New Strategy: Broaden Arms, Narrow Scope. *USA Today.*

Keech, William R., and Donald R. Matthews. 1976. *The Party's Choice.* Washington, D.C.: Brookings.

Keeter, Scott, and Cliff Zukin. 1983. *Uninformed Choice: The Failure of the New Presidential Nominating System.* New York: Praeger.

Kenney, Patrick J., and Tom W. Rice. 1985. Voter Turnout in Presidential Primaries: A Cross-Sectional Examination. *Political Behavior* 7:101-12.

———, and Tom W. Rice. 1990. Boarding the Bush Bandwagon: Political Momentum in the 1988 Republican Prenomination Campaign. Presented at the annual meeting of the Midwest Political Science Association, Chicago, Ill.

Kessel, John H. 1980. *Presidential Campaign Politics.* Homewood, Ill.: Dorsey.

———. 1988. *Presidential Campaign Politics,* 3rd ed. Chicago: Dorsey.

Kim, Jae-On, John R. Petrocik, and Stephen N. Enokson. 1975. Voter Turnout Among the American States: Systemic and Individual Components. *American Political Science Review* 69:107-23.

Kirkpatrick, Jeane Jordon. 1976. *The New Presidential Elite.* New York: Russell Sage.

———. 1978. *Dismantling the Parties.* Washington, D.C.: American Enterprise Institute.

Kirschten, Dick. February 2, 1988. The GOP's Wild Card. *National Journal,* 519-22.

Kritzer, Herbert M. 1980. The Representativeness of the 1972 Presidential Primaries. In *The Party Symbol,* ed. William Crotty. San Francisco: Freeman.

Kuttner, Robert. March 21, 1988. The Super Tuesday Fiasco: Red-Faced White Boys. *New Republic,* 9-10.

Ladd, Everett Carll. 1978. *Where Have All the Voters Gone?* New York: Norton.

Lengle, James I. 1981. *Representation and Presidential Primaries: The Democratic Party in the Post-Reform Era.* Westport, Conn.: Greenwood Press.

———. 1987. Democratic Party Reforms: The Past as Prologue to the 1988 Campaign. *Journal of Law and Politics* 4:233-73.

———, and Byron Shafer. 1976. Primary Rules, Political Power, and Social Change. *American Political Science Review* 70:25-40.

Levin, Sander. April 6, 1986. Primaries by Lot (letter to editor). *New York Times.*

Levitin, Teresa E., and Warren E. Miller. 1979. Ideological Interpretation of Presidential Elections. *American Political Science Review* 73:751-71.

Lichter, S. Robert, Daniel Amundson, and Richard Noyes. 1988. *The Video Campaign: Network Coverage of the 1988 Primaries.* Washington, D.C.: American Enterprise Institute.

Luntz, Frank I. 1988. *Candidates, Consultants and Campaigns.* New York: Basil Blackwell.

Maisel, Sandy. 1988. Spending Patterns in Presidential Nominating Campaigns, 1976-1988. Presented at annual meeting of the American Political Science Association, Washington, D.C.

Mann, Thomas E. 1985. Should the Presidential Nominating System Be Changed (Again)? In *Before Nomination: Our Primary Problems,* ed. George Grassmuck. Washington, D.C.: American Enterprise Institute.

Markus, Gregory B. 1979. *Analyzing Panel Data.* Beverly Hills: Sage.

Marshall, Thomas R. 1984. Issues, Personalities and Presidential Primary Voters. *Social Science Quarterly* 65:750-60.

Martz, Larry. March 7, 1988. Day of the Preachers. *Time,* 44-46.

Mashek, John W. February 21, 1988. Candidates Hope For Big Breaks from "Lesser" State Contests. *Atlanta Constitution.*

Mashek, John W., and Tom Baxter. March 10, 1988. Super Tuesday Debut Called a Success, But Will it Return in '92? *Atlanta Constitution.*

Mayer, William G. 1987. The New Hampshire Primary: A Historical Overview. In *Media and Momentum: The New Hampshire Primary and Nomination Politics,* eds. Gary R. Orren and Nelson W. Polsby. Chatham, N.J.: Chatham.

McQuaid, John. March 6, 1988. Bush v Dole: A Matter of Style. *New Orleans Times-Picayune.*

———. March 10, 1988. Southern Primary to Stay Despite Some Bad Reviews. *New Orleans Times-Picayune.*

Moran, Jack, and Mark Fenster. 1982. Voter Turnout in Presidential Primaries: A Diachronic Analysis. *American Politics Quarterly* 10:453-476.

Morris, William D., and Otto A. Davis. 1975. The Sport of Kings: Turnout in Presidential Preference Primaries. Presented at the annual meeting of the American Political Science Association, San Francisco, Calif.

Morrison, Donald. 1988. *The Winning of the White House 1988.* New York: Time.

Moxley, Warden. January 17, 1976. Roads to the Presidency: A Look Backward. *Congressional Quarterly Weekly Reports,* 93-95.

Nelson, Michael. 1989. *Congressional Quarterly's Guide to the Presidency.* Washington, D.C.: Congressional Quarterly.

Niemi, Richard G., and Herbert Weisberg. 1984. What Determines the Vote? In *Controversies in Voting Behavior,* eds. Richard G. Niemi and Herbert Weisberg. Washington, D.C.: Congressional Quarterly.

Norrander, Barbara. 1986a. Selective Participation: Presidential Primary Voters as a Subset of General Election Voters. *American Politics Quarterly* 14:35-53.

———. 1986b. Correlates of Vote Choice in the 1980 Presidential Primaries. *Journal of Politics* 48:156-67.

———. 1986c. Measuring Primary Turnout in Aggregate Analysis. *Political Behavior* 8:356-73.

———. 1989. Ideological Representativeness of Presidential Primary Voters. *American Journal of Political Science* 33:570-87.

———, and Gregg W. Smith. 1985. Type of Contest, Candidate Strategy and Turnout in Presidential Primaries. *American Politics Quarterly* 13:28-50.

O'Byrne, James. March 6, 1988. South Ready to Rise Again. *New Orleans Times-Picayune.*

Oreskes, Michael. March 2, 1988. Jackson Sets Sights on White Vote. *New York Times.*

———. March 10, 1988. Turnout in South Seen as Boon for the G.O.P. *New York Times.*

————. March 25, 1990. Democrats Approve Rules to Allow Earlier Primaries. *New York Times*.

Overacker, Louise. 1926. *The Presidential Primary*. New York: MacMillan.

Painton, Priscilla. February 26, 1988. Jackson Aims at Bigger Share of Delegate Pie. *Atlanta Constitution*.

————. March 3, 1988. For Jackson, Racial Issue Is Constant Opponent. *Atlanta Constitution*.

Patterson, Thomas E. 1980. *The Mass Media Election: How Americans Choose Their President*. New York: Praeger.

Phillips, Leslie. February 24, 1988. Candidates Court Cities, Snub Towns. *USA Today*.

Polsby, Nelson W. 1980. The News Media as an Alternative to Party in the Presidential Selection Process. In *Political Parties in the Eighties*, ed. Robert A. Goldwin. Washington, D.C.: American Enterprise Institute.

————. 1983. *Consequences of Party Reform*. New York: Oxford University Press.

————, and Aaron Wildavsky. 1976. *Presidential Elections*, 4th ed. New York: Scribner's Sons.

Pomper, Gerald M. 1963. *Nominating the President: The Politics of Convention Choice*. New York: Norton.

————. 1979. New Rules and New Games in Presidential Nominations. *Journal of Politics* 41:784-805.

Popkin, Samuel L. 1991. *The Reasoning Voter: Communication and Persuasion in Presidential Campaigns*. Chicago: University of Chicago Press.

Presidential Primaries: Proposals For a New System. July 8, 1972. *Congressional Quarterly Weekly Reports*, 1650-54.

Primary Stirs Hope for Regional Impact. April 1, 1989. *Seattle Times*, 11a.

The Primaries: Raw Vote and Regional Vote. July 10, 1976. *Congressional Quarterly Weekly Reports*, 1808.

Ranney, Austin. 1972. Turnout and Representation in Presidential Primary Elections. *American Political Science Review* 66:21-37.

————. 1975. *Curing the Mischief of Factions*. Berkeley: University of California Press.

————. 1977. *Participation in American Presidential Nominations, 1976*. Washington, D.C.: American Enterprise Institute.

————. 1978. *The Federalization of Presidential Primaries*. Washington, D.C.: American Enterprise Institute.

Reeves, Richard. March 9, 1988. Super Tuesday Was a Mess That Jeopardized America's Political Health. *Atlanta Constitution*.

Reiter, Howard L. 1985. *Selecting the President: The Nominating Precess in Transition*. Philadelphia: University of Pennsylvania Press.

Rheem, Donald L. July 28, 1988. Disgruntled with Primaries, Reformers Offer Suggestions: Get Rid of Super Tuesday—or Have Four More. *Christian Science Monitor*.

Rice, Tom W., and Patrick J. Kenney. 1984. Boosting State Economies: The Caucus-Convention vs. the Primary. *Presidential Studies Quarterly* 14:357-60.

Risen, James. March 4, 1988. Gephardt Voice Still Little Heard in South. *Los Angeles Times*.

Roberts, Steven V. January 19, 1988. Robertson Seeks the Faithful in Cross-State Tour of Iowa. *New York Times*.

Robinson, Michael J. 1977. Television and American Politics: 1956-1976. *Public Interest* 48:3-39.

————. 1980. Media Coverage in the Primary Campaign of 1976: Implications for Voters, Candidates, and Parties. In *The Party Symbol: Readings on Political Parties*, ed. William Crotty. San Francisco: Freeman.

————, and Margaret A. Sheehan. 1983. *Over the Wire and on TV*. New York: Russell Sage Foundation.

Rosenthal, Andrew. March 1, 1988. Negative Campaign Spots Move to the Southern Airwaves. *New York Times*.

————. September 29, 1989. Democrats Vote to Rescind Part of Dukakis-Jackson Pact. *New York Times*.

Rothenberg, Lawrence S., and Richard A. Brody. 1988. Participation in Presidential Primaries. *Western Political Quarterly* 41:253-71.

Rubin, Richard L. 1981. *Press, Party, and Presidency*. New York: Norton.

Runkel, David R., ed. 1989. *Campaign for President: The Managers Look at '88*. Dover, Mass.: Auburn.

Sack, Kevin. February 25, 1988. Presidential Hopefuls March on South Airport by Airport. *Atlanta Constitution*.

————. February 26, 1988. Gore Backers Urge Him to Focus Message, "Beat the Drum Everywhere." *Atlanta Constitution*.

————. February 28, 1988. Dukakis Turns Aggressor at Debate. *Atlanta Constitution*.

————. March 1, 1988a. Democratic Rivals Tear into Gephardt for 1981 Support of Reagan Tax Cut. *Atlanta Constitution*.

————. March 1, 1988b. Gephardt's Pocketbook Issues Give Him Edge, Democrats Say. *Atlanta Constitution*.

————. March 2, 1988. Candidates Begin Bombarding South with Tough TV Ads. *Atlanta Constitution*.

————. March 5, 1988. Gore Aims Ad Blitz at Gephardt, Trying to Finish Him Off in South. *Atlanta Constitution*.

————. March 10, 1988. Gore Mapping Dukakis Fight in the North. *Atlanta Constitution*.

————, and Hal Straus. February 17, 1988. Campaigns Seek to Juggle Money, Media Coverage. *Atlanta Constitution*.

Scammon, Richard M. 1962. *America Votes 4, 1960*. Pittsburgh: University of Pittsburgh Press.

————. 1966. *America Votes 6, 1964*. Washington, D.C.: Congressional Quarterly.

————, and Alice V. McGillivray. 1989. *America Votes 18, 1988*. Washington, D.C.: Congressional Quarterly.

Secter, Bob, and Cathleen Decker. March 8, 1988. Missouri: From Shoo-In to Showdown. *Los Angeles Times*.

Shafer, Byron E. 1983. *Quiet Revolution*. New York: Russell Sage.

Sharkansky, Ira. 1969. The Utility of Elazar's Political Culture. *Polity* 2:66-83.

Shepard, Scott, and Mike Christensen. February 25, 1988. Bush Denies Tricks Against Robertson. *Atlanta Constitution*.

The Shock of Super Tuesday. March 10, 1988. *New York Times*, 30a.

Silk, Mark. February 18, 1988. Dukakis Tries to Sell South on His "American Strategy." *Atlanta Constitution*.

————. March 6, 1988. Kemp Gets Maddox Endorsement. *Atlanta Constitution*.

Southern Days. March 9, 1988. *USA Today*, 7a.

Southern Legislative Conference. no date. Fact Sheet: SLC and the Southern Regional Primary.

Southern Legislative Conference. January 27, 1986. Early Southern Regional Primary Effort Focus of Press Club Newsmaker Breakfast. Press Release.

Southern Legislative Conference. February 7, 1986. Early Southern Regional Primary Moves Closer to Reality for 1988. Press Release.

Stanley, Harold W., and Charles D. Hadley. 1987. The Southern Regional Primary: Regional Intentions with National Implications. *Publius* 17:83-91.

————, and Charles D. Hadley. 1989. Super Tuesday Surveys: Insights and Hindsights. Presented at the annual meeting of the Midwest Political Science Association, Chicago, Ill.

————, and Richard G. Niemi. 1990. *Vital Statistics on American Politics,* 2nd ed. Washington, D.C.: Congressional Quarterly.

Stevenson, Adlai E., III. 1984. The Presidency—1984. *Presidential Studies Quarterly* 14:18-21.

Straus, Hal. March 1, 1987. Gephardt Targeting South in Presidential Bid. *Atlanta Constitution.*

————. February 20, 1988. Ahead in Southern Polls, Gephardt Moves Swiftly to Rebuild Organization. *Atlanta Constitution.*

————. March 1, 1988. Clergy Convert to Robertson for S.C. Vote. *Atlanta Constitution.*

————. March 4, 1988. Southern Campaign Heats Up While Endorsements Pile Up. *Atlanta Constitution.*

Surprise Harvest in Iowa. February 4, 1980. *Time,* 24-28.

Tolchin, Martin. February 12, 1991. Cutting Funds for '92 Candidates is Proposed, but to Stiff Resistance. *New York Times.*

Toner, Robin. March 25, 1990. Eyes to Left, Democrats Edge Toward the Center. *New York Times.*

Treadwell, David. April 19, 1986. Eight Dixie States Plan Same-Day Primary. *Los Angeles Times.*

Udall, Stewart L. January 10, 1988. Maybe the Party Will Thank Hart. *New York Times.*

U.S. Bureau of the Census. 1989. *Statistical Abstract of the United States 1989.* Washington, D.C.: Government Printing Office.

U.S. Department of Education. 1988. *Digest of Education Statistics 1988.* Washington, D.C.: Government Printing Office.

Walsh, Edward. December 5, 1987. The More Seed Money the Better. *Washington Post.*

Warner, Margaret Garrard. January 25, 1988. What Al Haig Really Wants. *Newsweek,* 19.

Warren, Ellen. March 11, 1988. Kemp Ends 11-Month Quest for White House. *San Jose Mercury News.*

Wattier, Mark J. 1983. Ideological Voting in 1980 Republican Presidential Primaries. *Journal of Politics* 45:1016-26.

Webb, Gary. August 17, 1989. March Presidential Primary Gaining Favor. *San Jose Mercury News.*

Weinraub, Bernard. February 13, 1988. Haig Drops Campaign for Presidency and Gives His Endorsement to Dole. *New York Times.*

White, Theodore H. 1961. *The Making of the President 1960.* New York: Atheneum.

Wicker, Tom. September 16, 1985. A Pair of Good Ideas. *New York Times.*

————. February 19, 1988. The Road to a Ticket. *New York Times.*

Wilcox, Clyde. 1991. Financing the 1988 Prenomination Campaigns. In *Nominating the President,* eds. Emmett Buell and Lee Sigelman. Knoxville: University of Tennessee Press.

Will, George F. January 12, 1986. Early Regional Primary Would Allow the South to Throw Its Weight Around. *Washington Post.*

Williams, Daniel C., Stephen J. Weber, Gordon A. Haaland, Ronald H. Mueller, and Robert E. Craig. 1976. Voter Decisionmaking in a Primary Election: An Evaluation of Three Models of Choice. *American Journal of Political Science* 22:37-49.

Winebrenner, Hugh. 1987. *The Iowa Precinct Caucuses*. Ames: Iowa State University Press.

Witcover, Jules. 1978. *Marathon: The Pursuit of the Presidency, 1972-1976*. New York: Signet.

Wolfinger, Raymond E., and Steven J. Rosenstone. 1980. *Who Votes?* New Haven: Yale.

———, Steven J. Rosenstone, and Richard A. McIntosh. 1981. Presidential and Congressional Voters Compared. *American Politics Quarterly* 9:245-56.

Wright, Gerald C., Robert S. Erikson, and John P. McIver. 1985. Measuring State Partisanship and Ideology with Survey Data. *Journal of Politics* 47:469-89.

Zeidenstein, Harvey. 1970. Presidential Primaries: Reflection of "The People's Choice"? *Journal of Politics* 32:856-74.

INDEX